Mastering phpMyAdmin 3.1 for Effective MySQL Management

Increase your MySQL productivity and control by discovering the real power of phpMyAdmin 3.1

Marc Delisle

BIRMINGHAM - MUMBAI

Mastering phpMyAdmin 3.1
for Effective MySQL Management

First published: March 2009

Production Reference: 1050309

Published by Packt Publishing Ltd.
32 Lincoln Road
Olton
Birmingham, B27 6PA, UK.

ISBN 978-1-847197-86-3

www.packtpub.com

Cover Image by Marc Delisle (Marc.Delisle@cegepsherbrooke.qc.ca)

Credits

Author

Marc Delisle

Reviewer

Kai "Oswald" Seidler

Acquisition Editor

Shilpa Dube

Development Editor

Shilpa Dube

Technical Editor

Gaurav Datar

Copy Editor

Sumathi Sridhar

Indexer

Rekha Nair

Production Editorial Manager

Abhijeet Deobhakta

Editorial Team Leader

Akshara Aware

Project Team Leader

Lata Basantani

Project Coordinator

Rajashree Hamine

Proofreaders

Mark Reardon

Joel T. Johnson

Production Coordinator

Rajni R. Thorat

Cover Work

Rajni R. Thorat

About the author

Marc Delisle, owing to his involvement with phpMyAdmin, is a member of the MySQL Developers Guild that regroups community developers. He began contributing to this popular MySQL web interface in December 1998, when he made its first multi-language version. As a developer and project administrator, he has been actively involved with this software project since 2001.

Since 1980 Marc has worked at Cegep de Sherbrooke, Québec, Canada, as an application programmer and network manager. He has also been teaching networking, security, and PHP/MySQL application development. In one of his classes, he was pleased to meet a phpMyAdmin user from Argentina. Marc lives in Sherbrooke with his wife, and they enjoy spending time with their four children.

This book is an update to Marc's first book on phpMyAdmin, published by Packt Publishing in 2004, followed by "Creating your MySQL Database: Practical Design Tips and Techniques", also by Packt Publishing.

I am truly grateful to Louay Fatoohi, who approached me for this book project, and to the Packt team whose sound comments were greatly appreciated during production. My thanks also go to Garvin Hicking, Alexander Marcus Turek, and Kai 'Oswald' Seidler — the reviewers for the successive editions of this book. Their sharp eyes helped in making this book clearer and more complete.

Finally, I wish to thank all contributors to phpMyAdmin's source code, translations, and documentation. The time they gave to this project still inspires me and continues to push me forward.

About the reviewer

Kai "Oswald" Seidler was born in Hamburg in 1970. He graduated from the Technical University of Berlin with a Diplom-Informatiker degree (the equivalent of a Master of Science degree) in Computer Science. In the '90s, he created and managed Germany's biggest IRCnet server — `irc.fu-berlin.de`, and co-managed one of the world's largest anonymous FTP servers — `ftp.cs.tu-berlin.de`.

He set up his first professional public web server in 1993. From 1993 to 1998, he was a member of Projektgruppe Kulturraum Internet — a research project on net culture and network organization. In 2002, he co-founded Apache Friends and created the multi-platform Apache web server bundle XAMPP. Around 2005, XAMPP became the most popular Apache stack worldwide.

In 2006, his third book, "Das XAMPP-Handbuch", was published by Addison Wesley.

To Carole, André, Corinne, Annie, and Guillaume, with all my love.

Table of Contents

Preface   **1**

Chapter 1: Introduction and Installation   **7**

Introducing phpMyAdmin   **7**

Web applications   7

PHP and MySQL:The leading open source duo   8

What is phpMyAdmin?   8

phpMyAdmin features   9

Installing phpMyAdmin   **10**

Required information   11

System requirements   11

Downloading the files   11

Installation procedure   12

Installation on a remote server using a Windows client   12

Installation on a local Linux server   13

Installation on local Windows servers (Apache, IIS)   13

Configuring phpMyAdmin   **13**

The config.inc.php file   14

Permissions on config.inc.php   14

Configuration principles   15

Web-based setup script   16

Manual creation of config.inc.php   22

Tips for editing config.inc.php on a Windows Client   22

Description of some configuration parameters   23

PmaAbsoluteUri   23

Server-specific sections   23

Upgrading phpMyAdmin   **26**

Summary   **26**

Chapter 2: Authentication and Security   27

MySQL authentication   27

Root user without password   27
Single-user authentication using config   28
     Testing the connection   28
Multi-user authentication   29
     Authentication types offered   29
     The control user   29
     Logging out   30
     HTTP authentication   30
     Cookie authentication   31
     Signon authentication   33
Multi-server configuration   34
     Servers defined in the configuration file   34
     Arbitrary server   35

Security   36

Directory-level protection   36
Error handling   37
IP-based access control   37
     Rules   37
     Order of interpretation for rules   38
     Simplified rule for root access   39
Restricting the list of databases   39
Protecting in-transit data   40
Swekey hardware authentication   40
     Configuration   41
     Usage   41
     Security note   42

Summary   42

Chapter 3: Interface Overview   43

Panels and windows   43

Login panels   43
Left and right panels   43
     Homepage   44
     Views   44
Query window   44
Starting page   45

General customization   45

Window titles configuration   45
Icon configuration   45
Natural sort order for database and table names   46
Site-specific header and footer   46

MySQL documentation links   47

Themes   48
    Theme configuration   48
    Theme selection   48

The color picker   49

Sliders   50

Character sets, collations and language   **50**

Collations   50

Unicode and UTF-8   51

Language selection   51

Effective character sets and collations   52

Left panel (navigation)   **53**

Logo configuration   54

Database and table list   54
    Light mode   55
    Full mode   56
    Table short statistics   57
    Table quick-access icon   58
    Nested display of tables within a database   58

Server-list choice   59

Handling many databases or tables   60
    Limits on the interface   60
    Improving fetch speed   61

Right panel (main)   **62**

Homepage   62

Database view   63

Table view   65

Server view   65

Icons for homepage and menu tabs   66

Query window   **66**

Summary   **67**

Chapter 4: First Steps   **69**

Database creation   **69**

No privileges?   69

First database creation is authorized   70

Creating our first table   **71**

Choosing the fields   71

Table creation   72

Choosing keys   74

Manual data insertion   **76**

Data entry panel tuning for CHAR and VARCHAR   77

Browse mode 78
  SQL query links 79
  Navigation bar 80
  Query results operations 82
  Sorting results 83
    Headwords 84
  Color-marking rows 84
  Limiting the length of each column 85
    Display options 85
  Browsing distinct values 85
  Browse-mode customization 86
Creating an additional table 87
Summary 88

Chapter 5: Changing Data 89
  Edit mode 89
  Moving to next field with the tab key 90
  Moving with arrows 91
  Handling NULL values 91
  Applying a function to a value 92
  Duplicating rows of data 93
  Multi-row editing 94
  Editing the next row 94
  Deleting data 95
  Deleting a single row 95
  Deleting many rows 96
  Deleting all the rows in a table 97
  Deleting all rows in many tables 98
  Deleting tables 98
  Deleting databases 98
  Summary 99

Chapter 6: Changing Table Structures 101
  Adding a field 101
  Vertical mode 102
  Horizontal mode 103
  Editing field attributes 103
  TEXT 104
  BLOB (Binary Large Object) fields 104
  Binary content uploads 105

ENUM and SET	**106**
DATE, DATETIME, and TIMESTAMP	**108**
Calendar pop up	108
TIMESTAMP options	110
Bit	**110**
Index management	**111**
Single-field indexes	111
Multi-field indexes and index editing	112
FULLTEXT Indexes	113
Table optimization—explaining a query	114
Detection of index problems	115
Summary	**116**
Chapter 7: Exporting Structure and Data (Backup)	**117**
Dumps, backups, and exports	**117**
Scope of the export	118
Database exports	**118**
The export subpanel	119
SQL	119
SQL options	122
The "Save as file" subpanel	126
File name template	126
Compression	127
Choice of character set	128
Kanji support	128
CSV	129
CSV for MS Excel	130
PDF	131
Microsoft Excel 2000	131
Microsoft Word 2000	132
LaTeX	133
XML	134
Native MS Excel (pre-Excel 2000)	134
Open document spreadsheet	135
Open document text	136
YAML	137
CodeGen	137
Texy! text	137
Table exports	**138**
Split-file exports	138

Selective exports	**139**
Exporting partial query results	139
Exporting and checkboxes	140
Multi-database exports	**140**
Saving the export file on the server	**141**
User-specific save directories	142
Memory limits	**142**
Summary	**142**
Chapter 8: Importing Structure and Data	**143**
Limits for the transfer	**144**
Time limits	144
Other limits	144
Partial imports	145
Temporary directory	145
Importing SQL files	**146**
Importing CSV files	**147**
Differences between SQL and CSV formats	147
Exporting a test file	148
CSV	148
CSV using LOAD DATA	149
Requirements	149
Using the LOAD DATA interface	150
Web server upload directories	**151**
Summary	**152**
Chapter 9: Searching Data	**153**
Daily usage of phpMyAdmin	**153**
Single-table searches	**153**
Entering the search subpage	153
Search criteria by field—query by example	154
Searching for empty / non-empty values	155
Print view	155
Wildcard search	156
Case sensitivity	157
Combining criteria	157
Search options	158
Selecting the fields to be displayed	158
Ordering the results	158
Applying a WHERE clause	158
Obtaining distinct results	159
Complete database search	**160**

Restricting search to a column 161
Summary **161**
Chapter 10: Table and Database Operations **163**
Table maintenance **164**
Changing table attributes **164**
Table storage engine 165
Table comments 165
Table order 166
Table collation 167
Impact of switching connection collation 168
Table options 168
Renaming, moving, and copying tables **169**
Appending data to a table 170
Multi-table operations **170**
Repairing an "in use" table 171
Database operations **171**
Renaming a database 172
Copying a database 172
Summary **172**
Chapter 11: The Relational System **173**
Relational MySQL **173**
InnoDB and PBXT 174
Linked-tables infrastructure **174**
Goal of the infrastructure 175
Location of the infrastructure 175
Installing linked-tables infrastructure 175
Multi-user installation 176
Single-user installation 178
Defining relations with the relation view **179**
Internal relations 180
Defining the relation 180
Defining the display field 181
Foreign key relations 182
Foreign keys without linked-tables infrastructure 185
Defining relations with the Designer **185**
Interface overview 186
Defining relations 187
Foreign key relations 189
Defining the display field 189
Exporting for PDF schema 190

Benefits of the defined relations — **190**
Foreign key information — 190
The drop-down list of foreign keys — 191
The browseable foreign-table window — 192
Referential integrity checks — 192
Automatic updates of metadata — 193
Column-commenting — **193**
Automatic migration — 194
Summary — **195**

Chapter 12: Entering SQL Commands — **197**
The SQL query box — **197**
The Database view — 197
The Table view — 198
The Fields selector — 199
Clicking into the query box — 199
The Query window — **200**
Query window options — 201
Session based SQL history — 201
Database based SQL history (permanent) — 201
Editing queries in the query window — 202
Multi-statement queries — **202**
Pretty printing (syntax-highlighting) — **203**
The SQL Validator — **204**
System requirements — 204
Making the Validator available — 205
Validator results — 205
Standard-conforming queries — 205
Non-standard-conforming queries — 206
Summary — **207**

Chapter 13: The Multi-Table Query Generator — **209**
Choosing tables — **210**
Column criteria — **211**
Field selector: Single-column or all columns — 211
Sorts — 211
Showing a column — 212
Updating the query — 212
Criteria — 212
Adjusting the number of criteria rows — 214
Adjusting the number of criteria columns — 216
Automatic joins — **216**

Executing the query	**217**
Summary	**218**
Chapter 14: Bookmarks	**219**
Comparing bookmark and query history features	**219**
Bookmark creation	**220**
Creating a bookmark after a successful query	220
Storing a bookmark before sending a query	222
Public bookmarks	223
The default initial query for a table	223
Multi-query bookmarks	224
Recalling from the bookmarks list	**225**
Bookmark execution	225
Bookmark manipulation	226
Bookmark parameters	**226**
Creating a parameterized bookmark	226
Passing a parameter value to a bookmark	227
Executing bookmarks by browsing the pma_bookmark table	**228**
Summary	**228**
Chapter 15: System Documentation	**229**
Structure reports	**229**
Using print view	229
The database print view	230
The selective database print view	230
The table print view	230
The data dictionary	231
Relational schema in PDF	**232**
Adding a third table to our model	232
Editing PDF pages	233
Page planning	233
Creating a new page	233
Editing a page	234
Displaying a page	236
A note about fonts used	238
Using the Designer for PDF layout	239
Summary	**239**
Chapter 16: MIME-Based Transformations	**241**
Display behavior in browse mode	**241**
Display options	242
Enabling transformations	**242**

The MIME column's settings   242
  MIME types   243
  Browser transformations   244
  Transformation options   244
Requirements for image generation   244
  The GD2 library   245
  The JPEG and PNG libraries   245
  Memory limits   245
Examples of transformations   **246**
  Clickable thumbnail (.jpeg or .png)   246
  Links to an image   247
  Date formatting   247
  Links from text   248
    text/plain: link   248
    text/plain: imagelink   249
  Preserving the original formatting   250
  Displaying parts of a text   251
  Download link   251
  Hexadecimal representation   252
  SQL pretty printing   252
  IP address   252
  External applications   252
    External application example: In-cell sort   254
Summary   **255**
Chapter 17: MySQL 5.0 and 5.1 Support   **257**
Views   **257**
  Manually creating a view   258
  Right panel and views   259
  Creating a view from results   260
  Renaming a view   261
  Performance hint   261
Routines—stored procedures and functions   **262**
  Creating a stored procedure   262
    Changing the delimiter   262
    Entering the procedure   263
  Testing the procedure   263
  Manipulation   264
  Manually creating a function   265
  Testing the function   266
  Exporting stored procedures and functions   266
Triggers   **267**

Manually creating a trigger   268
Testing the trigger   268
Information_schema   **269**
Profiling   **270**
Partitioning   **271**
Table creation   271
Operations   272
Exporting   272
Event scheduler   **272**
Activating the scheduler   272
Granting EVENT permission   273
Creating an event   273
Event manipulation   273
Exporting   274
BLOB streaming   **274**
System requirements   274
Configuration   275
Implementation limitations in phpMyAdmin   275
Creating the PBMS system tables   276
Table preparation   276
Uploading to BLOB repository   276
Streaming the data from repository   277
Changing repository data   278
Summary   **278**

Chapter 18: MySQL Server Administration   **279**
User and privileges management   **279**
The user overview   279
Privileges reload   280
Adding a user   281
User name   282
Host   282
Password   282
Database creation and rights   282
Global privileges   283
Resource limits   283
Editing a user   284
Edit privileges   284
Database-specific privileges   284
Changing the password   286
Changing login information or copying a user   286
Removing a user   287

Database information   **288**
Enabling statistics   288
Sorting statistics   289
Checking the database privileges   289
Dropping selected databases   289
Server information   **289**
Server status verification   290
   The general status page   290
   InnoDB status   291
Server variables   292
Server processes   292
Storage engines   293
Available character sets and collations   294
The binary log   294
Summary   **295**

Appendix A: History of phpMyAdmin   **297**
Early events   **297**
Project re-launch   **299**
Distributors   300
Evolution   **300**
GoPHP5 and the 3.x branch   **301**
Awards   **302**
Summary   **303**

Appendix B: Troubleshooting and Support   **305**
Base configuration   **306**
Solving common errors   **306**
#2003 - Can't connect to MySQL server   307
Named pipe problem (Windows)   307
MySQL said: Access denied   307
When using http authentication   307
MySQL said: Error 127, Table Must Be Repaired   308
BLOB column used in key specification without a key length   308
IIS: No Input File Specified   309
A "404: page not found" error when modifying a row   309
Not being able to create a database   309
Problems importing large files or uploading large BLOB files   310
MySQL root password lost   310
Duplicate field names when creating a table   310
Authentication window displayed more than once   311
Column size changed by phpMyAdmin   311
Seeing many databases that are not ours   311
Not being able to store a value greater than 127   311

FAQs	**312**
Help forums	**312**
Creating a SourceForge account	312
Choosing the thread title	312
Reading the answers	312
Support tracker	312
Bug tracker	313
Environment description	313
Bug description	313
Contributing to the project	**313**
The code base	314
Translation updates	314
Patches	314
Future phpMyAdmin versions	**314**
Summary	**314**
Index	**315**

Preface

Providing a powerful graphical interface for managing MySQL, phpMyAdmin is one of the most popular open source applications. While most developers use routine features of phpMyAdmin every day, few are aware of the power and potential its advanced features have. This book builds a solid understanding of the core capabilities of phpMyAdmin, and then walks you through every facet of this legendary tool.

Used by millions of developers, MySQL is the most popular open source database. It supports numerous large, dynamic websites and applications. MySQL has acquired this wide popularity by virtue of its open source nature, performance, reliability, robustness, and support for multiple platforms. However, this popularity has also been helped by the existence of phpMyAdmin—the industry standard administration tool that makes database management easy for both, the experienced developer and the novice one.

Bringing a web interface to MySQL has made phpMyAdmin an indispensable tool for MySQL and web developers, be they professionals or in the classroom. Every user can benefit from phpMyAdmin, by unlocking the full potential of this powerful application.

What this book covers

Chapter 1 gives us the reasons why we should use phpMyAdmin as a means of developing web applications. It then covers the downloading and installation procedures for phpMyAdmin.

Chapter 2 provides an overview of various authentication types used in MySQL. It then covers the security issues related to phpMyAdmin installation.

Chapter 3 gives us an overview of the phpMyAdmin interface. It includes the login panel, the left and the right panel including the Light and the Full mode, and the Query window.

Chapter 4 is all about database creation. It teaches us how to create a table, how to insert data manually, and how to sort the data.

Chapter 5 covers the aspects of data editing in phpMyAdmin. It teaches us handling NULL values, multi-row editing. Finally, it covers an important aspect of any database tool—data deletion.

Chapter 6 explores the subject of changing the structure of tables. Its primary focus is on editing field attributes and index management.

Chapter 7 deals with backups and exports. It lists various ways to trigger an export, available export formats, the options associated with export formats, and the various places where the export files may be sent.

Chapter 8 tells us how to bring back exported data created for backup and transfer purposes. It provides an overview of the various options available in phpMyAdmin to import data, and different mechanisms involved in importing SQL and CSV files. Finally, it covers the limitations that may be faced while importing files, and the ways to overcome them.

Chapter 9 presents the mechanisms that are useful for searching data effectively.

Chapter 10 covers ways to perform some operations that influence and can be performed on entire tables or databases as a whole. Finally, it deals with table maintenance operations for table repair and optimization.

Chapter 11 is where we start covering advanced features of phpMyAdmin. The chapter explains how to define inter-table relations. It also explains how to install the linked-tables infrastructure—a prerequisite for the advanced features.

Chapter 12 helps us enter our own SQL commands. The chapter also gives us an overview of Query window—the window used to edit an SQL query. Finally, it also helps us to obtain the history of typed commands.

Chapter 13 covers the multi-table query generator, which allows us to produce multi-table queries without actually typing them.

Chapter 14 covers Bookmarks—one of the features of the linked-tables infrastructure. It covers how to record bookmarks and how to manipulate them. Finally, it covers passing parameters to bookmarks, and executing bookmarks directly from the pma_bookmark table.

Chapter 15 gives an overview of how to produce documentation, which explains the structure of the databases, using the tools offered by phpMyAdmin.

Chapter 16 explains how to apply transformations to the data in order to customize its format at view time.

Chapter 17 covers phpMyAdmin's support for the MySQL features that are new in versions 5.0 and 5.1.

Chapter 18 is about the administration of a MySQL server, focusing on the management of user accounts and privileges. The chapter discusses how a system administrator can use phpMyAdmin's server management features for day-to-day user account maintenance, server verification, and server protection.

Appendix A provides a history of the phpMyAdmin project, from its roots back in 1998 through the project re-launch in 2001, and its subsequent evolution.

Appendix B explains how to troubleshoot phpMyAdmin by examining some of its error messages, and proposing appropriate solutions. It also explains how to interact with the development team for support, bug reports, and contributions.

What you need for this book

You need to have access to a server or workstation that has the following installed:

- MySQL version 5.0 or newer
- PHP version 5.0 or newer
- Web server software with PHP support (this book explains phpMyAdmin's installation on Apache and IIS)

Who is this book for

phpMyAdmin is a must have tool for everyone who needs to manage their MySQL databases and tables in an effective manner. This book is a must read for every serious phpMyAdmin user who would like to use this outstanding application to its fullest potential.

Conventions

In this book, you will find a number of styles of text that distinguish between different kinds of information. Here are some examples of these styles, and an explanation of their meaning.

Code words in text are shown as follows: "If we are using the `config` authentication type, no login panel is displayed."

A block of code will be set as follows:

```
$cfg['MySQLManualBase'] = 'http://www.mysql.com/doc/en';
$cfg['MySQLManualType'] = 'searchable';
```

When we wish to draw your attention to a particular part of a code block, the relevant lines or items will be shown in bold:

```
$cfg['Servers'][$i]['AllowDeny']['order'] = 'allow,deny';
```

Any command-line input or output is written as follows:

```
tar -xzvf phpMyAdmin-3.1.1-all-languages.tar.gz
```

New terms and **important words** are shown in bold. Words that you see on the screen, in menus or dialog boxes for example, appear in our text like this: "The **Home** link from the left panel is used to display this page".

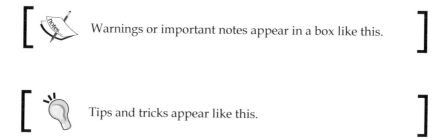

Warnings or important notes appear in a box like this.

Tips and tricks appear like this.

Reader feedback

Feedback from our readers is always welcome. Let us know what you think about this book—what you liked or may have disliked. Reader feedback is important for us to develop titles that you really get the most out of.

To send us general feedback, simply drop an email to feedback@packtpub.com, and mention the book title in the subject of your message.

If there is a book that you need and would like to see us publish, please send us a note in the **SUGGEST A TITLE** form on www.packtpub.com or email suggest@packtpub.com.

If there is a topic that you have expertise in and you are interested in either writing or contributing to a book, see our author guide on www.packtpub.com/authors.

Customer support

Now that you are the proud owner of a Packt book, we have a number of things to help you to get the most from your purchase.

Errata

Although we have taken every care to ensure the accuracy of our contents, mistakes do happen. If you find a mistake in one of our books—maybe a mistake in text or code—we would be grateful if you would report this to us. By doing so, you can save other readers from frustration, and help us to improve subsequent versions of this book. If you find any errata, please report them by visiting http://www.packtpub.com/support, selecting your book, clicking on the **let us know** link, and entering the details of your errata. Once your errata are verified, your submission will be accepted and the errata added to any list of existing errata. Any existing errata can be viewed by selecting your title from http://www.packtpub.com/support.

Piracy

Piracy of copyright material on the Internet is an ongoing problem across all media. At Packt, we take the protection of our copyright and licenses very seriously. If you come across any illegal copies of our works in any form on the Internet, please provide us with the location address or website name immediately so that we can pursue a remedy.

Please contact us at copyright@packtpub.com with a link to the suspected pirated material.

We appreciate your help in protecting our authors, and our ability to bring you valuable content.

Questions

You can contact us at questions@packtpub.com if you are having a problem with any aspect of the book, and we will do our best to address it.

1
Introduction and Installation

I wish you a warm welcome to this book! The goal of this first chapter is to:

- Know the position of this software product in the Web spectrum
- Be aware of all its features
- Become proficient at installing and configuring it

Introducing phpMyAdmin

This section describes the place of phpMyAdmin in the context of PHP/MySQL web applications and summarizes its features.

Web applications

The Web has evolved! In the last few years, the Web has changed dramatically. In its infancy, the Web was a medium used mainly to convey **static** information ("Look, my homepage is on the Web!"). Now, large parts of the Web carry information that is **dynamically generated** by application programs, on which enterprises, and even individuals, rely for their intranets and public websites.

Because of the clear benefits of databases—better accessibility and structuring of information—web applications are mostly database driven. While the front end used is usually a well- known (and quickly deployed) web browser, there is a database system at the back end. Application programs provide the interface between the browser and the database.

Those who are not operating a database-driven website, are not using the medium to its fullest capability. Also, they could be lagging behind competitors who have made the switch. So, it is not a question of whether we *should* implement a database driven site, but rather about *when* and *how* to implement it.

Why web applications? They improve user experience and involve them in the process by opening up possibilities such as:

- Gathering feedback about the site
- Letting users communicate with us and with each other through forums
- Ordering goods from our e-commerce site
- Enabling easily editable web-based information (content management)
- Designing and maintaining databases from the Web

Nowadays, **WWW** might stand for **World-Wide Wave**—a big wave that profoundly modifies the way developers think about user interface, data presentation, and most of all, the way data reaches users and comes back to the data center.

PHP and MySQL:The leading open source duo

When we look at the web applications platforms currently offered by host providers, we will see that the most prevalent is the PHP/MySQL combination.

Well supported by their respective homesites—`http://www.php.net` and `http://www.mysql.com`—this duo has enabled developers to offer a lot of readymade open source web applications, and most importantly, enabled in-house developers to quickly put in place solid web solutions.

MySQL, which is mostly compliant with the SQL:2003 standard, is a database system well known for its speed, robustness, and a small connection overhead. This is important in a web context where pages must be served as quickly as possible.

PHP, usually installed as a module inside the web server, is a popular scripting language in which applications are written to communicate with MySQL (or other database systems) on the back end and browsers on the front end. Ironically, the acronym's significance has evolved along with the Web evolution, from **Personal Homepage** to **Professional HomePage** to its current recursive definition: **PHP: Hypertext Processor**. A reference about the successive name changes can be seen in PHP's source code at `http://cvs.php.net/viewvc.cgi/php3/CHANGES?r1=1.23&r2=1.24`. Available on millions of Web domains, PHP drives its own wave of quickly developing applications.

What is phpMyAdmin?

phpMyAdmin (official homepage at `http://www.phpmyadmin.net`) is a web application written in PHP and contains (like most web applications) XHTML, CSS, and JavaScript client code. It provides a complete web interface for administering MySQL databases, and is widely recognized as the leading application in this field.

Being open source since its existence, it has enjoyed support from numerous developers and translators worldwide (being translated into 55 languages at the time of writing this book). The project is currently hosted on SourceForge.

Host providers everywhere are showing their trust in phpMyAdmin by installing it on their servers. The popular Cpanel (a website control application) interfaces with phpMyAdmin. In addition, we can install our own copy of phpMyAdmin inside our webspace as long as our provider respects the minimum requirements (see the *System Requirements* section later in this chapter).

phpMyAdmin features

The goal of phpMyAdmin is to offer complete web-based management of MySQL servers and data, and to keep up with MySQL and web standards evolution. While the product is not perfect, it currently includes the most commonly requested features and other extra features.

The development team constantly fine-tunes the product based on the reported bugs and requested features, releasing new versions regularly.

phpMyAdmin offers features that cover basic MySQL database and table operations. It also has an internal relational system that maintains metadata to support advanced features. Finally, system administrators can manage users and privileges from phpMyAdmin. It is important to note that phpMyAdmin's choice of available operations depends on the rights the user has on a specific MySQL server.

The basic features consist of:

- Database creation, deletion, renaming, and attribute changes
- Table creation, renaming, copying, and deletion
- Table structure maintenance, including indexes
- Special table operations (repair, optimization, and changing type)
- Data insertion, modification, deletion
- Data display in horizontal/vertical mode, and Print view
- Data navigation and sorting
- Binary data uploading
- Data search (table or database)
- Querying by example (multi-table)
- Batch loading of data (import)
- Exporting structure and data in various formats, with compression
- Multi-user and multi-server installation with web-based setup

The advanced features include:

- Field-level comments
- Foreign keys (with or without InnoDB)
- Browse foreign table
- Bookmarks of queries
- Data dictionary
- PDF relational schema and dictionary
- SQL queries history
- Connection to MySQL, using either the traditional `mysql` extension or the new `mysqli` extension (in PHP 5)
- Character-set support for databases, tables, and fields (with MySQL 4.1)
- Column contents transformation based on MIME type
- Visual Designer for relations
- Support for MySQL 5.0 features—views, procedures, triggers, profiling
- Support for MySQL 5.1 features—events and partitions
- Support for special storage engines—Maria, PBXT, and PBMS (BLOB streaming)
- Support for Swekey hardware authentication USB key
- Theme management to customize the look of the interface

The server administration features consist of:

- User and privileges management
- Database privileges check
- Verify server's runtime information and obtain configuration hints
- Full server export

Installing phpMyAdmin

It's time to install the product and to configure it minimally for first-time use.

Our reason for installing phpMyAdmin could be one of the following:

- Our host provider did not install a central copy
- Our provider installed it, but the version installed is not current
- We are working directly on our enterprise's web server

Required information

Some host providers offer an integrated web panel where we can manage accounts, including MySQL accounts, and also a file manager that can be used to upload web content. Depending on this, the mechanism we use to transfer phpMyAdmin to our webspace will vary. We will need some specific information (listed below) before starting the installation:

- The web server's name or address. Here, we will assume it to be www.mydomain.com.
- Our web server's account information (username, password). This information will be used either for FTP or SFTP transfer, SSH login, or web control panel login.
- The MySQL server's name or address. Often, this is localhost, which means that it is located on the same machine as the web server. We will assume this to be mysql.mydomain.com.
- Our MySQL server's account information (username, password).

System requirements

The up-to-date requirements for a specific phpMyAdmin version are always stated in the accompanying Documentation.html. For phpMyAdmin 3.1, the minimum PHP version required is PHP 5.2 with **session** support and the **Standard PHP Library (SPL)**. Moreover, the web server must have access to a MySQL server (version 5.0 or later)—either locally or on a remote machine. It is strongly recommended that the PHP mcrypt extension be present for improved performance in cookie authentication mode (more on this in Chapter 2). In fact, on a 64-bit server, this extension is required.

On the browser side, cookie support must be activated, whatever authentication mode we use.

Downloading the files

There are various files available in the **Download** section of http://www.phpmyadmin.net. There might be more than one version offered here and it is always a good idea to download the latest stable version. We only need to download one file, which works regardless of the platform (browser, web server, MySQL, or PHP version). For version 3.1, there are two groups of files—english and all-languages. If we need only the English interface, we can download a file containing "english"—for example, phpMyAdmin-3.1.0-english.zip. On the other hand, if we have the need for at least one other language, a choice containing "all-languages" would be appropriate.

If we are using a server supporting only PHP4—for which the PHP team has discontinued support since December 31, 2007—the latest stable version of phpMyAdmin is not a good choice for download. I recommend using version 2.11.x, which is the latest branch that supports PHP4.

The files offered have various extensions: `.zip`, `.tar.bz2`, `.tar.gz`, `.7z`. Download a file having an extension for which you have the corresponding extractor. In the Windows world, `.zip` is the most universal file format, although it is bigger than `.gz` or `.bz2` (common in the Linux/Unix world). In the following examples, we will assume that the chosen file was `phpMyAdmin-3.1.1-all-languages.zip`.

After clicking on the appropriate file, we will have to choose the nearest mirror site. The file will start to download, and we can save it on our computer.

Installation procedure

The next step depends on the platform you are using. The following sections detail the procedures for some common platforms. You may proceed directly to the relevant section.

Installation on a remote server using a Windows client

Using the File explorer, we double-click the `phpMyAdmin-3.1.1-all-languages.zip` file we just downloaded on the Windows machine. A file extractor should start, showing us all the scripts and directories inside a main `phpMyAdmin-3.1.1-all-languages` directory.

Use whatever mechanism your file extractor offers to save all the files, including subdirectories, to some location on your workstation. Here, we have chosen `c:\`. Therefore, a `c:\phpMyAdmin-3.1.1-all-languages` directory has been created for extraction.

Now, it's time to transfer the entire directory structure `c:\phpMyAdmin-3.1.1-all-languages` to the web server in our webspace. We use our favorite FTP software or the web control panel for the transfer.

The exact directory under which we transfer phpMyAdmin may vary. It could be our `public_html` directory or another directory where we usually transfer web documents. For further instructions about the exact directory to be used or the best way to transfer the directory structure, we can consult our host provider's help desk.

After the transfer is complete, these files can be removed as they are no longer needed on our Windows client.

Installation on a local Linux server

Let's say we chose phpMyAdmin-3.1.1-all-languages.tar.gz and downloaded it directly to some directory on the Linux server. We move it to our web server's document root directory (for example, /var/www/html) or to one of its subdirectories (for example, /var/www/html/utilities). We then extract it with the following shell command or by using any graphical file extractor that our window manager offers:

```
tar -xzvf phpMyAdmin-3.1.1-all-languages.tar.gz
```

We must ensure that the permissions and ownership of the directory and files are appropriate for our web server. The web server user or group must be able to read them.

Installation on local Windows servers (Apache, IIS)

The procedure here is similar to that described in the *Installation on a remote server using a Windows client* section, except that the target directory will be under our DocumentRoot (for Apache) or our wwwroot (for IIS). Of course, we do not need to transfer anything after modifications are made to config.inc.php (described in the next section), as the directory is already on the webspace.

Apache is usually run as a service. Hence, we have to ensure that the user under which the service is running has normal read privileges to access our newly created directory. The same principle applies to IIS, which uses the **IUSR_machinename** user. This user must have read access to the directory. You can adjust permissions in the **Security/permissions** tab of the directory's properties.

Configuring phpMyAdmin

Here, we learn how to prepare and use the configuration file containing the parameters to connect to MySQL, and which can be customized as per our requirements.

Before configuring, we can rename the directory phpMyAdmin-3.1.1-all-languages to something like phpMyAdmin, phpmyadmin, admin, or something easier to remember. This way, we and our users can visit an easily remembered URL to start phpMyAdmin. We can also use a symbolic link if our server supports this feature.

The config.inc.php file

This file contains valid PHP code, defining the majority of the parameters (expressed by PHP variables) that we can change to tune phpMyAdmin to our own needs. There are also normal PHP comments in it, and we can comment our changes.

 Be careful not to add any blank line at the beginning or end of the file; this would hamper the execution of phpMyAdmin.

Note that phpMyAdmin looks for this file in the first level directory — the same one where `index.php` is located.

In versions before 2.8.0, a generic `config.inc.php` file was included in the downloaded kit. Since 2.8.0, this file is no longer present in the directory structure. Since version 2.9.0, a `config.sample.inc.php` file is included, which can be copied over to `config.inc.php` to act as a starting point. However, it is recommended that you use the web-based setup script (explained in this chapter) instead, for a more comfortable configuration interface.

There is another file — `layout.inc.php` — containing some configuration information. As phpMyAdmin offers theme management, this file contains the theme-specific colors and settings. There is one `layout.inc.php` per theme, located in `themes/themename`, for example, `themes/original`. We will cover modifying some of those parameters in Chapter 4, under the *First steps* section.

Permissions on config.inc.php

In its normal behavior, phpMyAdmin verifies that the permissions on this file do not allow everyone to modify it. This means that the file should not be writable by the world. Also, it displays a warning if the permissions are not correct. However, in some situations (for example a NTFS file system mounted on a non-Windows server), the permission detection fails. In these cases, you should set this parameter to `false`:

```
$cfg['CheckConfigurationPermissions'] = false;
```

Configuration principles

phpMyAdmin's behavior, given that no configuration file is present, has changed in version 3.1.0. In versions 3.0 and earlier, the application used its default settings as defined in `libraries/config.default.php`, and tried to connect to a MySQL server on `localhost`—the same machine where the web server is running—with user `root` and no password. This is the default setup produced by most MySQL installation procedures, even though it is not really secure. However, if our freshly installed MySQL server were still to have the default root account, we would have logged on automatically and would have seen a warning given by phpMyAdmin about such lack of security.

> If the notion of MySQL `root` user eludes you, it might now be the time to browse `http://dev.mysql.com/doc/refman/5.1/en/privilege-system.html`, to learn the basics about MySQL's privilege system.

Since version 3.1.0, the development team has wanted to promote a more flexible login panel. This is why, in the situation of lacking a configuration file, phpMyAdmin displays the cookie based login panel by default (more details on this in Chapter 2):

We can verify this fact by opening our browser and visiting `http://www.mydomain.com/phpmyadmin`, and substituting the proper values for the domain part and the directory part.

If we are able to log in, it means that there is a MySQL server running on the same host as the web server (localhost), and we've just made a connection to it. However, not having created a configuration file means that we would be limited to managing this host only. Moreover, many advanced phpMyAdmin features (for example, query bookmarks, full relational support, column transformation, and so on) would not be activated.

> The cookie based authentication method uses Blowfish encryption for storing credentials in browser cookies. When no configuration file exists, a Blowfish secret key is generated and stored in session data, which can open the door to security issues. This is why the warning message is displayed: **The configuration file now needs a secret passphrase (blowfish_secret)**.

At this point, we have some choices:

- Use phpMyAdmin without a configuration file
- Use the web-based setup script to generate a `config.inc.php` file
- Create a `config.inc.php` file manually

These options are presented in the following sections. We should note that, even if we use the web-based setup script, we should familiarize ourselves with the `config.inc.php` file format, because the setup script does not cover all the possible configuration options.

Web-based setup script

The web-based setup mechanism is strongly recommended in order to avoid syntax errors that could result from the manual creation of the configuration file. Also, as this file must respect PHP's syntax, it's common for new users to experience problems in this phase of the installation.

> A warning is in order here: the current version has only a limited number of translation languages for the setup interface.

To access the setup script, we must visit `http://www.mydomain.com/phpmyadmin/ scripts/setup`. Here is what appears on the initial execution:

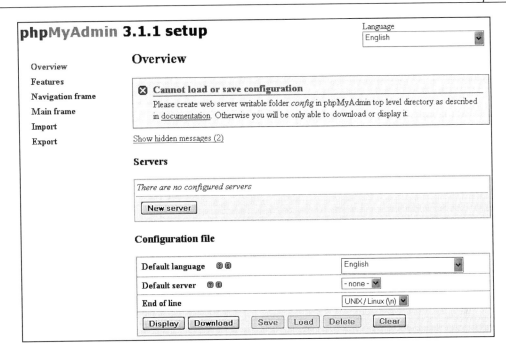

In most cases, the icons beside each parameter point to the respective phpMyAdmin official wikis and to the documentation, providing you with more information about this parameter and its possible values.

If **Show hidden messages** appears, and we click on this link, the following messages are revealed:

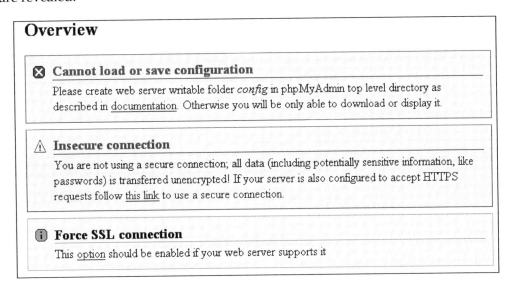

There are three warnings here. We will first deal with the second one—**Insecure connection**. This message appears if we are accessing the web server over HTTP, an insecure protocol. As we are possibly going to input confidential information, such as the user name and password in the setup phase, it's recommended that you communicate over HTTPS at least for this phase. HTTPS uses **SSL (Secure Socket Layer)** to encrypt the communication and make eavesdropping on the line impossible. If our web server supports HTTPS, we can simply follow the proposed link. It will restart the setup process, this time over HTTPS. We have made this assumption in our example.

The third warning encourages you to use the ForceSSL option, which would automatically switch to HTTPS when using phpMyAdmin (not related to the setup phase).

The first warning tells us that phpMyAdmin did not find a writable directory with the name config. This is normal as it was not present in the downloaded kit. Also, as the directory is not yet there, we observe that the **Save**, **Load,** and **Delete** buttons in the interface are grey. In this config directory, we can:

- Save the working version of the configuration file during the setup process
- Load a previously prepared config.inc.php file

It's not absolutely necessary that we create this configuration directory, as we can download the config.inc.php file produced by the setup procedure to our client machine. We can then upload it to phpMyAdmin in the first-level directory via the same mechanism (say FTP) that we used to upload phpMyAdmin. In any case, we'll create this directory.

The principle here is that the web server must be able to write to this directory. There is more than one way to achieve this. Here is one that would work on a Linux server—adding read, write, and execute permissions for everyone on this directory.

```
cd phpMyAdmin
mkdir config
chmod 777 config
```

Having done that, we refresh the page in our browser and we see:

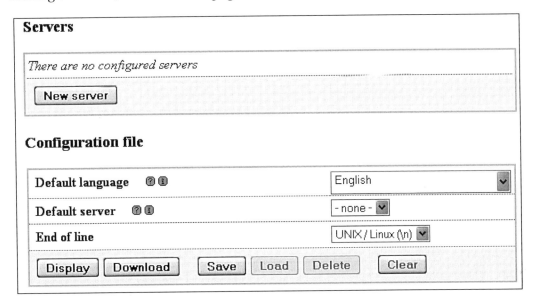

In the configuration dialog, a drop-down menu permits the user to choose the proper end-of-line format. This is according to the platform on which we plan to open later, with a text editor, the `config.inc.php` file.

A single copy of phpMyAdmin can be used to manage many MySQL servers. We will now define parameters describing our first MySQL server. We click **New server**, and the server configuration panel is shown.

A complete explanation of these parameters can be found in the following sections of this chapter and in Chapter 11. For now, we notice that the setup process has detected that PHP also supports the `mysqli` extension. Therefore, this is the one that is chosen by default. This extension is the programming library used by PHP to communicate with MySQL.

I encourage you to stay in the philosophy proposed by the interface, and keep **cookie** as the **Authentication type**. We assume that our MySQL server is located on localhost. Hence, we keep this value and all the proposed values intact, except for the following:

- **Verbose name of this server** — we enter **my server**
- **User for config auth** — we remove **root** and leave it empty

You can see that any parameter changed from its default value appears in a different color. Moreover, a small arrow becomes available, the purpose of which is to restore a field to its default value. Hence, you can feel free to experiment with changing parameters, knowing that you can easily revert to the proposed value. At this point, the panel should look like this:

Add a new server

| Basic settings | Signon login options | Server configuration | PMA database |

Enter server connection parameters

Verbose name of this server ② ①
Hostname where MySQL server is running
`my server`

Server hostname ② ①
`localhost`

Server port ② ①
Port on which MySQL server is listening, leave empty for default

Server socket ② ①
Socket on which MySQL server is listening, leave empty for default

Use SSL ② ①
☐

Connection type ② ①
How to connect to server, keep tcp if unsure
`tcp`

PHP extension to use ② ①
What PHP extension to use; you should use mysqli if supported
`mysqli`

Compress connection ② ①
Compress connection to MySQL server
☐

Authentication type ② ①
Authentication method to use
`cookie`

User for config auth ② ①
Leave empty if not using config auth

Password for config auth ② ①
Leave empty if not using config auth

Connect without password ② ①
Try to connect without password
☐

SweKey config file ② ①
The path for the config file for SweKey hardware authentication (not located in your document root; suggested: /etc/swekey.conf)

[Save] [Reset]

We then click **Save** and are brought back to the **Overview** panel. This save operation did not yet save anything to disk; changes were saved in memory. We are warned that a Blowfish secret key was generated. However, we don't have to remember it, as it's not keyed in during login process, but is used internally. For the curious, you can switch to the **Features** panel and click the **Security** tab to see which secret key was generated. Back to the **Overview** panel. Now our setup process knows about one MySQL server, and there are links that enable us to **Edit** or **Delete** these server settings:

Servers

#	Name	Authentication type	DSN	
1	my server	cookie	mysqli://localhost	Edit | Delete

New server

We can have a look at the generated configuration lines by using the **Display** button — then we can analyze these parameters using the explanations given in the *Description of some Configuration Parameters* section later in this chapter.

At this point, this configuration is still just in memory, so we need to save it. This is done via the **Save** button on the **Overview** panel. It saves `config.inc.php` in the special `config` directory that we created previously. This is a directory strictly used for configuration purposes. If, for any reason, it was not possible to create this `config` directory, you just have to **Download** the file and upload it to the web sever directory where phpMyAdmin is installed.

The last step is to copy `config.inc.php` from the `config` directory to the top-level directory — the one that contains `index.php`. By copying this file, it becomes owned by the user instead of the web server, ensuring that further modifications are possible. This copy can be done via FTP or through commands such as:

```
cd config
cp config.inc.php ..
```

 As a security measure, it's recommended that you change the permission on the `config` directory — for example, with the `chmod ugo-rwx config` command. This is to block any unauthorized reading and writing in this directory.

Other configuration parameters can be set with these web-based setup pages. To do so, we would have to:

1. Enable read and write access to the `config` directory
2. Copy the `config.inc.php` there
3. Ensure that read and write access are provided to this file for the web server
4. Start the web-based setup tool

You are invited to peruse the remaining menus to get a sense of the available configuration possibilities, either now, or later when we cover a related subject.

In order to keep this book's text lighter, we will only refer to the parameters' textual values in the following chapters.

Manual creation of config.inc.php

We can create this text file from scratch using our favorite text editor, or by using `config.sample.inc.php` as a starting point. The exact procedure depends upon which client operating system we are using. We can refer to the next section for further information.

The default values for all possible configuration parameters that can be located inside `config.inc.php` are defined in `libraries/config.default.php`. We can take a look at this file to see the syntax used as well as further comments about configuration. See the important note about this file in the *Upgrading phpMyAdmin* section of this chapter.

Tips for editing config.inc.php on a Windows Client

This file contains special characters (Unix-style end of lines). Hence, we must open it with a text editor that understands this format. If we use the wrong text editor, this file will be displayed with very long lines.

The best choice is a standard PHP editor. Another choice would be WordPad, Metapad, or UltraEdit. We should be careful not to add any characters (even blank lines) at the beginning or end of the file. This would disturb the execution of phpMyAdmin and generate the **Cannot send header output...** error message. If this happens, refer to Appendix B.

Every time the `config.inc.php` file is modified, it will have to be transferred again to our webspace. This transfer is done via an FTP or an SFTP client. You have the option to use a standalone FTP/SFTP client such as FileZilla, or save directly via FTP/SFTP if your PHP editor supports this feature.

Description of some configuration parameters

In this chapter and the next one, we will concentrate on the parameters that deal with connection and authentication. Other parameters will be discussed in the chapters where the corresponding features are explained.

PmaAbsoluteUri

The first parameter we will look at is `$cfg['PmaAbsoluteUri'] = '';`

PMA is a familiar abbreviation for **phpMyAdmin**. For configuration parameters, the chosen convention is to capitalize the first letter, producing `Pma` in this case. At some places in its code, phpMyAdmin sends an HTTP `Location` header and must know the absolute URI of its installation point. Using an absolute URI in this case is required by RFC 2616, section 14.30.

In most cases, we can leave this one empty, as phpMyAdmin tries to auto-detect the correct value. If we browse a table later, and then edit a row and click **Save**, we will receive an error message from our browser saying, for example, **This document does not exist**. This means that the absolute URI that phpMyAdmin built in order to reach the intended page was wrong, indicating that we must manually put the correct value in this parameter.

For example, we would change it to:

```
$cfg['PmaAbsoluteUri'] = 'http://www.mydomain.com/phpMyAdmin/';
```

Server-specific sections

The next section of the file contains server-specific configurations, each starting with:

```
$i++;
$cfg['Servers'][$i]['host']              = '';
```

If we examine only the normal server parameters (other parameters will be covered starting with Chapter 11), we see a section that looks like the following for each server:

```
$i++;
$cfg['Servers'][$i]['host']            = '';
$cfg['Servers'][$i]['port']            = '';
$cfg['Servers'][$i]['socket']          = '';
$cfg['Servers'][$i]['connect_type']    = 'tcp';
$cfg['Servers'][$i]['extension']       = 'mysqli';
$cfg['Servers'][$i]['compress']        = FALSE;
$cfg['Servers'][$i]['controluser']     = '';
$cfg['Servers'][$i]['controlpass']     = '';
$cfg['Servers'][$i]['auth_type']       = 'cookie';
$cfg['Servers'][$i]['user']            = '';
$cfg['Servers'][$i]['password']        = '';
$cfg['Servers'][$i]['only_db']         = '';
$cfg['Servers'][$i]['hide_db']         = '';
$cfg['Servers'][$i]['verbose']         = '';
```

In this section, we have to enter in `$cfg['Servers'][$i]['host']`, the hostname or IP address of the MySQL server—for example, `mysql.mydomain.com` or `localhost`. If this server is running on a non-standard port or socket, we fill in the correct values in `$cfg['Servers'][$i]['port']` or `$cfg['Servers'][$i]['socket']`. See the section on `connect_type` for more details about sockets.

The displayed server name inside phpMyAdmin's interface will be the one entered in `'host'` (unless we enter a non-blank value in the following parameter). For example:

```
$cfg['Servers'][$i]['verbose'] = 'Test server';
```

This feature can thus be used to hide the real server hostname as seen by the users.

extension

The traditional mechanism PHP uses to communicate with a MySQL server, as available in PHP before version 5, is the `mysql` extension. This extension is still available in PHP 5. However, a new extension called `mysqli` has been developed and should be preferred for PHP 5, because of its improved performance and its support of the full functionality of MySQL family 4.1.x. This extension is designed to work with MySQL version 4.1.3 and higher.

In phpMyAdmin version 2.6.0, a new library has been implemented. This has made possible the use of both extensions, choosing either one for a particular server. We indicate the extension we want to use in `$cfg['Servers'][$i]['extension']`.

PersistentConnections

Another important parameter (which is not server-specific but applies to all server definitions) is `$cfg['PersistentConnections']`. For every server we connect to using the `mysql` extension, this parameter, when set to TRUE, instructs PHP to keep the connection to the MySQL server open. This speeds up the interaction between PHP and MySQL. However, it is set to FALSE by default in `config.inc.php` because persistent connections are often a cause of resource depletion on servers. So you will find MySQL refusing new connections. For this reason, the option is not even available for the `mysqli` extension. Hence they setting it to TRUE here would have no effect if you are connecting with this extension.

connect_type, socket and port

Both the `mysql` and `mysqli` extensions automatically use a socket to connect to MySQL if the server is on `localhost`. Consider this configuration:

```
$cfg['Servers'] [$i] ['host']          = 'localhost';
$cfg['Servers'] [$i] ['port']          = '';
$cfg['Servers'] [$i] ['socket']        = '';
$cfg['Servers'] [$i] ['connect_type']  = 'tcp';
$cfg['Servers'] [$i] ['extension']     = 'mysql';
```

The default value for `connect_type` is `tcp`. However, the extension will use a socket because it concludes that this more efficient as the `host` is `localhost`. So in this case, we can use `tcp` or socket as the `connect_type`. To force a real tcp connection, we can specify `127.0.0.1` instead of `localhost` in the `host` parameter. Because the socket parameter is empty, the extension will try the default socket. If this default socket, as defined in `php.ini`, does not correspond to the real socket assigned to the MySQL server, we have to put the socket name (for example, `/tmp/mysql.sock`) in `$cfg['Servers'] [$i] ['socket']`.

If the hostname is not localhost, a tcp connection will occur — here, on the special port 3307. However, leaving the port value empty would use the default 3306 port:

$cfg['Servers'][$i]['host']   = 'mysql.mydomain.com';

$cfg['Servers'][$i]['port']   = '3307';

$cfg['Servers'][$i]['socket']   = '';

$cfg['Servers'][$i]['connect_type'] = 'tcp';

$cfg['Servers'][$i]['extension']   = 'mysql';

compress configuration

Starting with PHP 4.3.0 and MySQL 3.23.49, the protocol used to communicate between PHP and MySQL allows a compressed mode. Using this mode provides better efficiency. To take advantage of this mode, simply specify:

```
$cfg['Servers'][$i]['compress']     = TRUE;
```

Upgrading phpMyAdmin

Normally, upgrading is just a matter of installing the newer version into a separate directory and copying the previous version's `config.inc.php` to the new directory. If the previous version is phpMyAdmin 2.6.0 or older, we cannot copy its `config.inc.php` to the new version because the file format has changed too much.

> An upgrade path or the first-installation path, which should not be taken is to copy `libraries/config.default.php` to `config.inc.php`. This is because the default configuration file is version-specific, and is not guaranteed to work for the future versions.

New parameters appear from version to version. They are documented in `Documentation.html` and defined in `libraries/config.default.php`. If a configuration parameter is not present in `config.inc.php`, its value from `libraries/config.default.php` will be used. Therefore, we do not have to include it in `config.inc.php` if the default value suits us.

Special care must be taken to propagate the changes we might have made to the layout.inc.php files depending on the themes used. We may even have to copy our custom themes subdirectories if we added our own themes to the structure.

Summary

This chapter covers how the web has evolved as a means of delivering applications, and why we should use PHP/MySQL to develop these applications. The chapter also gives an overview of why phpMyAdmin is recognized as a leading application to interface MySQL from the Web and a brief list of its features. It then discusses common reasons for installing phpMyAdmin, steps for downloading it from the main site, basic configuration, uploading phpMyAdmin to our web server, and also about upgrading.

Now that the basic installation has been done, the next chapter will deal with the configuration subject in depth, by exploring the authentication and security aspects.

2
Authentication and Security

There are many ways of configuring authentication in phpMyAdmin—depending on our goals, the presence of other applications, and the level of security we need. This chapter explores the available possibilities.

MySQL authentication

When we type in a username and password, although it seems that we are logging in to phpMyAdmin, we are not! The authentication system is a function of the MySQL server. We are merely using phpMyAdmin (which is running on the web server) as an interface that sends our username and password information to the MySQL server. Strictly speaking, we do not log **in to** phpMyAdmin, but **through** phpMyAdmin.

This is why in user support forums about phpMyAdmin, people asking for help about authentication are often referred back to their MySQL server's administrator, because a lost MySQL user or password is not really a phpMyAdmin problem.

This section explains the various authentication modes offered by phpMyAdmin.

Root user without password

In many cases, MySQL's default installation leaves a server open to intrusion because it creates a MySQL account named `root` without a password. To counter this problem, phpMyAdmin 3.1.0 has introduced a server-specific configuration parameter, `$cfg['Servers'][$i]['AllowNoPasswordRoot']`, which by default is `false`. Generally, this directive should remain `false` to avoid this kind of access via phpMyAdmin, as hackers are actively probing the web for insecure MySQL servers. Go through the *Security* section for other ideas about protecting your server.

If this parameter is set to `false` and a login attempt is made with the `root` account and no password, an **Access denied** message is displayed.

Single-user authentication using config

For our first example, we will use the `config` authentication type, which is easy to understand. However, in the *Multi-user authentication* section, we will see more powerful and versatile ways of authenticating.

 Using the `config` authentication type leaves our phpMyAdmin open to intrusion, unless we protect it as explained in the *Security* section of this chapter.

Here we ask for `config` authentication, and enter our username and password for this MySQL server:

```
$cfg['Servers'][$i]['auth_type']  = 'config';
$cfg['Servers'][$i]['user']       = 'marc';
$cfg['Servers'][$i]['password']   = 'bingo';
```

We can then save the changes we made in `config.inc.php`.

Testing the connection

Now it's time to start phpMyAdmin and try connecting with the values we configured. This will test the following:

- The values we entered in the `config` file or on the web-based setup
- The setup of the PHP component inside the web server, if we did a manual configuration
- Communication between web and MySQL servers

We start our browser and point it to the directory where we installed phpMyAdmin, as in `http://www.mydomain.com/phpMyAdmin`. If this does not work, we try `http://www.mydomain.com/phpMyAdmin/index.php`. (This would mean that our web server is not configured to interpret `index.php` as the default starting document.)

If you still get an error, refer to Appendix B for troubleshooting and support. We should now see phpMyAdmin's homepage. Chapter 3 gives an overview of the panels seen now.

Multi-user authentication

We might want to allow a single copy of phpMyAdmin to be used by a group of persons, each having their own MySQL username and password, and seeing only the databases they have rights to. Or we might prefer to avoid having our username and password in clear text in `config.inc.php`.

Authentication types offered

Instead of relying on a username and password stored in `config.inc.php`, phpMyAdmin will communicate with the browser and get authentication data from it. This enables **true login** for all users defined in a specific MySQL server, without having to define them in the configuration file. There are three modes offered that allow a controlled login to MySQL via phpMyAdmin—`http`, `cookie`, and `signon`. We will have to choose the one that suits our specific situation and environment (more on this in a moment). The `http` and `cookie` modes may require that we first define a control user.

The control user

Defining the control user has two purposes:

- On a MySQL server previous to version 4.1.2 or running with `--skip-show-database`, the control user permits the use of multi-user authentication. This aspect is described in the current section.

- On all versions of MySQL server, this user is necessary to be able to use the advanced relational features of phpMyAdmin, which are described starting at Chapter 11.

To be able to use authentication types for every kind of MySQL user (in MySQL, user privileges may be expressed in various ways), we should define a control user and a password in the server-specific section of a server. If we do not define one, users who have been defined in MySQL with a syntax of `'user'@'hostname'` or `'user'@'%'`, will be able to function normally with phpMyAdmin's features like creating a database, while others won't.

For authentication purposes, the control user is a special user (the usual name we choose for it is `pma`) who has the rights to read some fields in the special mysql database (which contains all the user definitions). phpMyAdmin sends queries with this special control user only for the specific needs of authentication, and not for normal operation. The commands to create the control user are available in phpMyAdmin's `Documentation.html` and may vary from one version to the other. This documentation contains the most current commands.

When our control user is created in the MySQL server, we fill in the parameters as in the following example:

```
$cfg['Servers'][$i]['controluser']     = 'pma';
$cfg['Servers'][$i]['controlpass']      = 'bingo';
```

 I use the bingo password when I teach phpMyAdmin; it is recommended to avoid using the same password for your own installation.

Logging out

Since version 2.10, a mechanism is available to indicate phpMyAdmin, as to which URL it should pass control after a logout. This feature works for all authentication types. Here is an example:

```
$cfg['Servers'][$i]['LogoutURL']       = 'http://www.mydomain.com';
```

This directive must contain an absolute URL, including the protocol.

HTTP authentication

This mode—http—is the traditional mode offered in HTTP, in which the browser asks for the username and password, sends them to phpMyAdmin, and keeps sending them until all the browser's windows are closed.

To enable this mode, we simply use the following line:

```
$cfg['Servers'][$i]['auth_type']        = 'http';
```

This mode has some limitations:

- PHP, depending on the version, might not support HTTP authentication. It works when PHP is running as a module under Apache; for other cases, we should consult the PHP documentation for our version.

- If we want to protect phpMyAdmin's directory with a .htaccess file (see the *Security* section in this chapter), this will interfere with HTTP authentication type; we cannot use both.

- There is not a true logout, as we will have to close all browser windows to be able to login again with the same username.

Even considering those limitations, this mode may be a valuable choice for the following reasons:

- Some browsers can store the authentication information in an unencrypted form
- It is a bit faster than cookie processing

Cookie authentication

The `cookie` authentication mode is superior to `http` in terms of the functionalities offered. It offers true login and logout, and can be used with PHP running on any kind of web server. It presents a login panel (see the following figure) from within phpMyAdmin. This can be customized, as we have the application source code. However, as you may have guessed, for cookie authentication, the browser must accept cookies coming from the web server—true for all authentication modes starting with phpMyAdmin 2.8.0.

This mode stores the username typed in the login screen into a permanent cookie in our browser. The password is stored as a temporary cookie. In a multi-server configuration, the username and password corresponding to each server are stored separately. To protect the username and password secrecy against some attack methods that target cookie content, they are encrypted using the Blowfish mechanism. So, to use this mode, we have to define (once) in `config.inc.php`, a secret password that will be used to securely encrypt all passwords stored as cookies from this phpMyAdmin installation.

This is done by putting a secret password here:

```
$cfg['blowfish_secret'] = 'SantaLivesInCanada';
```

Then, for each server-specific section, use the following:

```
$cfg['Servers'][$i]['auth_type']        = 'cookie';
```

The next time we start phpMyAdmin, we will see the login panel as shown in the following figure:

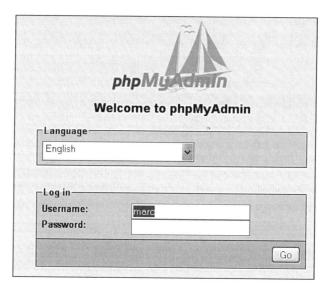

By default, phpMyAdmin displays (in the login panel) the last username for which a successful login was achieved for this particular server, as retrieved from the permanent cookie. If this behavior is not acceptable (if we would prefer that someone else who logs in from the same workstation should not see the previous username), we can set the following parameter to FALSE:

```
$cfg['LoginCookieRecall']        = FALSE;
```

A security feature was added in phpMyAdmin 2.6.0—a time limit for the validity of the entered password. This feature helps to protect the working session. After a successful login, our password is stored in a cookie, along with a timer. Every action in phpMyAdmin resets the timer. If we stay inactive for a certain number of seconds, as defined in $cfg['LoginCookieValidity'], we are disconnected and have to log in again. The default is 1800 seconds.

 The Blowfish algorithm used to protect the username and password requires many computations. To achieve the best possible speed, the PHP's mcrypt extension and its accompanying library must be installed on our web server. Otherwise, phpMyAdmin relies on an internally-coded algorithm, which works, but causes delays of several seconds on almost every operation done from phpMyAdmin! This is because the username and password information must be decoded on every mouse click to be able to connect to MySQL.

Signon authentication

Since version 2.10, the `signon` mode enables us to use the credentials from another application to authenticate to phpMyAdmin. Some applications have their own authentication mechanism, so it's convenient to be able to use this fact to avoid another cumbersome login panel. In order for this to work, this other application has to store the proper credentials into PHP's session data to be retrieved later by phpMyAdmin.

To enable this mode, we start with this directive:

```
$cfg['Servers'][$i]['auth_type'] = 'signon';
```

Let's suppose that the authenticating application has used a session named `FirstApp` to store the credentials. We tell this to phpMyAdmin:

```
$cfg['Servers'][$i] ['SignonSession'] = 'FirstApp';
```

We must take care of users that would try to access phpMyAdmin before the other application; in this case, phpMyAdmin will redirect users to the authenticating application. This is done with

```
$cfg['Servers'][$i] ['SignonURL'] = 'http://www.mydomain.com/
FirstApp';
```

How does the authenticating application store credentials in a format that phpMyAdmin can understand? An example is included as `scripts/signon.php`. In this script, there is a simple HTML form to input the credentials and logic that initializes the session—we would use `FirstApp` as a session name, and create the user, password, and host information into this session:

```
$_SESSION['PMA_single_signon_user'] = $_POST['user'];

$_SESSION['PMA_single_signon_password'] = $_POST['password'];

$_SESSION['PMA_single_signon_host'] = $_POST['host'];
```

> Note that `FirstApp` does not need to ask the MySQL's credentials to the user. These could be hard coded inside the application, as they are secret or there is a known correspondence between the credentials of this application and that of MySQL's.

The authenticating application then uses a way of its choosing—a link or a button—to let its users start phpMyAdmin.

Multi-server configuration

The `config.inc.php` file contains at least one server-specific section; however, we can add more, enabling a single copy of phpMyAdmin to manage many servers. Let us see how to configure more servers.

Servers defined in the configuration file

In the server-specific sections of the `config.inc.php` file, we see lines referring to `$cfg['Servers'][$i]` for each server. Here, the variable `$i` is used so that one can easily cut and paste whole sections of the configuration file to configure more servers. While copying such sections, we should take care that the `$i++;` instruction, which precedes each section and is crucial to delimit the server sections, is also copied.

Then, at the end of the sections, the following line controls what happens at startup:

```
$cfg['ServerDefault'] = 1;
```

The default value, 1, means that phpMyAdmin will connect by itself to the first server defined or present this server choice by default when using advanced authentication (more on this later in this chapter). We can specify any number, for the corresponding server-specific section. We can also enter the value 0, signifying no default server.

This configuration can also be done via web-based setup. Given here is an example of a multi-server definition, with the default server being set to **let the user choose**.

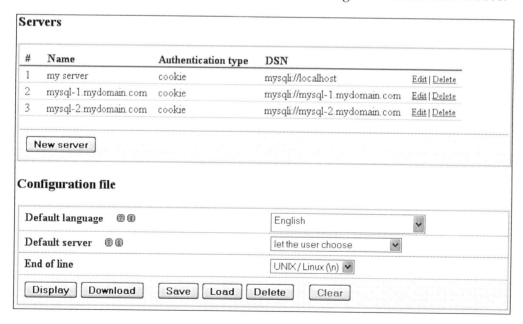

With no default server defined, phpMyAdmin will present a server choice:

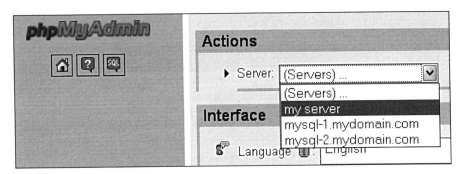

Arbitrary server

Another mechanism can be used if we want to be able to connect to an undefined MySQL server. First, we have to set the following parameter:

```
$cfg['AllowArbitraryServer']     = TRUE;
```

We also have to put back the default value of 1 into $cfg['ServerDefault']. Then, we need to use the cookie authentication type. We will be able to choose the server and enter a username and a password.

Allowing an arbitrary server means that any MySQL server accessible from our web server could be connected to via phpMyAdmin. Therefore, this feature should probably be used in conjunction with a reinforced security mechanism (see the Security section).

As seen here, we still can choose one of the defined servers in **Server Choice**. In addition, we can also enter an arbitrary server name, a username, and a password:

As the tooltip indicates, you can also enter a port number (of course separated from hostname/IP address by space), if this MySQL server is listening on a non-standard port.

Security

Security can be examined at various levels:

- How we can protect the phpMyAdmin installation directory
- Which workstations can access phpMyAdmin
- The databases that a legitimate user can see
- How in-transit data protection and access protection can be enforced via a physical USB key on the workstation

Directory-level protection

Suppose an unauthorized person is trying to execute our copy of phpMyAdmin. If we use the simple config authentication type, anyone knowing the URL of our phpMyAdmin will have the same effective rights to our data as we do. In this case, we should use the directory protection mechanism offered by our web server (for example, .htaccess, a file name with a leading dot) to add a level of protection.

If we decide on using http or cookie authentication types, our data would be safe enough. However, we should take normal precautions with our password (including its periodic change).

The directory where phpMyAdmin is installed contains sensitive data. Not only the configuration file but also all scripts stored there must be protected from alteration. We should ensure that apart from us, only the web server effective user has read access to the files contained in this directory, and that only we can write to them.

 phpMyAdmin's scripts never have to modify anything inside this directory, except when we use the **Save export file to server** feature (explained in Chapter 7).

Another possible attack is from other developers having an account on the same web server as we do. In this kind of attack, someone can try to open our config.inc.php file. As this file is readable by the web server, someone could try to include our file from their PHP scripts. This is why it is recommended to use PHP's open_basedir feature, possibly applying it to all directories from which such attacks could originate.

Error handling

Version 3.0 has introduced a new PHP error trapping behavior in phpMyAdmin, based on PHP's custom error handler mechanism. One of the benefits of this error handler is to avoid path disclosure, which is considered a security weakness. The default settings related to this are:

```
$cfg['Error_Handler'] = array();
$cfg['Error_Handler']['display'] = false;
```

You should let the default value for display to be false, unless you are developing a new phpMyAdmin feature and want to see all PHP errors and warnings.

IP-based access control

An additional level of protection can be added, this time verifying the **Internet Protocol (IP)** address of the machine from which the request to use phpMyAdmin is received.

To achieve this level of protection, we construct rules allowing or denying access, and specify the order in which these rules will be applied.

Rules

The format of a rule is:

```
<'allow' | 'deny'> <username> [from] <source>
```

`from` being optional, here are some examples:

Rule	Description
allow Bob from 1.2.3.4	User `Bob` is allowed access from IP address 1.2.3.4.
allow Bob from 1.2.3/24	User `Bob` is allowed from any address matching the network 1.2.3 (this is CIDR IP matching).
deny Alice from 4.5/16	User `Alice` cannot access when located on network 4.5.
allow Melanie from all	User `Melanie` can login from anywhere.

Rule	Description
`allow Julie from localhost`	Equivalent to 127.0.0.1
`deny % from all`	`all` can be used as an equivalent to 0.0.0.0/0, meaning any host. Here, the `%` sign means any user.

The source part can also be formed with the special names `localnetA`, `localnetB`, or `localnetC`. These represent the complete class A, B, or C network in which the web server is located. Note that phpMyAdmin relies on the `$_SERVER["SERVER_ADDR"]` PHP parameter for this feature. Usually we will have several rules. Let's say we wish to have the two rules that follow:

```
allow Marc from 45.34.23.12
allow Melanie from all
```

We have to put them in `config.inc.php` (in the related server-specific section) as follows:

```
$cfg['Servers'][$i]['AllowDeny']['rules'] =
  array('allow Marc from 45.34.23.12',
    'allow Melanie from all');
```

When defining a single rule or multiple rules, a PHP array is used. We must follow its syntax, enclosing each complete rule within single quotes and separating each rule from the next with a comma. Thus, if we have only one rule, we must still use an array to specify it like this:

```
$cfg['Servers'][$i]['AllowDeny']['rules'] =
  array('allow Marc from 45.34.23.12');
```

The next parameter explains the order in which rules are interpreted.

Order of interpretation for rules

By default, this parameter is empty:

```
$cfg['Servers'][$i]['AllowDeny']['order'] = '';
```

This means that no IP-based verification is made.

Suppose we want to allow access by default, denying access only to some username/ IP pairs. We should use:

```
$cfg['Servers'][$i]['AllowDeny']['order'] = 'deny,allow';
```

In this case, all `deny` rules will be applied first, followed by `allow` rules. If a case is not mentioned in the rules, access is granted. Being more restrictive, we'd want to deny by default. We can use:

```
$cfg['Servers'][$i]['AllowDeny']['order'] = 'allow,deny';
```

This time, all `allow` rules are applied first, followed by `deny` rules. If a case is not mentioned in the rules, access is denied. The third (and most restrictive) way of specifying rules order is:

```
$cfg['Servers'][$i]['AllowDeny']['order'] = 'explicit';
```

Now, `deny` rules are applied before `allow` rules. But for them to be accepted, a username/IP address must be listed in the `allow` rules, and not in the `deny` rules.

Simplified rule for root access

As the `root` user is present in almost all MySQL installations, it's often the target of attacks. Starting with phpMyAdmin 2.6.1, a parameter permits us to easily block all logins of the MySQL's `root` account, using the following:

```
$cfg['Servers'][$i]['AllowRoot']      = FALSE;
```

Restricting the list of databases

Sometimes it is useful to avoid showing in the left panel, all the databases a user has access to. phpMyAdmin offers two ways of restricting—`only_db` and `hide_db`.

To specify the list of what can be seen, the `only_db` parameter is used. It may contain a database name or a list of database names. Only these databases will be seen in the left panel:

```
$cfg['Servers'][$i]['only_db']        = 'payroll';
$cfg['Servers'][$i]['only_db']        = array('payroll', 'hr');
```

The database names can contain MySQL wildcard characters like _ and %. If an array is used to specify many databases, they will be displayed on the interface in the same order they are listed in the array.

Another feature of `only_db` is that you can use it not to restrict the list, but instead to put emphasis on certain names that will be displayed on top of the list. Here, the `myspecial` database name will appear first, followed by all other names:

```
$cfg['Servers'][$i]['only_db']        = array('myspecial', '*');
```

We can also indicate which database names must be hidden with the `hide_db` parameter. It contains a regular expression (`http://en.wikipedia.org/wiki/Regular_expression`) representing what to exclude. If we do not want users to see all databases whose names begin with 'secret', we would use:

```
$cfg['Servers'][$i]['hide_db']         = '^secret';
```

These parameters apply to all users for this server-specific configuration.

 These mechanisms do not replace the MySQL privilege system. Users' rights on other databases still apply, but they cannot use phpMyAdmin's left panel to navigate to their other databases or tables.

Protecting in-transit data

HTTP is not inherently immune to network sniffing (grabbing sensitive data off the wire). So, if we want to protect not only our username and password but all the data that travels between our web server and browser, we have to use HTTPS.

To do so, assuming that our web server supports HTTPS, we just have to start phpMyAdmin by putting `https` instead of `http` in the URL as follows:

```
https://www.mydomain.com/phpMyAdmin
```

If we are using `PmaAbsoluteUri` auto-detection:

```
$cfg['PmaAbsoluteUri'] = '';
```

phpMyAdmin will see that we are using HTTPS in the URL and react accordingly. If not, we must put the `https` part in this parameter as follows:

```
$cfg['PmaAbsoluteUri'] = 'https://www.mydomain.com/phpMyAdmin';
```

Also, since phpMyAdmin 2.7.0, we can automatically switch users to an HTTPS connection with this setting:

```
$cfg['ForceSSL'] = TRUE;
```

Swekey hardware authentication

Since version 3.1, support for the Swekey hardware authentication key has been merged to cookie-based authentication in phpMyAdmin. Reference for this USB key is available at `http://phpmyadmin.net/auth_key`. A Swekey can be used with all compatible web applications to add a level of security, based on the possession of this physical device. In the case of phpMyAdmin, it does not replace the normal MySQL authentication.

Configuration

The `contrib/swekey.sample.cont` sample file should be used as a starting point
to configure this feature. This file contains sample configuration commands and
comments from the vendor. The principle is simple—each Swekey device contains
a unique id, and this id must be associated with a MySQL username in the Swekey
configuration file. These lines are part of the sample file:

```
00000000000000000000000000000763A:root

000000000000000000000000000089E4:steve

0000000000000000000000000000231E:scott
```

This means that the person responsible with the phpMyAdmin configuration, tracks
which Swekey is given to each user and puts this information in the file. The vendor
does not need to be informed about this association. They only keep track of which
Swekey are sold and which are deactivated. Hence, Swekey can be passed from one
user to another, provided that the configuration is updated accordingly.

Other security-related directives are in the sample file, and it's recommended
to refrain from changing them—SERVER_CHECK, SERVER_RNDTOKEN, and
SERVER_STATUS in particular. This is because these directives access servers via https,
which is a guaranty of a secure channel between our web server and the vendor's.

Once modified, this file should be copied over to a directory outside the web server's
document root (suggested place is `/etc/swekey-pma.conf`). Then, a configuration
parameter in `config.inc.php` must be set as well:

```
$cfg['Servers'][$i]['auth_swekey_config'] = '/etc/swekey-pma.conf';
```

Usage

Let's see what happens now when phpMyAdmin is started and no Swekey is
connected to your workstation:

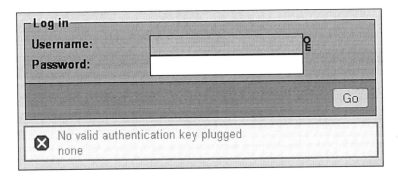

We notice three changes:

- The username field cannot be typed in
- A small key icon is displayed
- An error message appears

It's normal that the username field is deactivated, as user names are now taken from the Swekey configuration file. The icon can be clicked to reach the vendor's website. There is a testing mechanism on this site, to verify if a Swekey is connected. Drivers can also be downloaded in case the automatic installation did not work.

Now if you connect your Swekey, assuming that user `marc` has been defined and associated to this device, a reassuring panel is displayed:

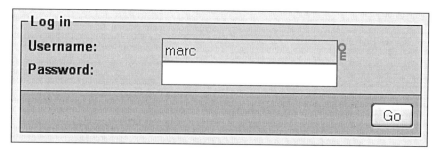

Security note

It would not make sense to rely on the protection offered by this device, if our users have access to a webspace on which they can install their own copy of phpMyAdmin. Obviously, phpMyAdmin has to be configured accordingly to make use of the Swekey. Hence, a user-installed copy of phpMyAdmin would circumvent the protection. This means that a host provider should permit access to his MySQL server, only from a web server on which he/she installed a controlled copy of phpMyAdmin, and on which other users cannot install their own copy.

Summary

This chapter gives us an overview of how to use a single copy of phpMyAdmin to manage multiple servers, and also the usage of authentication types to fulfill the needs of a users' group while protecting authentication credentials. The chapter also covers the ways of securing our phpMyAdmin installation.

We'll now have a look at all the panels and windows that comprise the user interface of phpMyAdmin.

3
Interface Overview

Before delving into task-oriented chapters, such as searching and the like, it's appropriate to have a look at the general organization of phpMyAdmin's interface. We'll also see configuration parameters and settings that influence the interface as a whole.

Panels and windows

The phpMyAdmin interface is composed of various panels and windows, each one having a specific function. We will first provide a quick overview of each panel, and then take a detailed look later in this chapter.

Login panels

The login panel that appears depends on the authentication type chosen. For the `http` type, it will take the form of our browser's HTTP authentication pop up screen. For the `cookie` type, the phpMyAdmin-specific login panel will be displayed. (This is covered in Chapter 2.) For the external authentication (`signon`), the login panel is handled by the external application itself. By default, a **Server** choice dialog and a **Language** selector are present on this panel.

However, if we are using the `config` authentication type, no login panel is displayed, and the first displayed interface contains the left and the right panels.

Left and right panels

These panels go together and are displayed during most of our working session with phpMyAdmin. The **left panel** is our navigation guide through the databases and tables. The **right panel** is the main working area where the data is managed and results appear. Its exact layout depends on the choices made from the left panel and the sequence of operations performed. For right-to-left languages like Hebrew, the navigation panel is located on the right side and the main panel is on the left.

Table	Action						Records[1]	Type	Collation	Size
columns_priv						✕	1	MyISAM	utf8_bin	6.6 KiB
db						✕	70	MyISAM	utf8_bin	33.9 KiB
func						✕	0	MyISAM	utf8_bin	1.0 KiB
help_category						✕	0	MyISAM	utf8_general_ci	1.0 KiB
help_keyword						✕	0	MyISAM	utf8_general_ci	1.0 KiB
help_relation						✕	0	MyISAM	utf8_general_ci	1.0 KiB
help_topic						✕	0	MyISAM	utf8_general_ci	1.0 KiB
host						✕	0	MyISAM	utf8_bin	1.0 KiB
proc						✕	2	MyISAM	utf8_general_ci	8.3 KiB
procs_priv						✕	0	MyISAM	utf8_bin	1.0 KiB
tables_priv						✕	8	MyISAM	utf8_bin	20.0 KiB
time_zone						✕	0	MyISAM	utf8_general_ci	1.0 KiB
time_zone_leap_second						✕	0	MyISAM	utf8_general_ci	1.0 KiB
time_zone_name						✕	0	MyISAM	utf8_general_ci	1.0 KiB

Homepage

The right panel can take the form of the homepage. The homepage will then contain various links related to MySQL operations or phpMyAdmin information, a **Language** selector, and possibly the themes selector.

Views

In the right panel, we can see the **Database** view — where we can take various actions about a specific database, or the **Table** view — where we can access many functions to manage a table. There is also a **Server** view, useful for both system administrators and non-administrator users. All these views have a top menu, which takes the form of tabs that lead to different subpages used to present information regrouped by common functions (table structure, privileges, and so on).

Please do not confuse the term view — used here in the interface sense — with the MySQL 5.0's notion of SQL views (covered in Chapter 17).

Query window

This is a distinct window that is usually opened from the left panel — and sometimes from the right panel when editing an SQL query. Its main purpose is to facilitate work on queries and display the results on the right panel.

Starting page

When we start phpMyAdmin, we will see the following (depending on the authentication type specified in config.inc.php, and on whether it has more than one server defined in it):

- One of the login panels
- The left and right panels with the homepage displayed in the right panel

General customization

This section describes settings that have an impact on many panels. These settings modify the appearance of titles in windows, of information icons, and how the list of tables is sorted. The whole visual style of all pages is controlled by the theme system, which is covered here altogether.

Window titles configuration

When the left and right panels are displayed, the window's title changes to reflect which MySQL server, database, and table are active. phpMyAdmin also shows some information about the web server's host name if $cfg['ShowHttpHostTitle'] is set to TRUE. What is displayed depends on another setting—$cfg['SetHttpHostTitle']. If this setting is empty (as it is by default), the true web server's host name appears in the title. We can put another string, such as "my Web server", and this will be shown instead of the true host name.

Seeing the web server's host name can come in handy when we have many phpMyAdmin windows open, thus being connected to more than one web server. Of course, each phpMyAdmin window can itself give access to many MySQL servers.

Icon configuration

When various warning, error, or information messages are displayed, they can be accompanied by an icon, if $cfg['ErrorIconic'] is set to TRUE. Another parameter, $cfg['ReplaceHelpImg'], when set to TRUE, displays a small icon containing a question mark at every place where documentation is available for a specific subject. These two parameters are set to TRUE by default, thus producing:

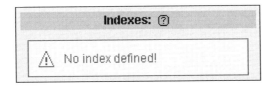

They can be independently set to FALSE. Setting both to FALSE would give:

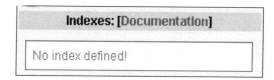

Natural sort order for database and table names

Usually, computers sort items in lexical order, which gives the following results for a list of tables:

```
table1
table10
table2
table3
```

phpMyAdmin implements "natural sort order" by default, as specified by $cfg['NaturalOrder'] being TRUE. Thus the database and table lists in left and right panels are sorted as:

```
table1
table2
table3
table10
```

Site-specific header and footer

Some users may want to display a company logo, a link to the helpdesk, or other information on the phpMyAdmin interface. In the main phpMyAdmin directory, for this purpose, we can create two scripts — config.header.inc.php and config.footer.inc.php. We can put our own PHP or XHTML code in these scripts, and it will appear either at the beginning (for header) or end of page (for footer) in case of the following:

- On the cookie login page
- On the right panel

For example, creating a config.footer.inc.php containing these lines:

```
<hr />
<em>All the information on this page is confidential.</em>
```

would produce the intended message on all pages:

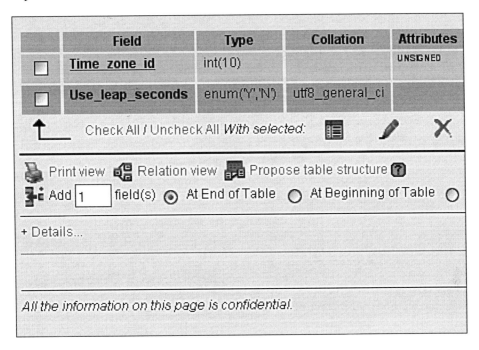

	Field	Type	Collation	Attributes
☐	**Time_zone_id**	int(10)		UNSIGNED
☐	**Use_leap_seconds**	enum('Y','N')	utf8_general_ci	

↑ Check All / Uncheck All *With selected:* ▦ ✎ ✕

🖨 Print view ◧ Relation view ▦ Propose table structure ⑦

🔧 Add 1 field(s) ⊙ At End of Table ○ At Beginning of Table ○

+ Details...

All the information on this page is confidential.

MySQL documentation links

phpMyAdmin displays links to the MySQL documentation at various places on its interface. These links refer to the exact point in the official MySQL documentation to learn about a MySQL command. We can customize the location, language, and manual type referred to, with the following configuration parameters:

```
$cfg['MySQLManualBase'] = 'http://www.mysql.com/doc/en';
$cfg['MySQLManualType'] = 'searchable';
```

You may take a look at http://www.mysql.com/documentation to see the languages in which the manual is available, and change the parameters accordingly. For the manual type, the most up-to-date possible values are explained as comments in config.inc.php. Users who prefer to keep a copy of this documentation on a local server would specify a local link here.

The $cfg['ReplaceHelpImg'] parameter controls how the links are displayed. Its default value of TRUE makes phpMyAdmin display small question-mark icons. However, if it has FALSE value, we are shown the **Documentation** link.

Themes

A theme system is available in phpMyAdmin starting with version 2.6.0. The color parameters and the various icons are located in a directory structure under the themes subdirectory. For each available theme, there is a subdirectory named after the theme. It contains:

- layout.inc.php for the theme parameters
- css directory with the various CSS scripts
- img directory containing the icons
- screen.png, a screenshot of this theme

The downloaded kit contains two themes, and more themes are available at http://phpmyadmin.net/home_page/themes.php.

Theme configuration

In config.inc.php, the $cfg['ThemePath'] parameter contains 'themes' by default, indicating which subdirectory the required structure is located in. This could be changed to point to another directory where our company's specific phpMyAdmin themes are located.

The default chosen theme is specified in $cfg['ThemeDefault'], and is set to 'original'. If no theme selection is available for users, this theme will be used.

 The original subdirectory should never be deleted; phpMyAdmin relies on it for normal operations.

Theme selection

On the **Home**page, we can offer a theme selector to users. Setting $cfg['ThemeManager'] to TRUE (the default) shows the selector:

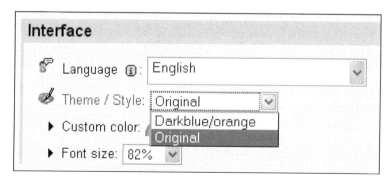

To help choose a suitable theme, the color palette icon next to **Theme/Style** brings us screenshots of the available themes. We can then click on **take it** under the theme we want. The chosen theme is remembered in a cookie. By default, the remembered theme applies to all servers we connect to. To make phpMyAdmin remember one theme per MySQL server, we set $cfg[ThemePerServer] to TRUE.

The color picker

Here is a feature—the custom color picker— that may seem frivolous but has its utility. We'll discuss first the *how* and then the *why*.

Located on the homepage, the small rainbow icon gives access to a picker, which controls the background color of both panels. The phpMyAdmin team merged the MooRainbow code from Djamil Legato (http://moorainbow.woolly-sheep.net) to offer this feature.

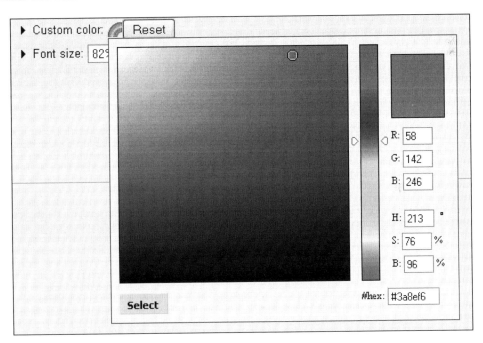

You can operate the picker in many ways—moving the slider, moving the mouse in the big square, or directly entering values in the fields. When you are done, you click **Select** to clear the picker.

The purpose of this feature is to help users who are working simultaneously on many MySQL servers, and like to have visual clues about each server. Another possible scenario—a busy database administrator—who takes calls from customers and opens many phpMyAdmin windows. He then assigns priorities using the color picker, say red for top priority—you get the idea.

Sliders

You'll see on some pages, a small plus sign followed by a controlling label—either **Options** or **Details**. A click on the label opens a slider to reveal a section of the interface, which is believed to be less often used in day-to-day work. As some persons prefer to immediately see the whole interface—at the expense of screen space—there is a configuration parameter that controls how the sliders are initially set:

```
$cfg['InitialSlidersState'] = 'closed';
```

The default value of closed means that sliders must be opened by a click on the label; you might have guessed that the reverse value is open. This Javascript feature comes from the Mootools library located at http://mootools.net.

Character sets, collations and language

A **character set** describes how symbols for a specific language or dialect are encoded. A **collation** contains rules to compare and sort the characters of a character set. The character set used to store our data may be different from the one used to display it, leading to data discrepancies. Thus, a need to transform the data arises.

Since MySQL 4.1.x, the MySQL server does the character recoding work for us. Also, MySQL enables us to indicate the character set and collation for each database, each table, and even each field. A default character set for a database applies to each of its tables, unless it is overridden at the table level. The same principle applies to every field.

Collations

When strings have to be compared and sorted, precise rules must be followed by the system (MySQL in this case). For example, is "A" equivalent to "a"? Is 'André' equivalent to "Andre"? A set of these rules is called a collation.

A proper choice of collation is important for obtaining the intended results when searching data (for example from phpMyAdmin's **Search** page), and also when sorting data.

For an introduction to collations, see `http://dev.mysql.com/doc/mysql/en/Charset-general.htm`, and for a more technical explanation of the algorithms involved, refer to `http://www.unicode.org/reports/tr10/`.

Unicode and UTF-8

> *Unicode is an industry standard designed to allow text and symbols […] to be consistently represented and manipulated by computers.*

For more information, visit `http://en.wikipedia.org/wiki/Unicode` and `http://www.unicode.org`.

Unicode currently supports more than 600 languages, which is its main advantage over other character sets available with ISO or Windows. This is especially important with a multi-language product like phpMyAdmin.

To represent or encode these Unicode characters, many **Unicode Transformation Formats (UTF)** exist. A popular transformation format is UTF-8, which uses one to four octets per character. For more details, visit `http://en.wikipedia.org/wiki/UTF-8`.

Note that the browser must support UTF-8 (as most current browsers do). The phpMyAdmin distribution kit includes a UTF-8 version of every language file in the `lang` subdirectory.

Language selection

A **Language** selector appears on the login panel (if any) and on the homepage. The default behavior of phpMyAdmin is to use the language defined in our browser's preferences, if there is a corresponding language file for this version.

The default language used — in case the program cannot detect one — is defined in `config.inc.php`, in the `$cfg['DefaultLang']` parameter with `'en-utf-8'`. This value can be changed. The possible values for language names are defined in the `libraries/select_lang.lib.php` script as an array.

Even if the default language is defined, each user (especially on a multi-user installation) can choose his/her preferred language from the selector. The user's choice will be remembered in a cookie whenever possible.

We can also force a single language by setting the $cfg['Lang'] parameter with a value, such as 'fr-utf-8'. Starting with version 2.7.0, another parameter, $cfg['FilterLanguages'], is available. Suppose we want to shorten the list of available languages to **English** and **Français — French**, as those are the ones used exclusively by our users. This is accomplished building a regular expression indicating which languages we want to display based on the ISO 639 codes of these languages. To continue with our example, we would use:

```
$cfg['FilterLanguages']   = '^(fr|en)';
```

In this expression, the caret (^) means **starting with** and the (|) means **or**. The expression indicates that we are restricting the list to languages whose corresponding ISO codes start with fr or en.

By default, this parameter is empty, meaning that no filter is applied to the list of available languages.

The small information icon beside **Language** gives access to phpMyAdmin's translator page, which lists, by language, the official translator and the contact information. This way, we can reach the translator for corrections, or to offer help on untranslated messages.

Effective character sets and collations

On the homepage, we can see the **MySQL charset** information and a **MySQL connection collation** selector. Here is the **MySQL charset** information:

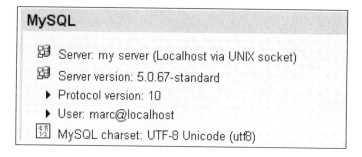

The character set information (as seen here after **MySQL charset**) comes directly from the $charset variable located in the language file that corresponds to the currently selected language. It is used to generate HTML information, which tells the browser what is the page's character set.

We can also choose which character set and collation will be used for our connection to the MySQL server using the **MySQL connection collation** dialog. This is passed to the MySQL server. MySQL then transforms the characters that will be sent to our browser into this character set. MySQL also interprets what it receives from the browser according to the character set information. Remember that all tables and fields have a character set information describing how their data is encoded.

Normally, the default value should work. However, if we are entering some characters using a different character set, we can choose the proper character set in this dialog.

The following parameter defines both the default connection collation and character set:

```
$cfg['DefaultConnectionCollation'] = 'utf8_unicode_ci';
```

Left panel (navigation)

The left panel contains the following elements:

- The logo (see the next section)
- The server list (if `$cfg['LeftDisplayServers']` is set to TRUE)
- The **Home** link or icon (takes you back to the phpMyAdmin homepage)
- A **Log out** link or icon
- A link or icon leading to the **Query window**
- Icons to display phpMyAdmin and MySQL documentation
- The databases and tables with statistics about the number of tables per database

If `$cfg['MainPageIconic']` is set to TRUE (the default), we see the **icons**. However, if it is set to FALSE, we see the **Home**, **Log out**, and **Query window** links.

The left panel can be resized by clicking and moving the vertical separation line in the preferred direction to reveal more data, in case the database or table names are too long for the default left panel size.

We can customize the appearance of this panel. Generally, all parameters are located in `themes/themename/layout.inc.php` unless stated otherwise. `$cfg['LeftWidth']` contains the default width of the left frame in pixels. The background color is defined in `$cfg['LeftBgColor']` with a default value of `'#D0DCE0'`. The `$cfg['LeftPointerColor']` parameter, with a default value of `'#CCFFCC'`, defines the pointer color. (The pointer appears when we are using the Full mode, discussed shortly.) To activate the left pointer for any theme being used, a master setting, `$cfg['LeftPointerEnable']`, exists in `config.inc.php`. Its default value is TRUE.

Logo configuration

The logo display behavior is controlled by a number of parameters. First, `$cfg['LeftDisplayLogo']` has to be set to TRUE, to enable any displaying of the logo. It is `true` by default. A click on this logo brings the interface to the page listed in the `$cfg['LeftLogoLink']` parameter, which is usually the main phpMyAdmin page (default value `main.php`), but can be any URL. Finally, the `$cfg['LeftLogoLinkWindow']` parameter indicates in which window the new page appears after a click on the logo. By default, it's on the main page (value `main`). However, it could be on a brand new window by using the value `new`.

The logo image itself comes from the `logo_left.png` file, which is located in each specific theme directory structure.

Database and table list

The following examples show that no database has been chosen yet:

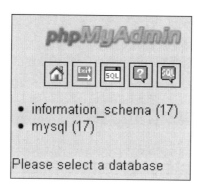

It is also possible to see the following screen:

This means that our current MySQL rights do not allow us to see any existing databases.

 A MySQL server always has at least one database (named **mysql**), but in this case, we do not have the right to see it. Moreover, as MySQL 5.0.2, a special database called **information_schema** appears at all times in the database list. It contains a set of views describing the metadata visible for the logged-in user.

We may have the right to create one, as explained in Chapter 4.

Light mode

The left panel can be shown in two ways—the Light mode and the Full mode. The Light mode is used by default, defined by a TRUE value in $cfg['LeftFrameLight']. This mode shows a drop-down list of the available databases, and only tables of the currently chosen database are displayed. It is more efficient than Full Mode; the reason is explained in the *Full Mode* section appearing later in the chapter. Here we have chosen the **mysql** database:

Clicking on a name opens the right panel in the **Database** view, and clicking on a table name opens the right panel in the **Table** view to browse this table. (see the *Right Panel* section for details.)

Tree display of database names

A user might be allowed to work on a single database — for example **marc**. Some system administrators offer a more flexible scheme by allowing user **marc** to create many databases, provided all have their names starting with **marc**, such as **marc_airline** and **marc_car**. In this situation, the left panel can be set to display a tree of these database names, like this:

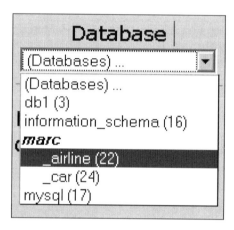

This feature is currently offered only in light mode, and is controlled by these parameters:

```
$cfg['LeftFrameDBTree']         = TRUE;
$cfg['LeftFrameDBSeparator']   = '_';
```

The default value of TRUE in $cfg['LeftFrameDBTree'] ensures that this feature is activated. A popular value for the separator is '_'.

Full mode

The previous examples were shown in Light mode, but setting the $cfg['LeftFrameLight'] parameter to FALSE produces a complete layout of our databases and tables using collapsible menus (if supported by the browser):

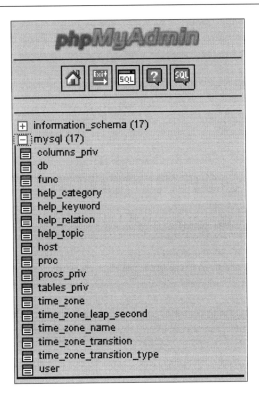

The number of tables per database is shown in brackets. The Full mode is not selected by default; it can increase network traffic and server load if our current rights give us access to a large number of databases and tables. Links must be generated in the left panel to enable table access and quick-browse access to every table. Also, the server has to count the number of rows for all tables.

Table short statistics

Moving the cursor over a table name displays comments about the table (if any), and the number of rows currently in it:

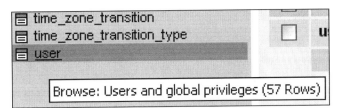

Table quick-access icon

Starting with version 3.0, it was established that the most common action on a table must be to browse it. Therefore, a click on the table name itself opens it in browse mode. The small icon beside each table name is a quick way to do another action on each table, and by default, it brings us to **Structure** view.

The `$cfg['LeftDefaultTabTable']` parameter controls this action. It has a default value of `'tbl_structure.php'`, which is the script showing the table's structure. Other possible values for this parameter are listed in `Documentation.html`.

Nested display of tables within a database

MySQL's data structure is based on two levels—databases and tables. This does not allow subdivisions of tables per project, a feature often requested by MySQL users. They must rely on having multiple databases, but this is not always allowed by their provider. To help them with this regard, phpMyAdmin introduces a **nested-levels** feature, based on the table naming.

Let's say we have access to the **db1** database, and we want to represent two projects, **marketing** and **payroll**. Using a special separator (by default a double underscore) between the project name and the table name, we create the **payroll__employees** and **payroll__jobs tables**, achieving a visually interesting effect:

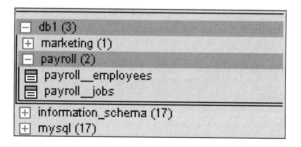

This feature is parameterized with `$cfg['LeftFrameTableSeparator']` (set here to `'__'`) to choose the characters that will mark each level change, and `$cfg['LeftFrameTableLevel']` (set here to `'1'`) for the number of sub-levels.

The nested-level feature is intended only for improving the left panel look. The proper way to reference the tables in MySQL statements stays the same—for example, `db1.payroll__jobs`.

Beginning with phpMyAdmin 2.6.0, a click in the left panel on the project name (here **payroll**) opens this project in the right panel, showing only those tables associated with that project.

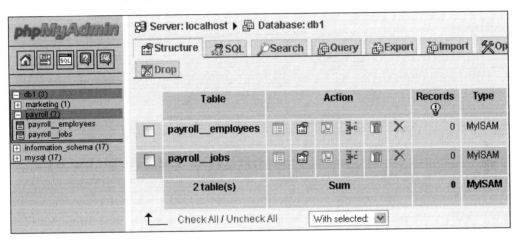

Server-list choice

If we have to manage multiple servers from the same phpMyAdmin window and often need to switch between servers, it might prove useful to always have the list of servers in the left panel.

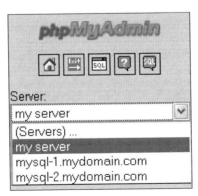

For this, the $cfg['LeftDisplayServers']$ parameter must be set to TRUE. The list of servers can have two forms—a drop-down list or links. Which form appears depends on $cfg['DisplayServersList']$. By default, this parameter is set to FALSE, so we see a drop-down list of servers. Setting $cfg['DisplayServersList']$ to TRUE produces a list of links to all defined servers:

Handling many databases or tables

This section describes some techniques to cope with a server holding a huge number of databases and tables.

Limits on the interface

Before phpMyAdmin 2.11, it was difficult to work with the interface if we had access to hundreds or even thousands of databases, or hundreds of tables in the same database. Loading of the navigation panel was slow, or did not work at all. In 2.11, the interface has been reworked to take care of this.

Two new parameters, shown here with their default values, establish a limit on the number of databases and tables displayed, by adding a page selector and navigation links:

```
$cfg['MaxDbList'] = 100;

$cfg['MaxTableList'] = 250;
```

The effect of $cfg['MaxDbList']$ can be seen on the main panel in **Server** view:

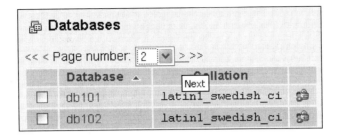

We can also see the effect in the navigation panel:

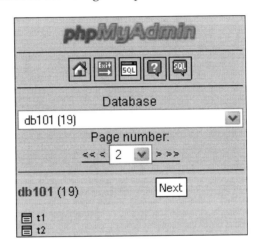

Improving fetch speed

Version 3.0 introduced two configuration parameters that have an effect on the speed of database names retrieval and table counting. The first one is

```
$cfg['Servers'][$i]['ShowDatabasesCommand'] = 'SHOW DATABASES';
```

Every time phpMyAdmin needs to obtain the list of databases from the server, it uses the command listed in this parameter. The default command SHOW DATABASES is fine in ordinary situations. However, on servers with many databases, speed improvements can be observed by trying other commands like one of these:

```
SHOW DATABASES LIKE '#user#\_%'

SELECT DISTINCT TABLE_SCHEMA FROM information_schema.SCHEMA_
PRIVILEGES'

SELECT SCHEMA_NAME FROM information_schema.SCHEMATA
```

In the first example, #user# is replaced by the current username.

In extreme situations (thousands of databases), a user who installs his own copy of phpMyAdmin should put `false` in this parameter. This would block any database names fetching, and would require to populate the `$cfg['Servers'][$i]['only_db']` parameter with this user's database list.

Another parameter that can help is `$cfg['Servers'][$i]['CountTables']`, which has a default value of `true`. Setting it to `false` would instruct phpMyAdmin to avoid counting the tables when producing the list of databases and tables in the navigation panel (in Full mode).

Right panel (main)

The right panel is the main working area, and all the possible views for it are explained in the following sections. Its appearance can be customized. The background color is defined in `$cfg['RightBgColor']`, and the default color is #F5F5F5. We can also select a background image by setting the URI of the image we want (for example, `http://www.domain.com/images/clouds.jpg`) in `$cfg['RightBgImage']`.

Homepage

The homepage may contain a varying number of links depending on the login mode and the user's rights. A normal user may see it as:

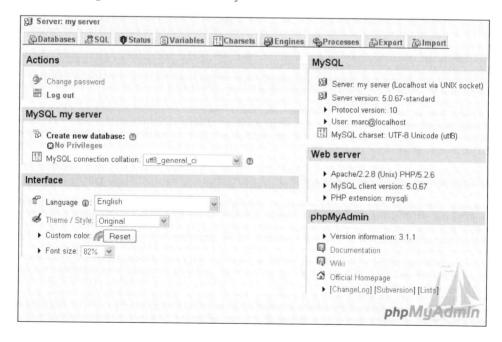

The **Home** link from the left panel is used to display this page. It shows the phpMyAdmin and MySQL versions, the MySQL server name, and the logged-in user. We also see that this user does not have the privileges to create a database. We see some links that relate to MySQL or phpMyAdmin itself. The **Log out** link might not be there if the user did not log in, as indicated by the configuration file's `$cfg['Servers'][$i]['auth_type']` parameter being set to `config`.

In this example, a normal user is allowed to change his/her password from the interface. To disallow this password change, we set `$cfg['ShowChgPassword']` to `FALSE`. Privileged users have more options on the homepage. They can always create databases and have more links to manage the server as a whole—for example the **Privileges** link (more on this in Chapter 18). Another setting, `$cfg['ShowPhpInfo']`, can be set to `TRUE` if we want to see the **Show PHP Information** link on the homepage.

Database view

phpMyAdmin goes into this view (shown in the screenshot that follows) every time we click on a database name from the left frame, or if the `USE` command followed by a database name is typed in a SQL box.

This is where we can see an overview of the database—the existing tables, a link to create a table, the tabs to the Database view subpages, and some special operations we might do on this database to generate documentation and statistics. There is a checkbox beside each table to make global operations on that table (covered in Chapter 10). The table is chosen by using the checkbox or by clicking anywhere on the row's background. We can also see each table's size, if `$cfg['ShowStats']` is set to `TRUE`. This parameter also controls the display of table-specific statistics in the Table view.

The initial screen that appears here is the database **Structure** subpage. We might want a different initial subpage to appear while entering the Database view. This is controlled by the `$cfg['DefaultTabDatabase']` parameter, and the available choices are given in the configuration file as comments.

Server: my server ▸ Database: mysql									
Structure **SQL** **Search** **Query** **Export** **Import** **Operations** **Privileges** **Drop**									
Table		Action				Records¹	Type	Collation	Size	Overhead
☐ columns_priv					×	1	MyISAM	utf8_bin	6.6 KiB	810 B
☐ db					×	69	MyISAM	utf8_bin	33.9 KiB	438 B
☐ func					×	0	MyISAM	utf8_bin	1.0 KiB	-
☐ help_category					×	0	MyISAM	utf8_general_ci	1.0 KiB	-
☐ help_keyword					×	0	MyISAM	utf8_general_ci	1.0 KiB	-
☐ help_relation					×	0	MyISAM	utf8_general_ci	1.0 KiB	-
☐ help_topic					×	0	MyISAM	utf8_general_ci	1.0 KiB	-
☐ host					×	0	MyISAM	utf8_bin	1.0 KiB	-
☐ proc					×	2	MyISAM	utf8_general_ci	8.3 KiB	5.1 KiB
☐ procs_priv					×	0	MyISAM	utf8_bin	1.0 KiB	-
☐ tables_priv					×	8	MyISAM	utf8_bin	20.0 KiB	8.3 KiB
☐ time_zone					×	0	MyISAM	utf8_general_ci	1.0 KiB	-
☐ time_zone_leap_second					×	0	MyISAM	utf8_general_ci	1.0 KiB	-
☐ time_zone_name					×	0	MyISAM	utf8_general_ci	1.0 KiB	-
☐ time_zone_transition					×	0	MyISAM	utf8_general_ci	1.0 KiB	-
☐ time_zone_transition_type					×	0	MyISAM	utf8_general_ci	1.0 KiB	-
☐ user					×	57	MyISAM	utf8_bin	6.4 KiB	188 B
17 table(s)		Sum				137	**MyISAM**	latin1_swedish_ci	**87.2 KiB**	**14.8 KiB**

The number of records is obtained using a quick method, the SHOW TABLE STATUS statement — not by using a SELECT COUNT(*) FROM TABLENAME. This quick method is usually accurate, except for InnoDB tables, which returns an approximate number of records. To help get the correct number of records, even for InnoDB, the `$cfg['MaxExactCount']` parameter is available. If the approximate number of records is lower than this parameter's value — by default, 20000 — the slower SELECT COUNT(*) method will be used.

> Do not put a value too high for this parameter. You would get correct results, but only after waiting for a few minutes, if there are hundreds of thousands of records in your InnoDB table.

A user might be surprised when seeing the term **KiB** in the **Size** and **Overhead** columns. phpMyAdmin has adopted the **International Electrotechnical Commission (IEC)** binary prefixes (see `http://en.wikipedia.org/wiki/Binary_prefix`). The displayed values are defined in each language file. Here is the definition for English:

```
$byteUnits = array('B', 'KiB', 'MiB', 'GiB', 'TiB', 'PiB', 'EiB');
```

Table view

This is a commonly used view, giving access to all table-specific subpages. Usually, the initial screen is the table's **Structure** screen, which shows all fields and (under the **Details** link) the indexes. Note that the header for this screen always shows the current database and table names. We also see the comments set for the table:

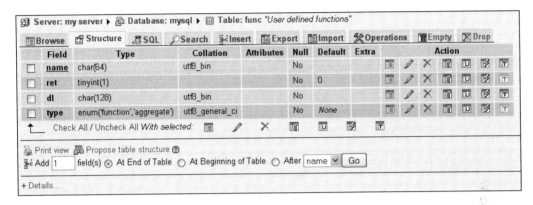

The $cfg['DefaultTabTable']$ parameter defines the initial subpage on the Table view. Some users prefer to avoid seeing the structure because in production they routinely run saved queries or enter the **Search** subpage (explained in Chapter 9).

Server view

This view is entered each time we go back to the **home**page. A privileged user will of course see more choices in the **Server** view. The **Server** view panel was created to group together related server management subpages, and enable easy navigation between them.

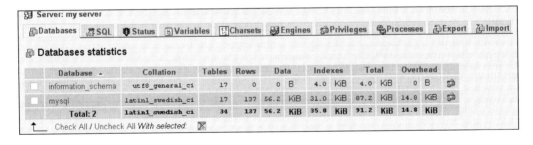

The default Server page is controlled by the `$cfg['DefaultTabServer']` parameter. This parameter defines the initial starting page as well. For multi-user installations, it is recommended to keep the default value (`main.php`), which displays the traditional homepage. We could choose to display server statistics instead by changing this parameter to `server_status.php`, or to see the user's list with `server_privileges.php`. Other possible choices are explained in the configuration file, and the server administration pages are explained in Chapter 18.

Icons for homepage and menu tabs

A configuration parameter, `$cfg['MainPageIconic']`, controls the appearance of icons at various places on the right panel:

- On the homepage
- At top of page when listing the **Server**, **Database**, and **Table** information
- On the menu tabs in Database, Table, and Server views

This parameter is set to TRUE by default producing, for example:

We can also display menu items without tabs by setting the `$cfg['LightTabs']` parameter to `true`, producing:

Query window

It is often convenient to have a distinct window in which we can type and refine queries, and which is synchronized with the right panel. This window is called the **Query window**. We can open this window by using the small SQL icon, or the **Query window** link from the left panel's icons or links zone.

This link or icon is displayed if `$cfg['QueryFrame']` is set to TRUE. The TRUE for `$cfg['QueryFrameJS']` tells phpMyAdmin to open a distinct window and update it using JavaScript commands; of course, this only works for a JavaScript-enabled browser. If this is set to FALSE, clicking on **Query window** will only open the right panel, and will display the normal SQL subpage.

The full usability of the **Query window** is only achieved with the distinct window mode.

The **Query window** itself has subpages, and it appears here over the right panel:

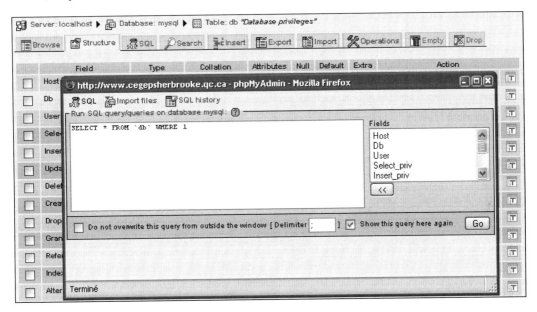

We can choose the dimensions (in pixels) of this window with `$cfg['QueryWindowWidth']` and `$cfg['QueryWindowHeight']`. Chapter 12 explains the **Query window** in more details, including the available SQL query history features.

Summary

This chapter covers:

- The language selection system
- The purpose of the left and right panels
- The contents of the left panel, including Light mode and Full mode
- The contents of the right panel, with its various views depending on the context
- The **Query** window and the customization of MySQL documentation links

The next chapter will guide you with simple steps to accomplish with a freshly-installed phpMyAdmin—initial table creation, data insertion and retrieval.

4
First Steps

Having seen the overall layout of phpMyAdmin's panel, we are ready to create a database, our first table, insert some data in it, and browse it. These first steps are intentionally simple, but they will give you the foundation on which more complex operations are achieved later. Moreover, at the end of the chapter, we will have at our disposition, the two basic tables on which the remaining of the exercises are based.

Database creation

Before creating a table, we must ensure that we have a database for which the MySQL server's administrator has given us the CREATE privilege. Various possibilities exist:

- The administrator has already created a database for us, and we see its name in the left panel; we don't have the right to create an additional database
- We have the right to create databases from phpMyAdmin
- We are on a shared host, and the host provider has installed a general Web interface (for example, Cpanel) to create MySQL databases and accounts

Note that a configuration parameter, $cfg['ShowCreateDb'], controls the display of the **Create new database** dialog. By default, it is set to true, which shows this dialog.

No privileges?

If you do not have the privilege to create a database, the homepage displays a **No privileges** message under the **Create new database** label. This means that you must work with the databases already created for you, or ask the MySQL server's administrator to give you the necessary CREATE privilege.

 If you are the MySQL server's administrator, refer to Chapter 18.

First database creation is authorized

If phpMyAdmin detects that we have the right to create a database, the homepage appears as shown in the following figure:

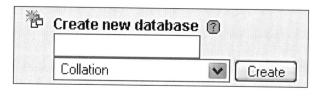

In the input field, a suggested database name appears if the $cfg['SuggestDBName'] parameter is set to TRUE—which is the default setting. The suggested database name is built according to the privileges we possess.

If we are restricted to the use of a prefix, the prefix might be suggested in the input field. (A popular choice for this prefix is the username.) Note that, in this case, the prefix is followed by an ellipsis mark. We should remove this ellipsis mark and complete the input field with an appropriate name.

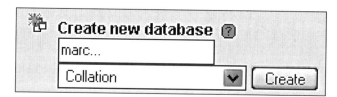

The **Collation** choice can be left unchanged for now; but with this dialog, we could pick a default character set and collation for this database. This setting can be changed later (see Chapter 10 for more explanation on this).

We will assume here that we have the right to create a database named **marc_book**. We enter **marc_book** in the input field and click on **Create**. Once the database is created, we will see the following screen:

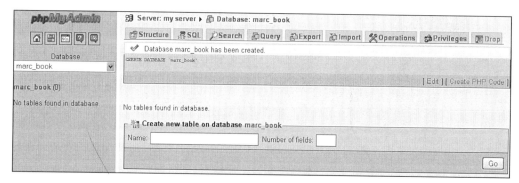

Notice the following:

- The main title of the right panel has changed to reflect the fact that we are now located in this database.

- A confirmation message regarding the creation is displayed.

- The left panel has been updated; we see **marc_book (0)**. Here, the name indicates that the **marc_book** database has been created, and the number **0** indicates that it contains no tables.

- By default, the SQL query sent to the server by phpMyAdmin to create the database is displayed in color.

> phpMyAdmin displays the query it generated, because `$cfg['ShowSQL']` is set to TRUE. Looking at the generated queries can be a good way of learning SQL.

As the generated queries could be large and take much on screen room, the `$cfg['MaxCharactersInDisplayedSQL']` acts as a limit. Its default value of `1000` should be a good balance between seeing too few and seeing too much of the queries, especially when doing large imports.

It is important to examine the phpMyAdmin feedback to ascertain the validity of the operations we make through the interface. This way, we can detect errors like typos in the names, or creation of a table in the wrong database.

Creating our first table

Now that we have a new database, it's time to create a table in it. The example table we will use is a table named **book**.

Choosing the fields

Before creating a table, we should plan the information we want to store. This is usually done during database design. In our case, a simple analysis leads us to the following book related data we want to keep:

- **International Standard Book Number (ISBN)**
- Title
- Number of pages
- Author identification

For now, it is not important to have the complete list of fields (or columns) for our **book** table. We will modify it by prototyping the application and refine it later. At the end of the chapter, we will add a second table, **author**, containing information about each author.

Table creation

We have chosen our table name and we know the number of fields. We enter this information in the **Create new table** dialog and click **Go** to start creating the table:

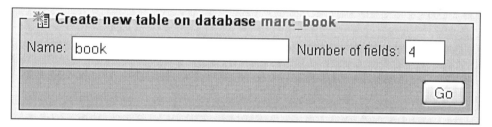

We then see a panel specifying field information. As we asked for four fields, we get four rows. Each row refers to information specific to one field. The following image represents the left side for this panel:

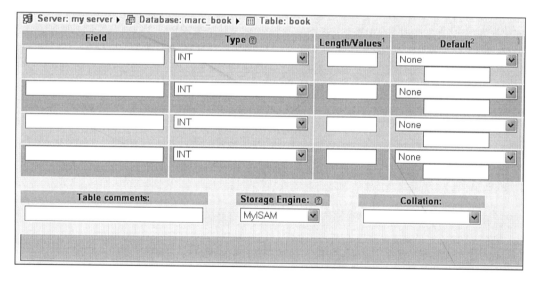

And the next one represents the right side.

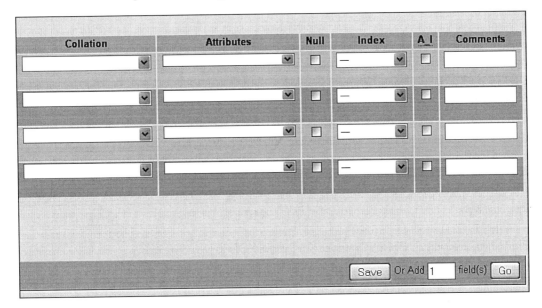

On pre-4.1 MySQL versions, the **Collation** and **Comments** columns might not be shown at this point. Please refer to Chapter 3, for collation issues, and to Chapter 11, for column commenting.

The MySQL documentation explains valid characters for the table and field names (if we search for **Legal names**). This may vary depending on the MySQL version. Usually, any character that is allowed in a file name (except the dot and the slash) is acceptable in a table name, and the length of the name must not exceed 64 characters. The 64-character limit exists for field names as well, but we can use any character.

We enter our field names under the **Field** column. Each field has a type, and the most commonly used types are located at the beginning of the drop-down list.

The **VARCHAR** (variable character) type is widely used when the field content is alphanumeric, because the contents will occupy only the space needed for it. This type requires a maximum length, which we specify. If we forget to do so, a small pop-up message reminds us later when we save. For the page count and the author identification, we have chosen **INT** type (integer), as depicted in the following screenshot:

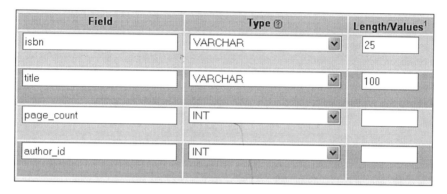

Field	Type ⑦	Length/Values[1]
isbn	VARCHAR	25
title	VARCHAR	100
page_count	INT	
author_id	INT	

There are other attributes for fields, but we will leave them empty in this example. You might notice the **Add 1 Field(s)** dialog at the bottom of the screen. We can use it to add some fields to this table creation panel by entering the appropriate value and hitting **Go**. The number of rows would change according to the new number of fields, leaving intact the information already entered about the first four fields. Before saving the page, let's define some keys.

Choosing keys

A table should normally have a primary key (a field with unique content that represents each row). Having a primary key is recommended for row identification, better performance, and possible cross-table relations. A good value here is the ISBN; so, in the **Index** dialog we select **PRIMARY** for the **isbn** field. Other possibilities for index type include **INDEX**, **UNIQUE**, and **FULLTEXT** (more on this in Chapter 6).

 Index management (also referred to as Key management) can be done at initial table creation, or later in the **Structure** subpage of Table view.

To improve the speed of the queries that we will make by author ID, we should add an index on this field. The right part of our screen now looks like this:

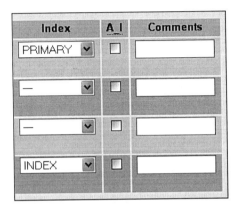

At this point, we could pick a different **Storage Engine** from the corresponding drop-down menu. However, for time being, we will just accept the default storage engine.

Now we are ready to create the table by clicking on **Save**. If all goes well, the next screen confirms that the table has been created; we are now in the **Structure** subpage of Table view.

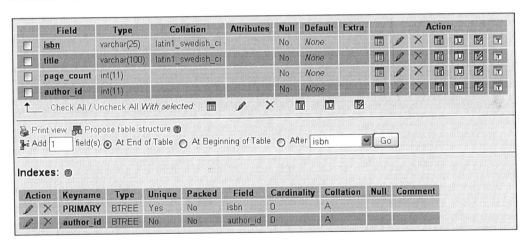

Should we forget to specify a value in the **Length** column for a **CHAR** or **VARCHAR**, phpMyAdmin would remind us before trying to create the table.

Of the various tabs leading to other subpages, some are not active, because it would not make sense to browse or search a table if there are no rows in it. However, it would be acceptable to export a table, as we can export a table's structure even if it contains no data.

Manual data insertion

Now that we have a table, let's put some data in it manually. Before we do that, here are some useful references on data manipulation within this book:

- Chapter 5 explains how to change data
- Chapter 8 explains how to import data from existing files
- Chapter 10 explains how to copy data from other tables
- Chapter 11 explains the relational system (in our case, we will want to link to the **author** table)

For now, click on the **Insert** link, which will lead us to the data-entry (or edit) panel. This screen has room to enter information for two rows, that is, two books in our example. This is because the default value of $cfg['InsertRows']$ is 2. In the lower part of the screen, the dialog **Restart insertion with 2 rows** can be used if the default number of rows does not suit our needs. But beware, any data already on screen would be lost. By default, the **Ignore** checkbox is ticked, which means that the second group of fields will be ignored. But as soon as we enter some information in one field of this group and exit the field, the **Ignore** box is unchecked.

We can enter the following sample information for two books:

- ISBN: 1-234567-89-0, title: A hundred years of cinema (volume 1), 600 pages, author ID: 1
- ISBN: 1-234567-22-0, title: Future souvenirs, 200 pages, author ID: 2

We start by entering data for the first and the second rows. The **Value** column width obeys the maximum length for the character fields. For this example, we keep the lower drop-down selector to its default value of **Insert as new row**. We then click on **Go** to insert the data. There is a **Go** button after each set of columns that represent a row, and another one on the lower part of the screen. All these have the same effect of saving the entered data.

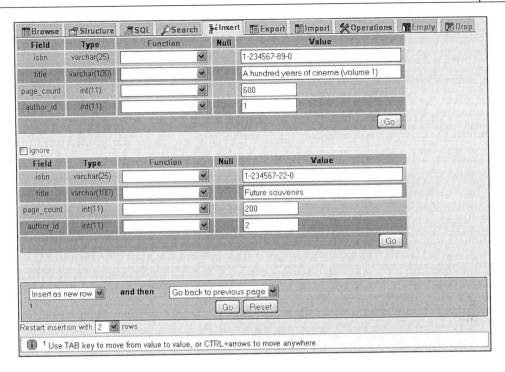

If our intention had been to enter data for more books after these two, we would have selected **Insert another new row** from the first drop-down before clicking on **Go**.

Data entry panel tuning for CHAR and VARCHAR

By default, phpMyAdmin displays an input field on a single line for the field types, CHAR and VARCHAR. This is controlled by setting $cfg['CharEditing'] to 'input'. Sometimes, we may want to insert line breaks (new lines) within the field. (This insertion might be done manually with the *Enter* key, or by copying and pasting lines of text from another on screen source.) This can be done by changing $cfg['CharEditing'] to 'textarea'. This is a global setting, and will apply to all the fields of all the tables, for all users of this copy of phpMyAdmin.

We can tune the number of columns and rows of this text area with:

```
$cfg['CharTextareaCols']    = 40;
$cfg['CharTextareaRows']    = 2;
```

Here, 2 for `$cfg['CharTextareaRows']` means that we should be able to see at least two lines before the browser starts to display a vertical scroll bar. These settings apply to all **CHAR** and **VARCHAR** fields. Applying those settings would generate a different **Insert** screen as follows:

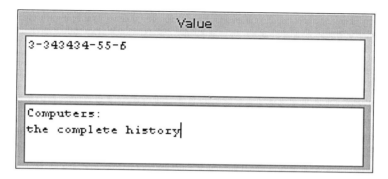

 With this entry mode, the maximum length of each field no longer applies visually. It would be enforced by MySQL at insert time.

Browse mode

There are many ways to enter this mode. In fact, it is used each time the query results are displayed. We can enter this mode by clicking on the table name on the navigation panel, or by clicking **Browse** when we are in Table view for a specific table.

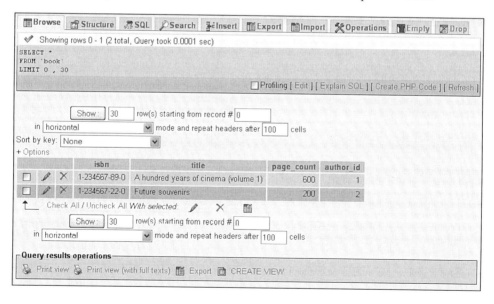

SQL query links

In the **Browse** results, the first part displayed is the query itself, along with a few links. The displayed links may vary depending on our actions and some configuration parameters.

The **Profiling** checkbox will be covered in Chapter 17.

The **Edit** link appears if $cfg['SQLQuery']['Edit']$ is set to TRUE. Its purpose is to open the **Query window**, so that you can edit this query (see Chapter 12 for more details).

Explain SQL is displayed if $cfg['SQLQuery']['Explain']$ is set to TRUE. We will see in Chapter 6, what this link can be used for.

The **Create PHP Code** link can be clicked to reformat the query to the syntax expected in a PHP script. It can then be copied and pasted directly at the place where we need the query in the PHP script we are working on. Note that after a click, this link changes to **Without PHP Code**, which would bring back the normal query display. This link is available if $cfg['SQLQuery']['ShowAsPHP']$ is set to TRUE.

Refresh is used to execute the same query again. The results might change, as a MySQL server is a multi-user server, and other users might be modifying the same tables. This link is shown if $cfg['SQLQuery']['Refresh']$ is set to TRUE.

All these four parameters have a default value of TRUE in config.inc.php.

Navigation bar

This bar is displayed at the top of results and also at the bottom. Column headers can be repeated at certain intervals among results depending on the value entered in **repeat headers after...**.

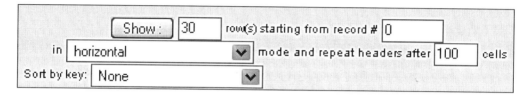

The bar enables us to navigate from page to page, displaying an arbitrary number of records (or rows), starting at some point in the results. As we entered browse mode by clicking **Browse**, the underlying query that generated the results includes the whole table. However, this is not always the case.

Notice that we are positioned at record number **0,** and are seeing records in **horizontal** mode.

The default display mode is 'horizontal', as defined in $cfg['DefaultDisplay']. We can also set this to 'vertical' if we usually prefer this mode. Even if our preferred mode is set in this configuration parameter, we can always use the **Show** dialog to change it on the fly.

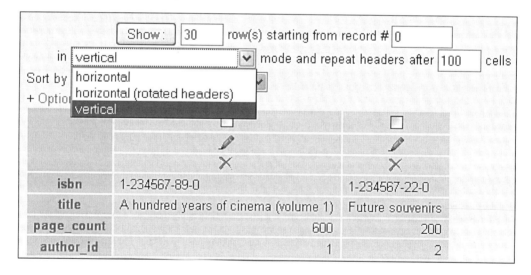

Another possibility is the 'horizontalflipped' choice, which rotates the column headers by 90 degrees. If we try this choice, another parameter, $cfg['HeaderFlipType'], plays a role. Its default value, css, displays true rotated headers. Not every browser supports this; however, Internet Explorer 7 does support this feature and produces:

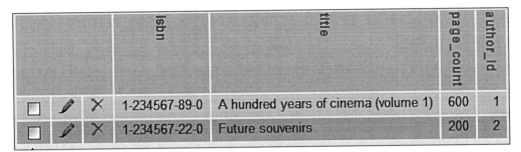

On other browsers, it seems the best we can achieve is by setting $cfg['HeaderFlipType'] to fake.

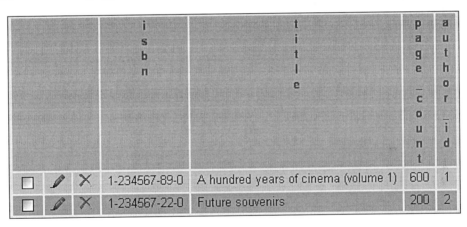

We are currently using a table containing a small number of rows. With larger tables, we could see a more complete set of navigation buttons. To simulate this, let's use the **Show** dialog to change the default number of rows from **30** to **1**; we then click **Show**. We can see that the navigation bar adapts itself:

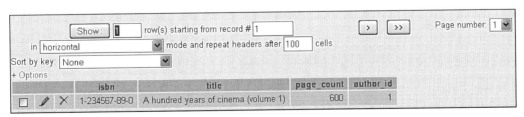

This time, there are buttons labeled **<<**, **<**, **>**, and **>>** for easy access to the first page, previous page, next page, and the last page of the results respectively. The buttons appear only when necessary; for example, the **first page** button is not displayed if we already are on the first page. These symbols are displayed in this manner, as the default setting of $cfg['NavigationBarIconic'] is TRUE. A FALSE here would produce a different set of labels.

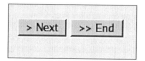

There is also a **Page number** drop-down menu, to go directly to one of the pages located near the current page. As there can be hundreds or thousands of pages, this menu is kept small, with only a few page numbers before and after the current page.

By design, phpMyAdmin always tries to give quick results, and one way to achieve this result is to add a LIMIT clause in SELECT. If a LIMIT clause is already there in the original query, phpMyAdmin will respect it. The default limit is 30 rows, set in $cfg['MaxRows']. The multiple users on the server help keep the server load to a minimum.

Another button is available on the navigation bar, but must be activated by setting $cfg['ShowAll'] to TRUE. It would be very tempting for users to use this button often. Hence, on a multi-user installation of phpMyAdmin, it is recommended that the button be disabled (FALSE). When enabled, the navigation bar is augmented with a **Show all** button. Clicking on this button retrieves all the rows of the current results set, which might hit the execution time limit in PHP or a memory limit in the server or browser.

 If we enter a big number in the **Show...rows** dialog, the same results will be achieved (and we may face the same problems).

Query results operations

A section labeled **Query results operations** is located under the results. It contains links to print the results (with or without the FULL TEXT columns), to export these results (see *Exporting Partial Query Results* section in Chapter 7), or to create a view from this query (more on this in Chapter 17).

Sorting results

In SQL, we can never be sure of the order in which the data is retrieved, unless we explicitly sort the data. Some implementations of the retrieving engine may show results in the same order as the one in which data was entered, or according to a primary key. However, a sure way to get results in the order we want is by sorting them explicitly.

When browsing results are displayed, any column header can be clicked to sort on this column, even if it is not part of an index. Let's click on the **author_id** column header.

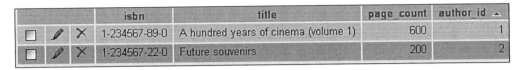

We can confirm that the sorting has occurred, by watching the SQL query at the top of screen; it contains an **ORDER BY** clause.

We now see a small red triangle pointing upwards beside the **author_id** header. This means that the current sort order is 'ascending'. Moving the mouse cursor over the **author_id** header makes the red triangle change direction, to indicate what will happen if we click on the header — a sort by descending **author_id**.

Another way to sort is by key. The **Sort** dialog shows all the keys already defined. Here we see a key named **PRIMARY** — the name given to our primary key on the **isbn** field when we checked **Primary** for this field at creation time:

This might be the only way to sort on multiple fields at once (for multi-fields indexes).

The default initial sort order is defined in $cfg['Order'] with ASC for ascending, DESC for descending. The sort order can also be or SMART, which means that fields of type DATE, TIME, DATETIME, and TIMESTAMP would be sorted in descending order, whereas other field types will be sorted in ascending order.

Headwords

Because we can change the number of records displayed on a page, it is quite possible that we do not see the whole data. In this case, it would help to see headwords—indications about the first and last row of displayed data. This way, you can click **Next** or **Previous** without scrolling to the bottom of the window.

However, which column should phpMyAdmin base his headwords generation on? A simple assumption has been made: if you click on a column's header to indicate your intention of sorting on this column, phpMyAdmin uses this column's data as a headword. For our current book table, we do not have enough data to clearly notice the benefits of this technique. However, we can nonetheless see that after a sort, the top part of the screen now contains this message:

```
Showing rows 0 - 1 (2 total, Query took 0.0006 sec) [author_id: 1 - 2]
```

Here, the message between square brackets means that **author_id** number **1** is on the first displayed row and number **2** is on the last one.

Color-marking rows

When moving the mouse between rows, the row background color may change to the color defined in `$cfg['BrowsePointerColor']`. This parameter can be found in `themes/themename/layout.inc.php`. To enable this, browse pointer for all themes— `$cfg['BrowsePointerEnable']` — must be set to TRUE (the default) in `config.inc.php`.

It may be interesting to visually mark some rows to highlight their importance for personal comparison of data, or when showing data to people. Highlighting is done by clicking the row. Clicking again removes the mark on the row. The chosen color is defined by `$cfg['BrowseMarkerColor']` (see `themes/themename/layout.inc.php`). This feature must be enabled by setting `$cfg['BrowseMarkerEnable']` to TRUE, this time in `config.inc.php`. This sets the feature for all the themes. We can mark more than one row. Marking the row also activates the checkbox for this row.

			isbn	title	page_count	author_id
☑	🖉	✕	1-234567-89-0	A hundred years of cinema (volume 1)	600	1
☐	🖉	✕	1-234567-22-0	Future souvenirs	200	2

Limiting the length of each column

In the previous examples, we always saw the full contents of each column, as each column had the number of characters within the limit defined by $cfg['LimitChars']$. This is a limit enforced on all non-numeric fields. If this limit was lower (say 10), the display would be as follows:

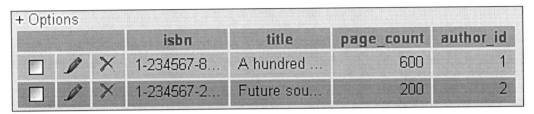

This would help us see more columns at the same time (at the expense of seeing less of each column).

Display options

In order to see the full texts, we will now make use of the **Options** slider, which reveals some display options. The option that concerns us at the moment is the **Partial Texts/Full Texts** pair; we can choose **Full Texts** to see all of the text that was truncated. Even if we elect not to change the $cfg['LimitChars']$ parameter, there will be a time when asking for full texts will be useful (when we work with TEXT field type—more on this in Chapter 6).

Browsing distinct values

There is a quick way to display all distinct values and the number of occurrences for each value for each field. This feature is available on the **Structure** page. For example, we want to know how many different authors we have in our book table and how many books each one wrote. On the line describing the field we want to browse (here **author_id**) we click the **Browse distinct values** icon or link.

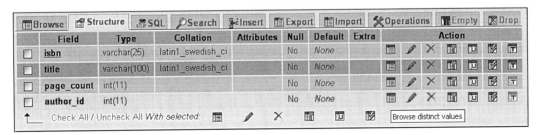

We have a limited test set, but can nonetheless see the results.

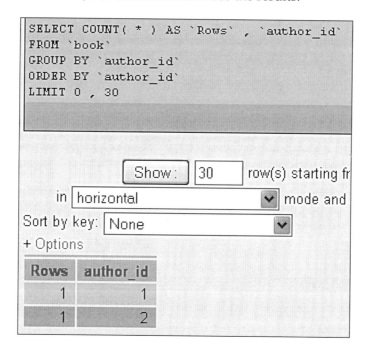

Browse-mode customization

Following are additional more parameters that control the appearance of results. These parameters—except $cfg['RepeatCells']—are located in themes/themename/layout.inc.php.

- $cfg['Border']: The HTML tables used to present results have no border by default because this parameter is set to 0; we can put a higher number (for example 1 or 2) to add borders to the tables

- $cfg['ThBgcolor']: The tables mentioned have headers with #D3DCE3 as the default background color

- $cfg['BgcolorOne'], $cfg['BgcolorTwo']: When displaying rows of results, two background colors are used alternately; by default, those are #CCCCCC and #DDDDDD.

- $cfg['RepeatCells']: When many rows of data are displayed, we may lose track of the meaning of each column. By default, at each 100th cell, the column headers are displayed

Creating an additional table

In our (simple) design, we know that we need another table—the **author** table. The **author** table will contain:

- Author identification
- Full name
- Phone number

To create this table, we must go back to the Database view. We click on **marc_book** in the navigation panel, and request the creation of another table with three fields as indicated in the following screenshot:

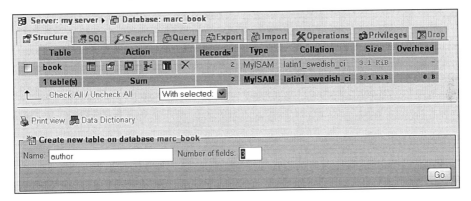

Using the same techniques used when creating the first table, we type this in:

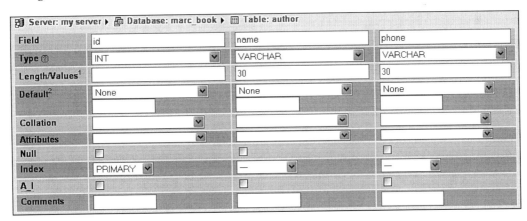

As we have three fields or less, the display is now in vertical mode (see the *Vertical Mode* section in Chapter 6 for more details).

The field name **id**, which is our primary key in this new table, relates to the `author_id` field from the `book` table. After saving the table structure, we enter some data for authors 1 and 2. Use your imagination for this!

Summary

This chapter explains how to create a database and tables, and how to enter data manually in the tables. It also covers how to confirm the presence of data by using the browse mode, which includes the SQL query links, navigation bar, sorting options, and row marking.

The next chapter explains how to edit data rows and covers the various aspects of deletion of rows, tables, and databases.

5

Changing Data

Data is not static, it changes often. This chapter focuses on editing and deleting data and its supporting structures—tables and databases.

Edit mode

When we browse a table or view results from a search on any single-table query, small icons appear on the left or right of each table row as shown in the following screenshot:

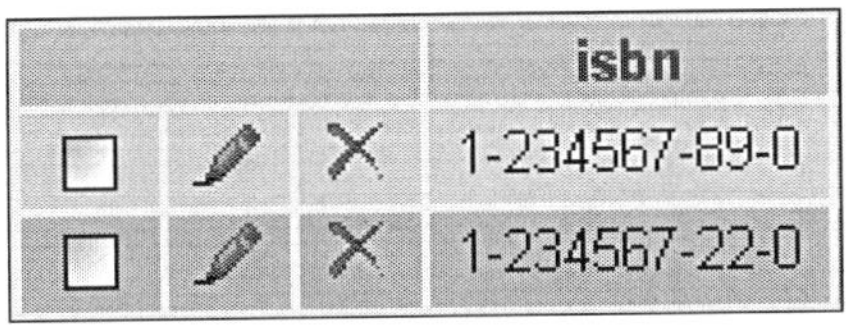

The row can be edited with the pencil-shaped icon and deleted with the X-shaped icon. The exact form and location of these controls are governed by:

```
$cfg['PropertiesIconic']    = TRUE;
$cfg['ModifyDeleteAtLeft']  = TRUE;
$cfg['ModifyDeleteAtRight'] = FALSE;
```

We can decide whether to display them on the left side, the right side, or on both sides. The $cfg['PropertiesIconic'] parameter can have the values TRUE, FALSE, or both. TRUE displays icons as seen in the previous image, FALSE displays **Edit** and **Delete** (or their translated equivalent) as links, and both displays the icon and the text.

The small checkbox beside each row is explained in the *Multi-Row Edit* and the *Deleting Many Rows* sections later in this chapter.

Clicking on the **Edit** icon or link brings the following panel, which is similar to the data entry panel (except for the lower part):

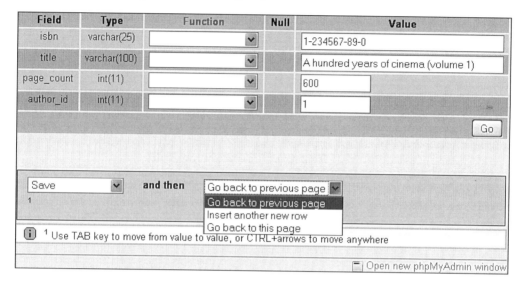

In this panel, we can change data by typing directly (or by cutting and pasting via the normal operating system mechanisms). We can also revert to the original contents using the **Reset** button.

By default, the lower drop-down menus are set to **Save** (so that we make changes to this row) and **Go back to previous page** (so that we can continue editing another row on the previous results page). We might want to stay on the current page after clicking **Go** — in order to save and then continue editing — we can choose **Go back to this page**. If we want to insert yet another new row after saving the current row, we just have to choose **Insert another new row** before saving. The **Insert as new row** choice — below the **Save** choice — is explained in the *Duplicating Rows of Data* section later in this chapter.

Moving to next field with the tab key

People who prefer to use the keyboard can use the *Tab* key to go to the next field. Normally, the cursor goes from left to right and from top to bottom, so it would travel into the fields in the **Function** column (more on this in a moment). However, to ease data navigation in phpMyAdmin, the normal order of navigation has been altered. The *Tab* key first goes through each field in the **Value** column, and then through each one in the **Function** column.

Moving with arrows

Another way of moving between fields is with the *Ctrl+arrows* keys. This method might be easier than using the *Tab* key when many fields are on screen. For this to work, the `$cfg['CtrlArrowsMoving']` parameter must be set to `true`, which is the default value.

 On a Mac OS X 10.5 with Spaces enabled, *Ctrl+arrows* are the default shortcut to switch between virtual desktops; so this technique cannot be used for moving between fields.

Handling NULL values

If the table's structure permits a NULL value inside a field, a small checkbox appears in the field's **Null** column. Checking it puts a NULL value in the field. A special mechanism has also been added to phpMyAdmin to ensure that, if data is typed into the **Value** column for this field, the **Null** checkbox is cleared automatically. (This is possible in JavaScript-enabled browsers.)

Here, we have modified the structure of the **phone** field in the `author` table, to permit a NULL value (refer *Editing field attributes* section in Chapter 6). The **Null** checkbox is not checked here:

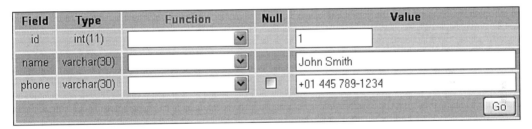

Field	Type	Function	Null	Value
id	int(11)			1
name	varchar(30)			John Smith
phone	varchar(30)		☐	+01 445 789-1234
				Go

The data is erased after checking the **Null** box, as shown in the following screenshot:

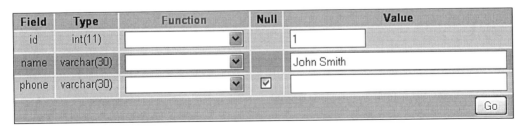

Field	Type	Function	Null	Value
id	int(11)			1
name	varchar(30)			John Smith
phone	varchar(30)		☑	
				Go

The **Edit** panel will appear this way if this row is ever brought on screen again.

Applying a function to a value

The MySQL language offers some functions that we may apply to data before
saving. Some of these functions appear in a drop-down menu beside each field,
if `$cfg['ShowFunctionFields']` is set to TRUE.

The function list is defined in the `$cfg['Functions']` array. The most
commonly used functions for a certain data type are displayed first in the list.
Some restrictions are defined in the `$cfg['RestrictColumnTypes']` and
`$cfg['RestrictFunctions']` arrays, to control which functions are displayed first.

Here are the definitions that restrict the function names to be displayed for the
VARCHAR type:

```
$cfg['RestrictColumnTypes'] = array(
        'VARCHAR'         => 'FUNC_CHAR',   [...]

$cfg['RestrictFunctions'] = array(
        'FUNC_CHAR'       => array(
            'ASCII',
            'CHAR',
            'SOUNDEX',
            'LCASE',
            'UCASE',
            'PASSWORD',
            'OLD_PASSWORD',
            'MD5',
            'SHA1',
            'ENCRYPT',
            'COMPRESS',
            'UNCOMPRESS',
            'LAST_INSERT_ID',
            'USER',
            'CONCAT'
        ),   [...]
```

As depicted in the following screenshot, we apply the **UPPER** function to the title
when saving **this row**:

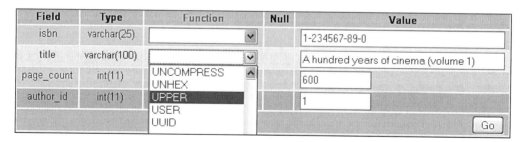

To gain some screen space (to be able to see more of the data), this feature may be disabled by setting $cfg['ShowFunctionFields']$ to FALSE. Moreover, the **Function** column header is clickable, so we can disable this feature on the fly.

When the feature is disabled—either by clicking or via the configuration parameter—a **Show: Function** link appears in order to display this **Function** column with a single click.

Field	Type	Null	Value
isbn	varchar(25)		1-234567-89-0
title	varchar(100)		A hundred years of cinema (volume 1)
page_count	int(11)		600
author_id	int(11)		1
			Go

Duplicating rows of data

During the course of data maintenance (for permanent duplication or for test purposes), we often have to generate a copy of a row. If this is done in the same table, we must respect the rules of key uniqueness.

An example is in order here. Our author has written Volume 2 of his book about cinema.Hence, the fields that need a slight change are the ISBN, title, and page count. We bring the existing row on screen, change these three fields, and choose **Insert as new row**, as shown in the following screenshot:

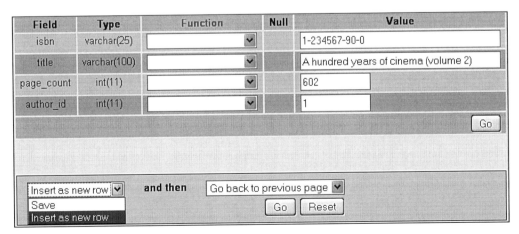

When we click **Go**, another row is created with the modified information, leaving the original row unchanged:

			isbn	title	page_count	author_id
☐	🖉	✕	1-234567-89-0	A hundred years of cinema (volume 1)	600	1
☐	🖉	✕	1-234567-22-0	Future souvenirs	200	2
☐	🖉	✕	1-234567-90-0	A hundred years of cinema (volume 2)	602	1

Multi-row editing

The multi-row edit feature enables us to use checkboxes on the rows we want to edit, and use the **Edit** link (or the pencil-shaped icon) in the **With selected** menu. The **Check All / Uncheck All** links can also be used to quickly check or uncheck all the boxes. We can also click anywhere on the row's data to activate the corresponding checkbox.

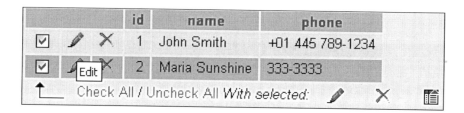

This brings up an Edit panel containing all the chosen rows. The editing process may continue while the data from these rows is seen, compared, and changed.

 When we mark some rows with the checkboxes, we can also perform two other actions on them—delete (see the *Deleting Many Rows* section in this chapter) and export (see Chapter 7).

Editing the next row

Sequential editing is possible on tables that have a primary key on an integer field. Our `author` table meets the criteria. Let's see what happens when we start editing the row having the **id** value **1**:

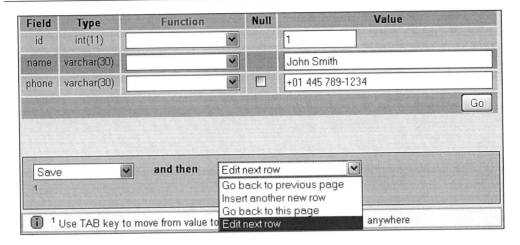

The editing panel appears, and we can edit author number **1**. However, in the drop-down menu, the **Edit next row** choice is available. If chosen, the next author – the first one whose primary key value is greater than the current primary key value – will be available for edit.

Deleting data

phpMyAdmin's interface enables us to delete the following:

- Single rows of data
- Multiple rows of a table
- All the rows in a table
- All the rows in multiple tables

Deleting a single row

We can use the small X-shaped icon beside each row to delete the row. If the value of $cfg['Confirm']$ is set to TRUE, every MySQL DELETE statement has to be confirmed before execution. This is the default, since it might not be prudent to allow a row to be deleted with just one click!

The form of the confirmation varies depending on the browser's ability to execute JavaScript. A JavaScript-based confirmation pop up would look like the following screenshot:

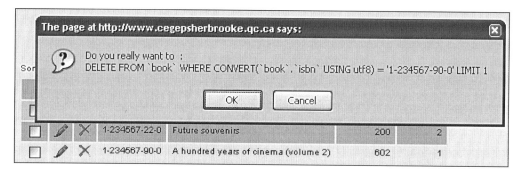

If JavaScript has been disabled in our browser, a distinct panel appears.

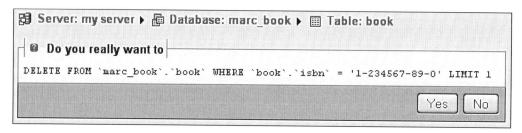

The actual DELETE statement will use whatever information is needed to ensure the deletion of only the intended row. In our case, a primary key had been defined and was used in the WHERE clause. In the absence of a primary key, a longer WHERE clause will be generated based on the value of each field. The generated WHERE clause might even prevent the correct execution of the DELETE operation, especially if there are TEXT or BLOB fields. This is because the HTTP transaction, used to send the query to the web server, may be limited in length by the browser or the server. This is another reason why defining a primary key is strongly recommended.

Deleting many rows

A feature added to phpMyAdmin in version 2.5.4 is the multi-row delete. Let's say we examine a page of rows and decide that some rows have to be destroyed. Instead of deleting them one-by-one with the **Delete** link or icon—and because sometimes the decision to delete must be made while examining a group of rows—there are checkboxes beside rows in Table view mode:

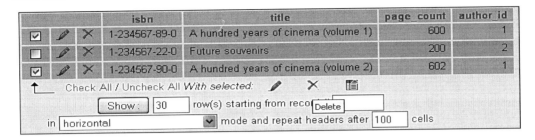

These are used with the **With selected** X-shaped icon. A confirmation screen appears listing all the rows that are about to be deleted. It is also possible to click anywhere on the row's data to activate the corresponding checkbox.

Deleting all the rows in a table

To completely erase all the rows in a table (leaving its structure intact), we go to the Database view and click on the database name in the left panel. We then click on the trash can icon located on the same line as the table we want to empty:

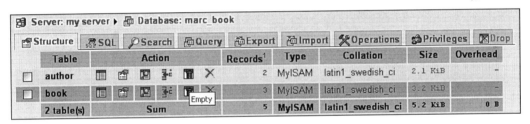

We get a message confirming the TRUNCATE statement (the MySQL statement used to quickly empty a table). For our exercise, we won't delete this precious data!

Emptying a table can also be done in Table view with the **Empty** link located on the top menu:

Deleting data, either row-by-row or by emptying a table, is a permanent action. No recovery is then possible except by using a backup.

Deleting all rows in many tables

The first screenshot under the previous section, shows a checkbox to the left of each table name. We can choose some tables. Then, in the **With selected** menu, choose the **Empty** operation as shown in the following screen:

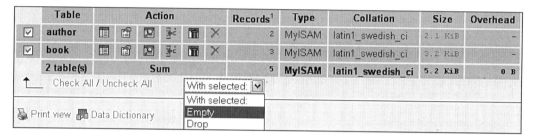

Of course, this decision must not be taken lightly!

Deleting tables

Deleting a table erases the data and the table's structure. We can delete tables using the **Drop** link in Table view:

In the Database view, we can delete a specific table by using the X-shaped icon for that table. The same mechanism also exists for deleting more than one table (with the drop-down menu and the **Drop** action).

[

The **Empty** and **Drop** actions are marked in red, to better indicate the inherent danger of these actions on data.
]

Deleting databases

We can delete an entire database (including all its tables) using the **Drop** link in Database view.

By default, $cfg['AllowUserDropDatabase']$ is set to FALSE. So, this link is hidden to unprivileged users until this setting is manually changed to TRUE.

To help us think twice, a special message—**You are about to DESTROY a complete database!**—appears before a database is deleted.

 The database mysql, containing all user and privilege definitions, is highly important. Therefore, the **Drop** button is deactivated for this database, even for administrators.

Summary

This chapter examines concepts, such as:

- Editing data
- Including the null field and using the *Tab* key
- Applying a function to a value
- Duplicating rows of data
- Deleting data, tables, and databases

The next chapter will cover another kind of change—modifications to a table's structure. This includes:

- Adding columns
- Handling special data types such as DATE, ENUM and BIT columns
- Managing indexes

6

Changing Table Structures

When developing an application, requirements about data structure often change because of new or modified needs. Developers must accommodate these changes through judicious table structure editing. This chapter explores the subject of changing the structure of tables. Specifically, it shows how to add a column to an existing table and edit the attributes of a column. We then build on these notions to introduce more specialized column types, and to explain their handling through phpMyAdmin. Finally, we cover the topic of index management.

Adding a field

Suppose that we need a new field to store a book's language and, by default, the books on which we keep data are written in English. We can call the field **language**, which will contain code composed of two characters (**en** by default).

In the **Structure** subpage of the Table view for the **book** table, we can find the **Add field** dialog. Here, we specify how many new fields we want, and where they will go.

The positions of the new fields in the table matter only from a developer's point of view. We usually group the fields logically, so that we can find them more easily in the list of fields. The exact position of the fields will not play a role in the intended results (output from the queries), as these results can be adjusted regardless of the table structure. Usually, the most important fields (including the keys) are located at the beginning of the table. However, it is a matter of personal preference.

We want to put the new field **At End of Table**. So, we check the corresponding radio button and click on **Go**.

Other possible choices would be **At Beginning of Table** and **After** (where we would have to choose from the drop-down menu, the field after which the new field must go).

We see the familiar panel for the new fields, repeated for the number of fields asked for. We fill it in. However, as we want to enter a default value this time, we do these two actions:

- Change the Default drop-down menu from **None** to **As defined:**
- Enter a default value, **en**

We then click on Save.

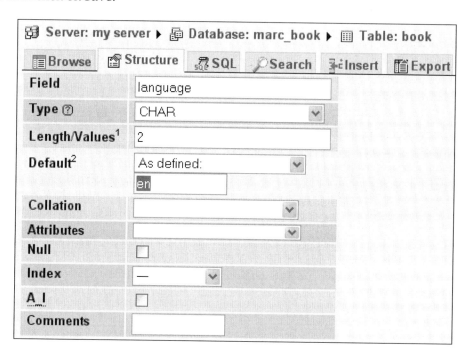

Vertical mode

The previous panel appeared in vertical mode because the default for `$cfg['DefaultPropDisplay']` is 3. This means that for three columns or less, the vertical mode is used, and for more than three, horizontal mode would be automatically selected. Here, we can use a number of our choosing.

If we set `$cfg['DefaultPropDisplay']` to `'vertical'`, the panel to add new fields (along with the panel to edit a field's structure) will be always presented in vertical order. The advantages of working in vertical mode become obvious, especially when there are more choices for each field, as explained in Chapter 16.

Horizontal mode

The $cfg['DefaultPropDisplay']$ parameter can also take a value of `'horizontal'`. Let's see how the panel appears in this mode when we ask for three new fields:

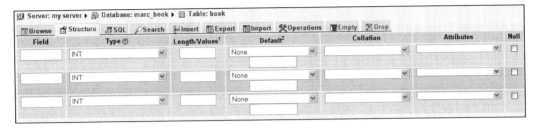

Editing field attributes

On the **Structure** subpage, we can make further changes to our table. For this example, we set `$cfg['PropertiesIconic']` to `'both'`, to see the icons along with their text explanation:

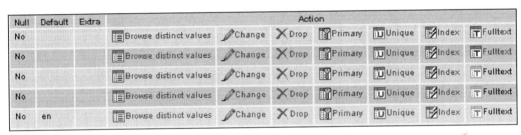

This panel does not allow every possible change to fields. It specifically allows:

- Changing one field structure, using the **Change** link on a specific field
- Removing a field, using **Drop** operation
- Adding a field to an existing **Primary** key
- Setting a non-unique **Index** or a **Unique** index on a field
- Setting a **Fulltext** index (offered only if the field type allows it)

These are quick links that may be useful in some situations, but they do not replace the full index management panel. Both of these are explained in this chapter.

We can use the checkboxes to choose fields and. Also, with the appropriate **With selected** icons, we can edit the fields or do a multiple field deletion with **Drop**. The **Check All / Uncheck All** option permits us to easily check or uncheck all boxes.

TEXT

We will now explore how to use the **TEXT** field type and the relevant configuration values to adjust for the best possible phpMyAdmin behavior. First, we add to the **book** table a **TEXT** field called **description**.

There are three parameters that control the layout of the text area that will be displayed in **Insert** or **Edit** mode for the **TEXT** fields. First, the number of columns and rows for each field is defined by:

```
$cfg['TextareaCols']           = 40;
$cfg['TextareaRows']           = 7;
```

This gives (by default) the following space to work on a **TEXT** field.

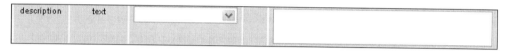

The settings impose only a visual limit on the text area, and a vertical scroll bar is created by the browser if necessary.

Although **MEDIUMTEXT**, **TEXT**, and **LONGTEXT** columns can accommodate more than 32K of data, some browsers cannot always edit them with the text area—the mechanism offered by HTML. In fact, experimentation has convinced the phpMyAdmin development team to have the product display a warning message if the contents are larger than 32K. The message warns users that the contents may not be editable.

The last parameter has an impact for **LONGTEXT** fields. Setting `$cfg['LongtextDoubleTextarea']` to TRUE, doubles the available editing space.

BLOB (Binary Large Object) fields

BLOB fields are generally used to hold binary data (such as images and sounds), even though the MySQL documentation implies that TEXT fields could be used for this purpose. The MySQL 5.1 manual says: "In some cases, it may be desirable to store binary data such as media files in BLOB or TEXT columns". However, another phrase: "BLOB columns are treated as binary strings (byte strings)", seems to indicate that binary data should really be stored in BLOB fields. Thus, phpMyAdmin's intention is to work with BLOB fields to hold all binary data.

We will see in Chapter 16 that there are special mechanisms available to go further with **BLOB** fields, including being able to view some images directly from within phpMyAdmin. Furthermore, Chapter 17 covers BLOB streaming support.

First, we add a **BLOB** field and **cover_photo** to our **book** table. If we now browse the table, we can see the field length information, **[BLOB – 0 B]**, for each **BLOB** field.

isbn	title	page_count	author_id	language	description	cover_photo
1-234567-89-0	A hundred years of cinema (volume 1)	600	1	en		[BLOB - 0 B]
1-234567-22-0	Future souvenirs	200	2	en		[BLOB - 0 B]
1-234567-90-0	A hundred years of cinema (volume 2)	602	1	en		[BLOB - 0 B]

This is because the **Show BLOB** display option (do you remember the **Options** slider?) has no check mark by default. So, it blocks the display of **BLOB** contents in Browse mode. This behavior is intentional. Usually, we cannot do anything with binary data represented in plain text.

Binary content uploads

If we edit one row, we see the **Binary – do not edit** warning and a **Browse...** button. The exact caption on this button depends on the browser. Even though editing is not allowed, we can easily upload a text or binary file's contents into this **BLOB** column.

Let's choose an image file using the **Browse** button—for example, the `logo_left.png` file in a test copy of the `phpMyAdmin/themes/original/img` directory located on our client workstation. We now click **Go**.

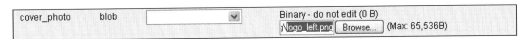

We need to keep in mind some limits for the upload size. Firstly, the **BLOB** field size is limited to 64K. Hence, phpMyAdmin reminds us of this limit with the **Max: 65,536 Bytes** warning. Also, there could be limits inherent to PHP itself (see Chapter 8 for more details). We have now uploaded an image inside this field for a specific row.

isbn	title	page_count	author_id	language	description	cover_photo
1-234567-89-0	A hundred years of cinema (volume 1)	600	1	en		[BLOB - 6.7 KiB]

If we put a check mark for the **Show BLOB** display option, we now see the following in the **BLOB** field:

 To really see the image from within phpMyAdmin, refer to Chapter 16.

The $cfg['ProtectBinary']$ parameter controls what can be done while editing binary fields (**BLOB**s and any other field with the binary attribute). The default value **blob** blocks the **BLOB** fields from being edited but allows us to edit other fields marked binary by MySQL. A value of **all** would block even binary fields from being edited. A value of FALSE would protect nothing, thus allowing us to edit all the fields. If we try the last choice, we see the following in the **Edit** panel for this row:

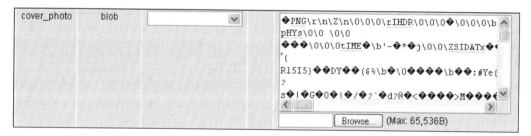

There are chances that this is not our favorite image editor! In fact, data may be corrupted even if we save this row without touching the **BLOB** field. But the possibility of setting $cfg['ProtectBinary']$ to FALSE exists, as some users put text in their **BLOB** fields, and they need to be able to modify this text.

MySQL **BLOB** data types are actually similar to their corresponding **TEXT** data types. However, we should keep in mind that a **BLOB** has no character set, whereas a **TEXT** column has a character set that impacts sorting and comparison. This is why phpMyAdmin can be configured to allow editing of **BLOB** fields.

ENUM and SET

Both these field types are intended to represent a list of possible values. The difference is that the user can choose only one value from a defined list of values with **ENUM**, and more than one value with **SET**. With **SET**, all the multiple values go into one cell; but multiple values do not imply the creation of more than one row of data.

We add a field named **genre** to the **book** table and define it as an **ENUM**. For now, we choose to put short codes in the value list and make one of them, **F**, into the default value as shown in the following screenshot:

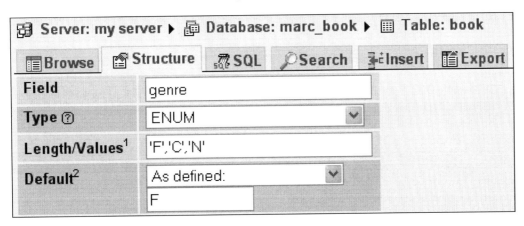

In the value list, we have to enclose each value within single quotes, unlike in the default value field. In our design, we know that these values stand for **Fantasy**, **Child**, and **Novel**. However, for now, we want to see the interface's behavior with short code. In the **Insert** panel, we now see a radio box interface.

If we decide to have more self-describing code, we can go back to **Structure** mode and change the values definition for the **genre** field. We also have to change the default value to one of the possible values, to avoid getting an error message while trying to save this field structure's modification.

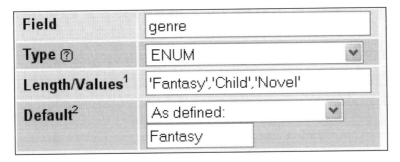

With the modified value list, the **Insert** panel now looks as follows:

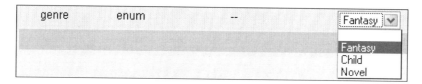

Observe that the radio buttons have been replaced by a drop-down list because the possible values are longer.

If we want more than one possible value selected, we have to change the field type to **SET**. The same value list may be used. However, using our browser's multiple value selector (control-click on a Windows or Linux desktop, command-click on a Mac), we can select more that one value as shown in the screenshot:

For the previous example, we would store only the **genre** code in the **book** table in a normalized data structure, and would rely on another table to store the description for each code. We would not be using **SET** or **ENUM** in this case.

DATE, DATETIME, and TIMESTAMP

We could use a normal character field to store date or time information. But **DATE**, **DATETIME**, and **TIMESTAMP** are more efficient for this purpose. MySQL checks the contents to ensure valid date and time information, and offers special functions to work on these fields.

Calendar pop up

As an added benefit, phpMyAdmin offers a calendar pop up for easy data entry.

We will start by adding a **DATE** field — **date_published** — to our **book** table. If we go into **Insert** mode, we should now see the new field where we could type a date. A **Calendar** icon is also available:

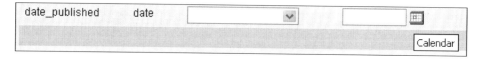

This icon brings a pop-up window, synchronized to this **DATE** field. If there is already a value in the field, the pop up is displayed accordingly. In our case, there is no value in the field, so the calendar shows the current date.

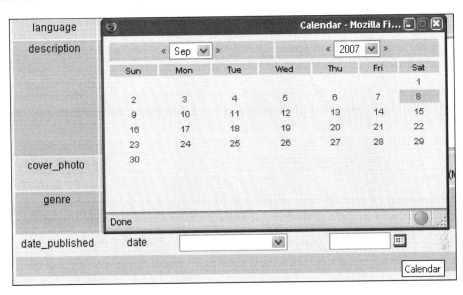

Small symbols on each side of the month and year headers permit easy scrolling through months and years. A simple click on the date we want transports it to our **date_published** field.

For a **DATETIME** or **TIMESTAMP** field, the pop up offers the ability to edit the time part.

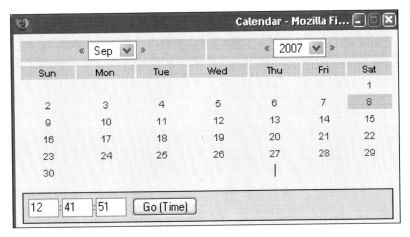

TIMESTAMP options

Starting with MySQL 4.1.2, there are more options that can affect a **TIMESTAMP** column. Let's add to our **book** table, a column named **stamp** of type **TIMESTAMP**. In the **Default** drop-down, we could choose **CURRENT_TIMESTAMP**; but we won't for this exercise. However in the **Attributes** column, we choose **on update CURRENT_TIMESTAMP**.

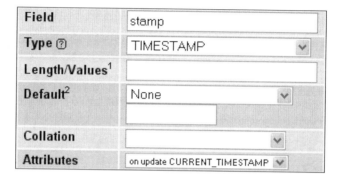

Bit

MySQL 5.0.3 introduced true bit-field values. These take the same amount of space in the database as the number of bits in their definition. Let's say we have three pieces of information about each book, and each piece can only be true (1) or false (0):

- Book is hard cover
- Book contains a CD-ROM
- Book is available only in electronic format

We'll use a single **BIT** field to store these three pieces of information. Therefore, we add a field having a length of **3** (which means 3 bits) to the book table:

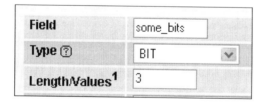

To construct and subsequently interpret the values we store in this field, we have to think in binary, respecting the position of each bit within the field. To indicate that a book is hard cover, does not contain a CD-ROM, and is available only in electronic format, we would use a value of 101.

phpMyAdmin handles `BIT` fields in a binary way. For example, if we edit one row and set a value of `101` to the `some_bits` column, the following query is sent at save time:

```
UPDATE `marc_book`.`book` SET `some_bits` = b '101'

WHERE `book`.`isbn` = '1-234567-89-0' LIMIT 1;
```

The highlighted part of this query shows that the column really receives a binary value. At browse time, the exact field value (which in decimal is 5 — a meaningless value for our purposes) is redisplayed in its binary form **101**, which helps to interpret each discrete bit value.

Index management

phpMyAdmin has a number of index management options, which will be covered in this section.

Single-field indexes

We have already seen how the **Structure** panel offers a quick way to create an index on a single field, thanks to some quick links such as **Primary**, **Index**, and **Unique**. Under the field list (in the **Details** slider), there is a section of the interface available to manage indexes:

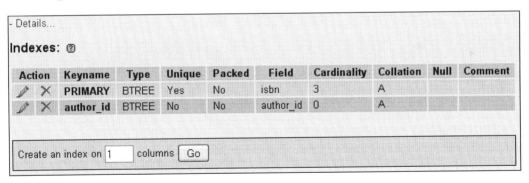

This section has links to edit or delete every index. Here, the **Field** part lists only one field per index, and we can see that the whole field participates in the index. This is because there is no size information after each field name, contrary to what will be seen in our next example.

We will now add an index on the title. However, we want to restrict the length of this index to reduce the space used by the on-disk index structure. The **Create an index on 1 columns** option is appropriate. So, we click **Go**. In the next screen, we specify the index details as shown here:

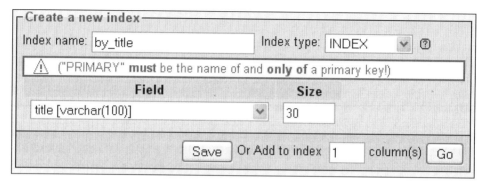

Here is how to fill in this panel:

- **Index name**: A name we invent
- **Index type**: We can choose INDEX or UNIQUE
- **Field**: We select the field that is used as the index, which is the title field
- **Size**: We enter **30** instead of **100** (the complete length of the field) to save space in the table's physical portion that holds index data

After saving this panel, we can confirm from the following screenshot that the index is created and does not cover the entire length of the title field:

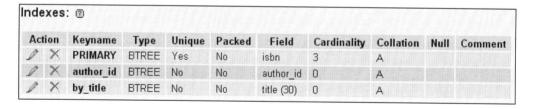

Action	Keyname	Type	Unique	Packed	Field	Cardinality	Collation	Null	Comment
✎ ✗	**PRIMARY**	BTREE	Yes	No	isbn	3	A		
✎ ✗	**author_id**	BTREE	No	No	author_id	0	A		
✎ ✗	**by_title**	BTREE	No	No	title (30)	0	A		

Multi-field indexes and index editing

In the next example, we assume that in a future application we will need to find the books written by a specific author in a specific language. It makes sense to expand our **author_id** index, adding the **language** field to it.

We click the **Edit** link (small pencil) on the line containing the **author_id** index; this shows the current state of this index. The interface has room to add another field to this index. We could use the **Add to index 1 column(s)** feature should we need to add more than one field. In the field selector, we select **language**. This time we do not have to enter a size, as the whole field will be used in the index. For better documentation, we change the **Index name** (**author_language** is appropriate).

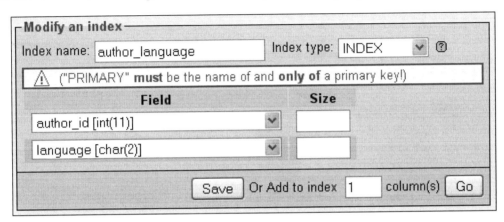

We save this index modification. In the list of indexes, we can confirm our index modification.

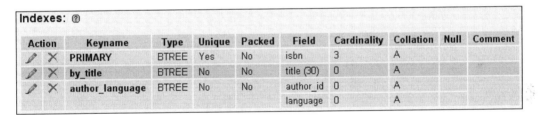

Action	Keyname	Type	Unique	Packed	Field	Cardinality	Collation	Null	Comment
✎ ✗	PRIMARY	BTREE	Yes	No	isbn	3	A		
✎ ✗	by_title	BTREE	No	No	title (30)	0	A		
✎ ✗	author_language	BTREE	No	No	author_id	0	A		
					language	0	A		

FULLTEXT Indexes

This special type of index allows for fulltext searches. It is supported only on `MyISAM` tables for the **VARCHAR** and **TEXT** fields. We can use the **Fulltext** quick link in the fields list or go to the index management panel and choose **Fulltext** in the drop-down menu.

We add a FULLTEXT index on the description field, so that we are able to locate a book from words present in its description.

Table optimization—explaining a query

In this section, we want to get some information about the index that MySQL uses for a specific query, and the performance impact of not having defined an index.

Let's assume we want to use the following query:

```
SELECT  *
FROM `book`
WHERE author_id = 2 AND language = 'es'
```

We want to know, which books written by the author whose id is 2, are in the es language—our code for Spanish.

To enter this query, we use the **SQL** link from the database or the table menu, or the SQL query window (see Chapter 12). We enter this query in the query box and click **Go**. Whether the query finds any results, is not important right now.

 You could obtain the same query by following explanations from Chapter 9 to produce a search for **author_id 2** and language **es**.

> ✔ MySQL returned an empty result set (i.e. zero rows). (Query took 0.0006 sec)
> ```
> SELECT *
> FROM `book`
> WHERE `author_id` =2
> AND `language` = 'es'
> LIMIT 0 , 30
> ```
> ☐ Profiling [Edit] [Explain SQL] [Create PHP Code] [Refresh]

Let's look at the links: **[Edit] [Explain SQL] [Create PHP Code] [Refresh]**

We will now use the **[Explain SQL]** link to get information about which index (if any) has been used for this query:

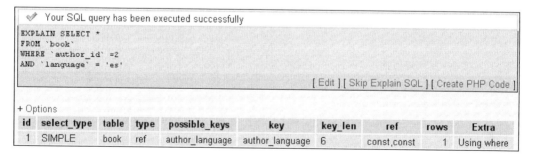

> ✔ Your SQL query has been executed successfully
> ```
> EXPLAIN SELECT *
> FROM `book`
> WHERE `author_id` =2
> AND `language` = 'es'
> ```
> [Edit] [Skip Explain SQL] [Create PHP Code]

+ Options

id	select_type	table	type	possible_keys	key	key_len	ref	rows	Extra
1	SIMPLE	book	ref	author_language	author_language	6	const,const	1	Using where

We can see that the EXPLAIN command has been passed to MySQL, telling us that the possible_keys used is author_language. Thus, we know that this index will be used for this type of query. If this index had not existed, the result would have been quite different.

id	select_type	table	type	possible_keys	key	key_len	ref	rows	Extra
1	SIMPLE	book	ALL	NULL	NULL	NULL	NULL	3	Using where

Here, **possible_keys (NULL)** and the **type (ALL)** mean that no index would be used, and all rows would need to be examined to find the desired data. Depending on the total number of rows, this could have a serious impact on the performance. We can ascertain the exact impact by examining the query timing that phpMyAdmin displays on each result page (**Query took x sec**), and comparing it with or without the index. However, the difference in time can be minimal if we only have limited test data, compared to a real table in production.

Detection of index problems

To help users maintain an optimal index strategy, phpMyAdmin tries to detect some common index problems. For example, let's access the book table and add an index on the **isbn** column. When we display this table's structure, we get a warning:

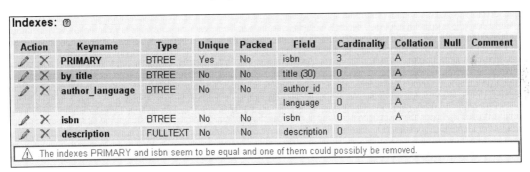

Indexes: ⓘ

Action	Keyname	Type	Unique	Packed	Field	Cardinality	Collation	Null	Comment
✎ ✕	PRIMARY	BTREE	Yes	No	isbn	3	A		
✎ ✕	by_title	BTREE	No	No	title (30)	0	A		
✎ ✕	author_language	BTREE	No	No	author_id	0	A		
					language	0	A		
✎ ✕	isbn	BTREE	No	No	isbn	0	A		
✎ ✕	description	FULLTEXT	No	No	description	0			

⚠ The indexes PRIMARY and isbn seem to be equal and one of them could possibly be removed.

The intention here is to warn us about an inefficient index structure when considering the whole table. We don't need to have two indexes on the same column.

Summary

In this chapter, we get an overview of:

- How to add fields, including special field types such as TEXT, BLOB, ENUM, and SET
- How to use a calendar pop up for DATE, DATETIME, and TIMESTAMP fields
- How to upload binary data into a BLOB field
- How to manage indexes (multi-field and full-text), and get feedback from MySQL about which indexes are used in a specific query

In Chapter 7, we'll learn how to export a tables structure and data for backup purposes, or to use as a gateway to another application.

Exporting Structure and Data (Backup)

Keeping good backups is crucial to a project. Backups consist of up-to-date backups and intermediary snapshots taken during development and production phases. The export feature of phpMyAdmin can generate backups, and can also be used to send data to other applications.

Dumps, backups, and exports

Let's first clarify some vocabulary. In MySQL documentation, you will encounter the term **dump**, and in other applications, the term **backup** or **export**. All these terms have the same meaning in the phpMyAdmin context.

MySQL includes **mysqldump**—a command-line utility that can be used to generate export files. But the shell access needed for command-line utilities is not offered by every host provider. Also, access to the export feature from within the Web interface is more convenient. This is why phpMyAdmin (since version 1.2.0) offers the export feature with more export formats than mysqldump. This chapter will focus on phpMyAdmin's export features.

Before starting an export, we must have a clear picture of the intended goal of the export. The following questions may be of help:

- Do we need the complete database or just some tables?
- Do we need just the structure, just the data, or both?
- Which utility will be used to import back the data? (Not every export format can be imported by phpMyAdmin.)
- Do we want only a subset of the data?
- What is the size of the intended export, and of the link speed between us and the server?

Scope of the export

When we click an **Export** link from phpMyAdmin, we can be in one of these views or contexts — Database view, Table view, or Server view (more on this later in Chapter 18). According to the current context, the resulting export's scope will be a complete database, a single table, or even a multi-database export as in the case of Server view. We will first explain database exports and all the relevant export types. Then we'll go on with table and multi-database exports, underlining the difference for these modes of exporting.

Database exports

In the Database view, click the **Export** link. The default export panel looks like this:

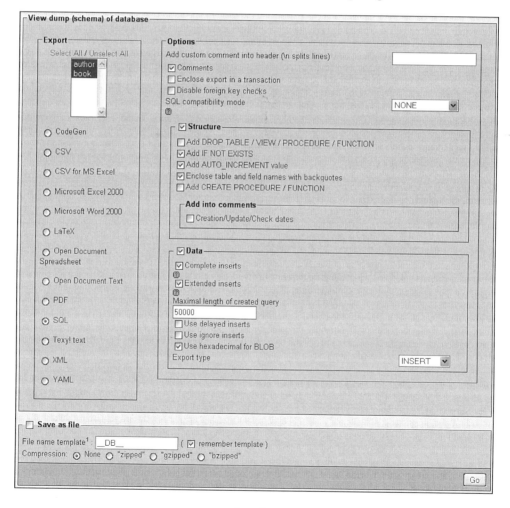

The default values selected here depend on `config.inc.php`, more specifically on the `$cfg['Export']` array of parameters. For example, the `$cfg['Export']['format']` parameter is set to `'sql'`, so that the **SQL** export mode is chosen by default.

The export panel has three subpanels. The top panel **Export** and the bottom panel **Save as file** are always there. However, the third panel varies (using dynamic menu techniques) in order to show the options for the export mode chosen (which is SQL here).

The export subpanel

This subpanel contains a table selector, from where we choose the tables and the format that we want. The SQL format is useful for our needs, as it creates standard SQL commands that would work on any SQL server. Other possible formats include LaTeX, PDF, Microsoft Excel 2000, Microsoft Word 2000, **Comma-Separated Values (CSV)**, YAML, CodeGen, Texy! text, Open Document Spreadsheet, Open Document Text, and XML. Another format, Native MS Excel, is available after further software installation and configuration. (See the section on *Native MS Excel* in this chapter.)

We shall now discuss the formats (and the options available once they have been chosen) that can be selected with the **Export** subpanel.

 Even if we can export from phpMyAdmin into all these formats, only the SQL and CSV formats can be imported back using the current phpMyAdmin version. Use only these two formats for backup.

SQL

We will start by clicking **Select All**; we want all the tables. We know that the tables are small, so the on screen export will not be too large. For the moment, let's deselect the **Extended inserts** checkbox. We then click **Go**, which produces the following output:

```
-- phpMyAdmin SQL Dump
-- version 3.1.1
-- http://www.phpmyadmin.net
--
-- Host: localhost
-- Generation Time: Dec 21, 2008 at 12:55 PM
-- Server version: 5.0.67
-- PHP Version: 5.2.6

SET SQL_MODE="NO_AUTO_VALUE_ON_ZERO";
```

```
--
-- Database: `marc_book`
--


-- ------------------------------------------------------------


--
-- Table structure for table `author`
--

CREATE TABLE IF NOT EXISTS `author` (
  `id` int(11) NOT NULL,
  `name` varchar(30) NOT NULL,
  `phone` varchar(30) default NULL,
  PRIMARY KEY  (`id`)
) ENGINE=MyISAM DEFAULT CHARSET=latin1;


--
-- Dumping data for table `author`
--

INSERT INTO `author` (`id`, `name`, `phone`) VALUES(1, 'John Smith',
'+01 445-789-1234');
INSERT INTO `author` (`id`, `name`, `phone`) VALUES(2, 'Maria
Sunshine', '333-3333');


-- ------------------------------------------------------------


--
-- Table structure for table `book`
--

CREATE TABLE IF NOT EXISTS `book` (
  `isbn` varchar(25) NOT NULL,
  `title` varchar(100) NOT NULL,
  `page_count` int(11) NOT NULL,
  `author_id` int(11) NOT NULL,
  `language` char(2) NOT NULL default 'en',
  `description` text NOT NULL,
  `cover_photo` blob NOT NULL,
  `genre` set('Fantasy','Child','Novel') NOT NULL default 'Fantasy',
  `date_published` datetime NOT NULL,
  `stamp` timestamp NOT NULL default '0000-00-00 00:00:00' on update
CURRENT_TIMESTAMP,
```

```
    `some_bits` bit(3) NOT NULL,
    PRIMARY KEY (`isbn`),
    KEY `by_title` (`title`(30)),
    KEY `author_language` (`author_id`,`language`),
    KEY `isbn` (`isbn`),
    FULLTEXT KEY `description` (`description`)
) ENGINE=MyISAM DEFAULT CHARSET=latin1;


--
-- Dumping data for table `book`
--

INSERT INTO `book` (`isbn`, `title`, `page_count`, `author_
id`, `language`, `description`, `cover_photo`, `genre`, `date_
published`, `stamp`, `some_bits`) VALUES('1-234567-89-0',
'A hundred years of cinema (volume 1)', 600, 1, 'en', '',
0x89504e470d0a1a0a0000000d494844, '', '0000-00-00 00:00:00', '2008-12-
20 14:14:35', b'011');
INSERT INTO `book` (`isbn`, `title`, `page_count`, `author_id`,
`language`, `description`, `cover_photo`, `genre`, `date_published`,
`stamp`, `some_bits`) VALUES('1-234567-22-0', 'Future souvenirs', 200,
2, 'en', '', '', '', '0000-00-00 00:00:00', '0000-00-00 00:00:00',
'\0');
INSERT INTO `book` (`isbn`, `title`, `page_count`, `author_id`,
`language`, `description`, `cover_photo`, `genre`, `date_published`,
`stamp`, `some_bits`) VALUES('1-234567-90-0', 'A hundred years of
cinema (volume 2)', 602, 1, 'en', '', '', '', '0000-00-00 00:00:00',
'0000-00-00 00:00:00', '\0');
```

In this export example, the data for one of the books (starting with 0x8950) has been truncated for brevity. In fact, it would contain the full hexadecimal representation of the cover_photo field of this book.

The first part of the export comprises comments (starting with the characters, --) that detail the utility (and version) that created the file, the date, and other environment information. We then see the CREATE and INSERT queries for each table.

phpMyAdmin generates ANSI-compatible comments in the export file. These comments start with --. They help with importing the file back on other ANSI SQL-compatible systems. In versions prior to 2.6.0, the MySQL-specific character, '#', was used.

SQL options

SQL options are used to define exactly what information the export will contain. We may want to see the structure, the data, or both. Selecting **Structure** generates the section with CREATE queries, and selecting **Data** produces INSERT queries:

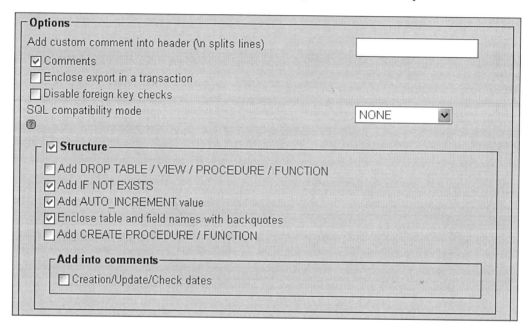

The general SQL options are:

- **Add custom comment into header**: We can add our own comments for this export (for example, **Monthly backup**), which will show in the export headers (after the PHP version number). If the comment has more than one line, we must use the special character \n to separate each line.

- **Comments**: Removing the check mark here causes the export to have no comments at all.

- **Enclose export in a transaction**: Starting with MySQL 4.0.11, we can use the START TRANSACTION statement. This command, combined with SET AUTOCOMMIT=0 at the beginning and COMMIT at the end, asks MySQL to execute the import (when we will re-import this file) in one transaction, ensuring that all the changes are done as a whole.

- **Disable foreign key checks**: In the export file, we can add DROP TABLE statements. However, normally a table cannot be dropped if it is referenced in a foreign key constraint. This option overrides the verification by adding SET FOREIGN_KEY_CHECKS=0 to the export file.

- **SQL compatibility mode:** This lets us choose the flavor of SQL that we export. We must know about the system onto which we intend to import this file. Among the choices are **MySQL 3.23**, **MySQL 4.0**, **Oracle**, and **ANSI**.

The options in **Structure** section are:

- **Add DROP TABLE / DROP VIEW**: Adds a DROP TABLE IF EXISTS statement before each CREATE TABLE statement, for example: DROP TABLE IF EXISTS `author`;. This way, we can ensure that the export file is executed on a database in which the same table already exists, updating its structure but destroying the previous table contents. A DROP VIEW is used for views.

- **Add IF NOT EXISTS**: Adds the IF NOT EXISTS modifier to CREATE TABLE statements, avoiding an error during import if the table already exists.

- **Add AUTO_INCREMENT value**: Puts auto-increment information from the tables into the export, ensuring that the inserted rows in the tables will receive the next exact auto-increment ID value.

- **Enclose table and field names with backquotes**: Backquotes are the normal ways of protecting table and field names that may contain special characters. In most cases, it is useful to have them. However, backquote are not recommended, if the target server (where the export file will be imported) is running a MySQL version older than 3.23.6, which does not support backquotes.

- **Add CREATE PROCEDURE / FUNCTION**: This includes all procedures and functions found in this database, in the export.

- **Add into comments**: This adds information (in the form of SQL comments), which cannot be directly imported, but which nonetheless is valuable and human-readable table information. The amount of information here varies depending on the relational system settings (see Chapter 11). In fact, with an activated relational system, we would get the following choices:

Add into comments:
- [ ] Creation/Update/Check dates
- [ ] Relations
- [ ] MIME type

Selecting **Relations** and **MIME type** would produce an additional section in the structure export.

```
--
-- COMMENTS FOR TABLE 'book':
--    'isbn'
--         'book number'
--    'page_count'
--         'approximate'
--    'author_id'
--         'see author table'
--


--
-- MIME TYPES FOR TABLE 'book':
--    'cover_photo'
--         'image_jpeg'
--    'date_released'
--         'text_plain'
--    'description'
--         'text_plain'
--


-- RELATIONS FOR TABLE 'book':
--    'author_id'
--         'author' -> 'id'
--
```

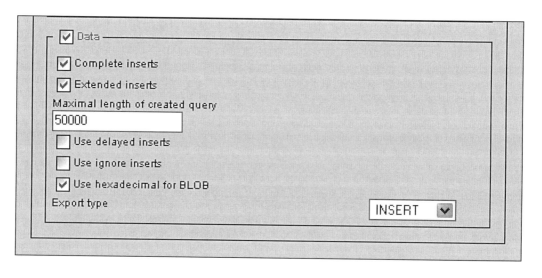

The options available in the **Data** section are:

- **Complete inserts**: Generates the following export for the `author` table:

```
    INSERT INTO 'author' ('id', `name`, `phone`)
VALUES (1, 'John Smith', '+01 445 789-1234');
    INSERT INTO 'author' ('id', `name`, `phone`)
VALUES (2, 'Maria Sunshine', '+01 455 444-5683');
```

  Notice that every column name is present in every statement. The resulting file is bigger, but will prove more portable on various SQL systems with the added benefit of being better documented.

- **Extended inserts**: Packs the whole table data into a single `INSERT` statement:

```
    INSERT INTO 'author' VALUES (1, 'John Smith',
     '+01 445 789-1234'), (2, 'Maria Sunshine', '+01 455 444-
                        5683');
```

  This method of inserting data is faster than using multiple `INSERT` statements, but is less convenient because it makes reading the resultant file harder. **Extended inserts** also produces a smaller file, but each line of this file is not executable in itself because each line does not have an `INSERT` statement. If you cannot import the complete file in one operation, you cannot split the file with a text editor and import it chunk by chunk.

- **Maximal length of created query**: The single `INSERT` statement generated for **Extended inserts** might become too big and could cause problems. Hence, we set a limit to the number of characters for the length of this statement.

- **Use delayed inserts**: Adds the `DELAYED` modifier to `INSERT` statements. This accelerates the `INSERT` operation because it is queued to the server, which will execute it when the table is not in use. Please note that this is a MySQL non-standard extension, and it's available only for `MyISAM`, `ISAM`, `MEMORY`, and `ARCHIVE` tables.

- **Use ignore inserts**: Normally, at import time, we cannot insert duplicate values for unique keys, as this would abort the insert operation. This option adds the `IGNORE` modifier to `INSERT` and `UPDATE` statements, thus skipping the rows that generate duplicate key errors.

- **Use hexadecimal for BLOB**: This option makes phpMyAdmin encode the contents of BLOB fields in `0x` format. Such a format is useful because, depending on the software that will be used to manipulate the export file (for example a text editor or mail program), handling a file containing 8-bit data can be problematic. However, using this option will produce an export of the `BLOB` that can be twice the size, or even more.

- **Export type**: The choices are **INSERT**, **UPDATE**, and **REPLACE**. The most well-known of these types is the default **INSERT** — using `INSERT` statements to import back our data. At import time, however, we could be in a situation where a table already exists and contains valuable data, and we just want to update the fields that are in the current table we are exporting. **UPDATE** generates statements like `UPDATE 'author' SET 'id' = 1, 'name' = 'John Smith', 'phone' = '111-1111' WHERE 'id' = '1';` updating a row when the same primary or unique key is found. The third possibility, **REPLACE**, produces statements like `REPLACE INTO 'author' VALUES (1, 'John Smith', '111-1111');` These act like an `INSERT` statement for new rows and update existing rows, based on primary or unique keys.

The "Save as file" subpanel

In the previous examples, the results of the export operation were displayed on screen, and of course, no compression was made on the data. We can choose to transmit the export file via HTTP by checking the **Save as file** checkbox. This triggers a **Save** dialog into the browser, which ultimately saves the file on our local station.

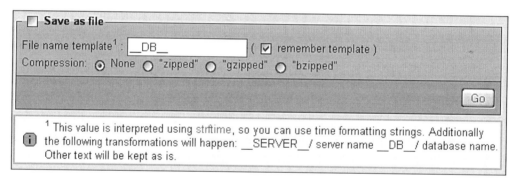

File name template

The name of the proposed file will obey the **File name template**. In this template, we can use the special **__SERVER__**, **__DB__**, and **__TABLE__** placeholders. These placeholders will be replaced by the current server, database, or table name (for a single-table export). Note that there are two underscore characters before and after the words. We can also use any special character from the PHP `strftime` function; this is useful for generating an export file based on the current date or hour. Finally, we can put any other string of characters (not part of the `strftime` special characters), which will be used literally. The file extension is generated according to the type of export. In this case, it will be `.sql`. Here are some examples for the template:

- **__DB__** would generate **marc_book.sql**
- **__DB__-%Y%m%d** would give **marc_book-20071206.sql**

The **remember template** option, when activated, stores the entered template settings into cookies (for database, table, or server exports) and brings them back the next time we use the same kind of export.

The default templates are configurable, via the following parameters:

```
$cfg['Export']['file_template_table']      = '__TABLE__';
$cfg['Export']['file_template_database']    = '__DB__';
$cfg['Export']['file_template_server']      = '__SERVER__';
```

Compression

To save transmission time and get a smaller export file, phpMyAdmin can compress to ZIP, GZIP, or BZIP2 formats. phpMyAdmin has native support for the ZIP format. However, the GZIP and BZIP2formats work only if the PHP server has been compiled with the --with-zlib or --with-bz2 configuration option respectively. The following parameters control which compression choices are presented in the panel:

```
$cfg['ZipDump']      = TRUE;
$cfg['GZipDump']     = TRUE;
$cfg['BZipDump']     = TRUE;
```

A system administrator installing phpMyAdmin for a number of users could choose to set all these parameters to FALSE, so as to avoid the potential overhead incurred by a lot of users compressing their exports at the same time. This situation usually causes more overhead than if all the users were transmitting their uncompressed files at the same time.

In older phpMyAdmin versions, the compression file was built in the web server memory. Some problems caused by this were:

- File generation depended on the memory limits assigned to running PHP scripts.
- During the time the file was generated and compressed, no transmission occurred. Hence, users were inclined to think that the operation was not working and that something had crashed.
- Compression of large databases was impossible to achieve.

The $cfg['CompressOnFly'] parameter (set to TRUE by default) was added to generate (for gzip and bzip2 formats) a compressed file containing more headers. Now, the transmission starts almost immediately. The file is sent in smaller chunks so that the whole process consumes much lesser memory.

Choice of character set

This section explains a little-known feature—the possibility of choosing the exact character set for our exported file.

This feature is activated by setting $cfg['AllowAnywhereRecoding'] to TRUE. We can see here the effect on the interface.

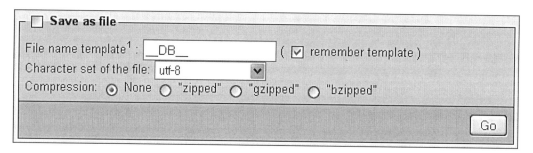

When this parameter is switched on, phpMyAdmin verifies that the conditions for recoding are met. For the actual encoding of data, the PHP component of the web server must support the iconv or the recode module. If this is not the case and the parameter has been set to TRUE, the following error message will be generated:

Couldn't load the iconv or recode extension needed for charset conversion. Either configure PHP to enable these extensions or disable charset conversion in phpMyAdmin.

If this message is displayed, consult your system's documentation (PHP or the operating system) for the installation procedures.

Another parameter ($cfg['RecodingEngine']) specifies the actual recoding engine—the choices being auto, iconv, and recode. If it is set to auto, phpMyAdmin will first try the iconv module and then the recode module.

Kanji support

If phpMyAdmin detects the use of the Japanese language, it checks whether PHP supports the mb_convert_encoding() multibyte strings function. If it does, additional radio buttons—**export**, **import**, and **query box**— are displayed on the following pages, so that we can choose between the EUC-JP and SJIS Japanese encodings.

Here is an example taken from the **Export** page:

CSV

This format is understood by a lot of programs, and you may find it useful for exchanging data. Note that it is a data-only format—no SQL structure here.

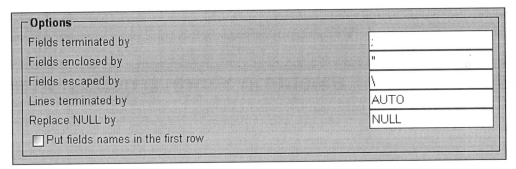

The available options are:

- **Fields terminated by**: We put a comma here, which means that a comma will be placed after each field.

- **Fields enclosed by**: We place an enclosing character here (like the quote) to ensure that a field containing the terminating character (comma) is not taken for two fields.

- **Fields escaped by**: If the export generator finds the **Fields enclosed by** character inside a field, the **Fields escaped by** character will be placed before it in order to protect it. For example, `"John \"The Great\" Smith"`.

- **Lines terminated by**: This decides the character that ends each line. We should use the proper line delimiter here depending on the operating system on which we will manipulate the resulting export file. The default value of this option comes from the $cfg['Export']['csv_terminated'] parameter, which contains 'AUTO' by default. The 'AUTO' value produces a value of \r\n if the browser's OS is Windows and \n otherwise. However, this might not be the best choice if the export file is intended for a machine with a different OS.

- **Replace NULL by**: This determines which string occupies the place in the export file of any NULL value found in a field.

- **Put fields names in the first row**: This gets some information about the meaning of each field. Some programs will use this information to name the column.

Finally, we select the **author** table.

The result is:

```
"id","name","phone"
"1","John Smith","+01 445 789-1234"
"2","Maria Sunshine","+01 455 444-5683"
```

CSV for MS Excel

This export mode produces a CSV file intended for Microsoft Excel. We can select the exact Microsoft Excel edition.

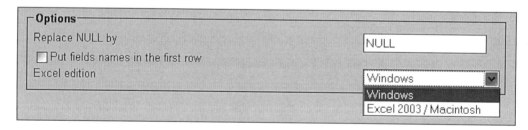

PDF

Since version 2.8.0, it's possible to create a PDF report of a table by exporting in PDF. This feature works on only one table at a time, and we must click the **Save as file** checkbox for normal operation. We can add a title for this report, and it also gets automatically paginated. In versions 2.8.0 to 2.8.2, this export format does not support non-textual (BLOB) data as in the book table. If we try it in this table, it will produce the wrong results.

Here, we test it on the author table.

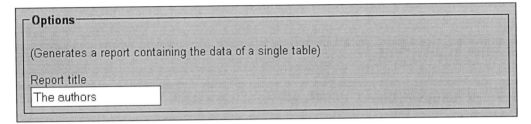

PDF is interesting because of its inherent vectorial nature — the results can be zoomed. Let's have a look at the generated report, as seen from the Acrobat Reader:

Microsoft Excel 2000

This export format directly produces an .xls file suitable for all software that understand the Excel 2000 format. We can specify which string should replace a NULL value. The **Put field names in the first row** option, when activated, generates the table's column names as the first line of the spreadsheet. Again, the **Save as file** checkbox should be checked. This produces a file, where each table's column becomes a spreadsheet column.

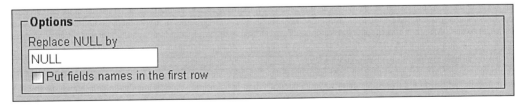

Microsoft Word 2000

This export format directly produces a .doc file suitable for all software that understand the Word 2000 format. We find options similar to those in the Microsoft Excel 2000 export, and a few more. We can independently export the table's **Structure** and **Data**.

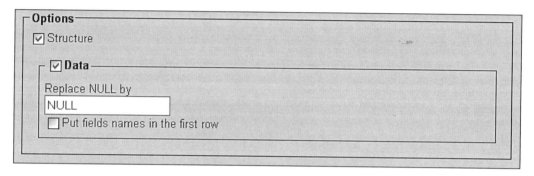

Note that, for this format and the Excel format, we can choose many tables for one export. However, unpleasant results happen if one of these tables has non-textual data. Here are the results for the **author** table:

Database marc_book

Table structure for table author

Field	Type	Null	Default
id	int(11)	Yes	
name	varchar(30)	Yes	
phone	varchar(30)	Yes	NULL

Dumping data for table author

1	John Smith	+01 445-789-1234
2	Maria Sunshine	333-3333

LaTeX

LaTeX is a typesetting language. phpMyAdmin can generate a `.tex` file that represents the table's structure and/or data in a sideways tabular format. Note that this file is not directly viewable, and must be processed further or converted for the intended final media.

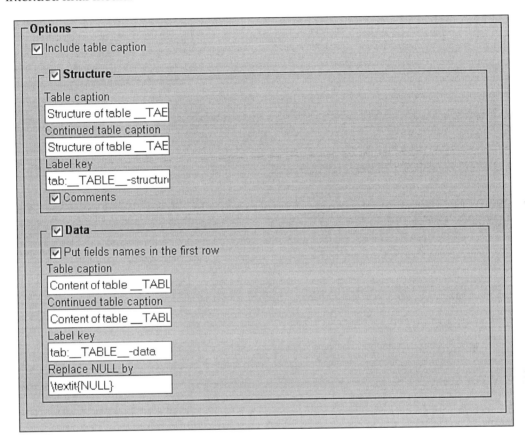

The available options are:

- **Include table caption**: Display captions in the tabular output.

- **Structure** and **Data**: The familiar choice to request structure, data, or both.

- **Table caption**: The caption to go on the first page.

- **Continued table caption**: The caption to go on, page after page.

- **Relations**, **Comments**, **MIME-type**: Other structure information we want as output. These choices are available if the relational infrastructure is in place (see Chapter 11 for details).

XML

This format is very popular these days for data exchange. Choosing **XML** in the **Export** interface yields no choice for options. What follows is the output for the **author** table.

```
<?xml version="1.0" encoding="utf-8" ?>
<!--
-
- phpMyAdmin XML Dump
- version 3.1.1
- http://www.phpmyadmin.net
-
- Host: localhost
- Generation Time: Dec 21, 2007 at 01:13 PM
- Server version: 5.0.67
- PHP Version: 5.2.6
-->

<!--
- Database: 'marc_book'
-->
<marc_book>
  <!-- Table author -->
    <author>
        <id>1</id>
        <name>John Smith</name>
        <phone>+01 445-789-1234</phone>
    </author>
    <author>
        <id>2</id>
        <name>Maria Sunshine</name>
        <phone>333-3333</phone>
    </author>
</marc_book>
```

Native MS Excel (pre-Excel 2000)

phpMyAdmin offers an experimental module to export directly into a .xls format—the native spreadsheet format understood by MS Excel and OpenOffice Calc. When this support is activated (more on this in a moment), we see a new export choice, **Native MS Excel**, and the same options as those for Microsoft Excel 2000.

We can optionally put our field names in the first row of the spreadsheet, with **Put fields names at first row**.

This functionality relies on the PEAR module `Spreadsheet_Excel_Writer`, which is currently at version 0.9.1 and generates Excel 5.0 format files. This module is documented at `http://pear.php.net/package/Spreadsheet_Excel_Writer`, but the complete installation in phpMyAdmin's context is documented here:

1. Ensure that the PHP server has PEAR support. (The `pear` command will fail if we do not have PEAR support.) PEAR itself is documented at `http://pear.php.net`.

2. If we are running PHP in safe mode, we have to ensure that we are allowed to include the PEAR modules. Assuming that the modules are located under `/usr/local/share/pear`, we should have the line `safe_mode_include_dir = /usr/local/share/pear` in `php.ini`.

3. We then install the module with `pear -d preferred_state=beta install -a Spreadsheet_Excel_Writer` (because the module is currently in beta state). This command fetches the necessary modules over the Internet and installs them into our PEAR infrastructure.

4. We need a temporary directory, under the main phpMyAdmin directory, for the `.xls` generation. It can be created on a Linux system with `mkdir tmp ; chmod o+rwx tmp`.

5. We set the `$cfg['TempDir']` parameter in `config.inc.php` to `'./tmp'`.

We should now be able to see the new **Native MS Excel data** export choice.

Open document spreadsheet

This spreadsheet format is a subset of the open document (`http://en.wikipedia.org/wiki/OpenDocument`), which was made popular with the `OpenOffice.org` office suite. We need to choose only one table to be exported in order to have a coherent spreadsheet. Here is our author table, exported into a file named `author.ods`, and subsequently looked at from OpenOffice:

Open document text

This is another subset of the open document standard, this time oriented towards text processing. The available options are as shown in the following screenshot:

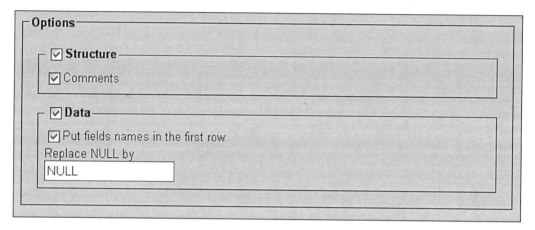

Our `author` table is now exported and viewed from OpenOffice.

Database marc_book

Table structure for table author

Field	Type	Null	Default	Comments
id	int(11)	Yes		
name	varchar(30)	Yes		
phone	varchar(30)	Yes	NULL	

Dumping data for table author

id	name	phone
1	John Smith	+01 445-789-1234
2	Maria Sunshine	333-3333

YAML

YAML stands for **YAML Ain't Markup Language**. YAML is a human-readable data serialization format; its official site is http://www.yaml.org. This format has no option that we can choose from within phpMyAdmin. Here is the YAML export for the author table:

```
1:
   id: 1
   name: John Smith
   phone: +01 445-789-1234

2:
   id: 2
   name: Maria Sunshine
   phone: 333-3333
```

CodeGen

This choice might some day support many formats related to code development. Currently, it can export in NHibernate **Object-relation mapping (ORM)** format. For more details, please refer to http://en.wikipedia.org/wiki/Nhibernate.

Texy! text

Texy! is a formatting tool (http://texy.info/en/) with its own simplified syntax. Here is an example of export in this format:

```
===Database marc_book

== Table structure for table author
|------
|Field|Type|Null|Default
|------
|//**id**//|int(11)|Yes|NULL
|name|varchar(30)|Yes|NULL
|phone|varchar(30)|Yes|NULL

== Dumping data for table author
|1|John Smith|+01 445 789-1234
|2|Maria Sunshine|333-3333
```

Table exports

The **Export** link in the Table view brings up the export subpanel for a specific table. It is similar to the database export panel, but there is no table selector. However, there is an additional section for split exports before the **Save as file** subpanel.

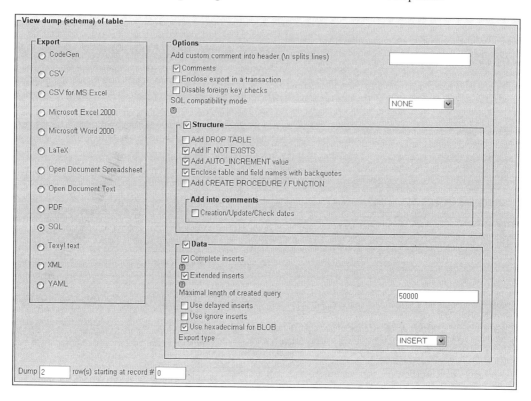

Split-file exports

The **Dump 2 row(s) starting at record # 0** dialog enables us to split the file into chunks. Depending on the exact row size, we can experiment with various values for the number of rows to find how many rows can be put in a single export file before the memory or execution time limits are hit in the web server. We could then use names like book00.sql and book01.sql for our export files.

Selective exports

At various places in phpMyAdmin's interface, we can export the results that we see, or select the rows that we want to export.

Exporting partial query results

When results are displayed from phpMyAdmin (here, the results of a query asking for the books from **author_id 2**), an **Export** link appears at the bottom of the page.

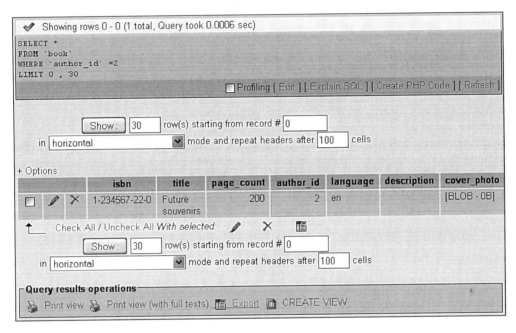

Clicking on this link brings up a special export panel containing the query on the top, along with the other table export options. An export produced via this panel would contain only the data from this result set.

> The results of single-table queries can be exported in all the available formats, while the results of multi-table queries can be exported only in the CSV, XML, and LaTeX formats.

Exporting and checkboxes

Anytime we see the results (when browsing or searching, for example), we can check the boxes beside the rows that we want, and use the **With selected: export** icon to generate a partial export file with just those rows.

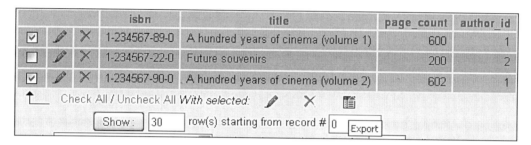

Multi-database exports

Any user can export the databases to which he/she has access, in one operation.

On the homepage, the **Export** link brings us to the screen shown on the following page. These has the same structure as the other export pages, except for the databases list.

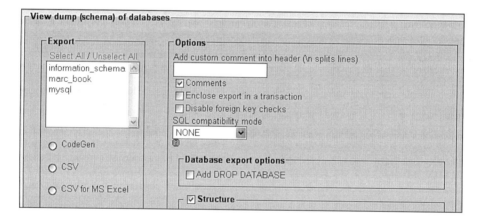

 Exporting large databases may or may not work. It depends on their size, the options chosen, and the web server's PHP component settings (especially memory size and execution time).

Saving the export file on the server

Instead of transmitting the export file over the network with HTTP, it is possible to save it directly on the file system of the web server. This could be quicker and less sensitive to execution time limits because the entire transfer from the server to the client browser is bypassed. Eventually, a file transfer protocol such as FTP or SFTP can be used to retrieve the file, as leaving it on the same machine would not provide good backup protection.

A special directory has to be created on the web server before saving an export file on it. Usually, this is a subdirectory of the main `phpMyAdmin` directory. We will use `save_dir` as an example. This directory must have special permissions. First, the web server must have write permissions for this directory. Also, if the web server's PHP component is running in safe mode, the owner of the phpMyAdmin scripts must be the same as that of `save_dir`.

On a Linux system, assuming that the web server is running as group apache, and the scripts are owned by a user "marc", the following commands would do the trick:

```
# mkdir save_dir
# chown marc.apache save_dir
# chmod g=rwx save_dir
```

 The proper ownership and permissions mask depend highly on the chosen web server and the **SAPI (Server Application Programming Interface)** (see http://en.wikipedia.org/wiki/Server_Application_Programming_Interface) used, which influences how directories and files are created and accessed. PHP could be using the scripts' owner as the accessing user, or the web server's user/group itself.

We also have to define the `'./save_dir'` directory name in `$cfg['SaveDir']`. We are using a path relative to the `phpMyAdmin` directory here, but an absolute path would work just as well.

The **Save as file** section will appear with a new **Save on server...** section:

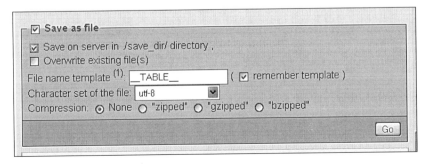

After clicking **Go**, we will get a confirmation message or an error message (if the web server does not have the required permissions to save the file).

 For saving a file again, using the same file name, check the **Overwrite existing file(s)** box.

User-specific save directories

We can use the special string, %u, in the $cfg['SaveDir'] parameter. This string will be replaced by the logged-in user name. For example, using

```
$cfg['SaveDir'] = './save_dir/%u';
```

This would give us an on screen choice, **Save on server in ./save_dir/marc/ directory**. These directories (one per potential user) must exist and must bear the proper permissions, as already seen in the previous section.

Memory limits

Generating an export file uses a certain amount of memory, depending on the size of the tables and on the chosen options. The $cfg['MemoryLimit'] parameter can contain a limit (in bytes) for the amount of memory used by the PHP script that is running. By default, the parameter is set to 0, meaning that there is no limit. Note that, if PHP has its safe mode activated, changing $cfg['MemoryLimit'] has no effect. Instead, the enforced limit comes from the memory_limit directive in php.ini.

Summary

In this chapter, we examine the various ways to trigger an export—from the Database view, the Table view, or a results page. We also list the various available export formats, their options, the possibility of compressing the export file, and the various places where it might be sent.

In the next chapter, we'll have the opportunity of importing back our structure and data, provided the chosen format is supported by phpMyAdmin.

8
Importing Structure and Data

In this chapter, we will learn how to bring back exported data that we create for backup or transfer purposes. Exported data may also come from authors of other applications, and could contain the whole foundation structure of these applications and some sample data.

The current phpMyAdmin version (3.1) can import files containing MySQL statements (usually having a `.sql` suffix, but not necessarily so) and CSV files (comma-separated values, although the separator is not necessarily a comma) directly. Future versions might be able to import files in more formats. There is also an interface to the MySQL LOAD DATA INFILE statement, enabling us to load text files containing data, also called CSV. The binary field upload covered in Chapter 6 can be said to belong to the import family.

[Importing and uploading are synonyms in this context.]

The import feature can be accessed from several panels:

- The **Import** menu available from the homepage, the Database view, or the Table view
- The **Import files** menu offered inside the **Query window** (as explained in Chapter 12)

A feature was added in version 2.11.0: an import file may contain the DELIMITER keyword. This enables phpMyAdmin to mimic the mysql command-line interpreter. The DELIMITER separator is used to delineate the part of the file containing a stored procedure, as these procedures can themselves contain semicolons.

The default values for the Import interface are defined in $cfg['Import'].

Before examining the actual import dialog, let's discuss some limits issues.

Limits for the transfer

When we import, the source file is usually on our client machine; so, it must travel to the server via HTTP. This transfer takes time and uses resources that may be limited in the web server's PHP configuration.

Instead of using HTTP, we can upload our file to the server using a protocol such as FTP, as described in the *Web Server Upload Directories* section. This method circumvents the web server's PHP upload limits.

Time limits

First, let's consider the time limit. In `config.inc.php`, the `$cfg['ExecTimeLimit']` configuration directive assigns, by default, a maximum execution time of 300 seconds (five minutes) for any phpMyAdmin script, including the scripts that process data after the file has been uploaded. A value of `0` removes the limit, and in theory, gives us infinite time to complete the import operation. If the PHP server is running in safe mode, modifying `$cfg['ExecTimeLimit']` will have no effect. This is because the limits set in `php.ini` or in user-related web server configuration file (such as `.htaccess` or virtual host configuration files) take precedence over this parameter.

Of course, the time it effectively takes depends on two key factors:

- Web server load
- MySQL server load

> The time taken by the file, as it travels between the client and the server, does not count as execution time because the PHP script only starts to execute after the file has been received on the server. Therefore, the `$cfg['ExecTimeLimit']` parameter has an impact only on the time used to process data (like decompression or sending it to the MySQL server).

Other limits

The system administrator can use the `php.ini` file or the web server's virtual host configuration file to control uploads on the server.

The `upload_max_filesize` parameter specifies the upper limit or the maximum file size that can be uploaded via HTTP. This one is obvious, but another less obvious parameter is `post_max_size`. As HTTP uploading is done via the POST method, this parameter may limit our transfers. For more details about the POST method, please refer to `http://en.wikipedia.org/wiki/Http#Request_methods`.

The memory_limit parameter is provided to avoid web server child processes from grabbing too much of the server memory—phpMyAdmin also runs as a child process. Thus, the handling of normal file uploads, especially compressed dumps, can be compromised by giving this parameter a small value. Here, no preferred value can be recommended; the value depends on the size of uploaded data. The memory limit can also be tuned via the $cfg['MemoryLimit'] parameter in config.inc.php, as seen in Chapter 7.

Finally, file uploads must be allowed by setting file_uploads to On. Otherwise, phpMyAdmin won't even show the **Location of the textfile** dialog. It would be useless to display this dialog, as the connection would be refused later by the PHP component of the web server.

Partial imports

If the file is too big, there are ways in which we can resolve the situation. If we still have access to the original data, we could use phpMyAdmin to generate smaller CSV export files, choosing the **Dump n rows starting at record # n** dialog. If this were not possible, we will have to use a text editor to split the file into smaller sections. Another possibility is to use the upload directory mechanism, which accesses the directory defined in $cfg['UploadDir']. This feature is explained later in this chapter

In recent phpMyAdmin versions, the **Partial import** feature can also solve this file size problem. By selecting the **Allow interrupt...** checkbox, the import process will interrupt itself if it detects that it is close to the time limit. We can also specify a number of queries to skip from the start, in case we successfully import a number of rows and wish to continue from that point.

Temporary directory

On some servers, a security feature called open_basedir can be set up in a way that impedes the upload mechanism. In this case, or for any other reason, when uploads are problematic, the $cfg['TempDir'] parameter can be set with the value of a temporary directory. This is probably a subdirectory of phpMyAdmin's main directory, into which the web server is allowed to put the uploaded file.

Importing SQL files

Any file containing MySQL statements can be imported via this mechanism. The dialog is available in the Database view or the Table view, via the **Import** subpage, or in the **Query** window.

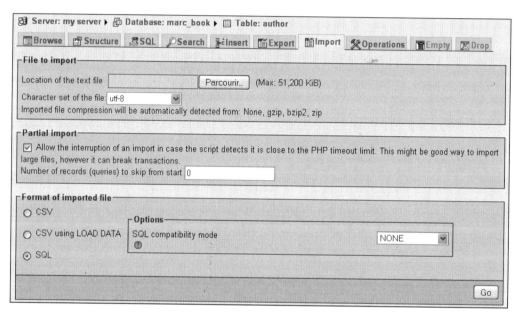

There is no relation between the currently selected table (here **author**) and the actual contents of the SQL file that will be imported. All the contents of the SQL file will be imported, and it is those contents that determine which tables or databases are affected. However, if the imported file does not contain any SQL statements to select a database, all statements in the imported file will be executed on the currently selected database.

Let's try an import exercise. First, we make sure that we have a current SQL export of the **book** table (as explained in Chapter 7). This export file must contain the structure and the data. Then we drop the **book** table—yes, really! We could also simply rename it. (See Chapter 10 for the procedure.)

Now it is time to import the file back. We should be on the **Import** subpage, where we can see the **Location of the text file** dialog. We just have to hit the **Browse** button and choose our file.

phpMyAdmin is able to detect which compression method (if any) has been applied to the file. Depending on the phpMyAdmin version, and the extensions that are available in the PHP component of the web server, there is variation in the formats that the program can decompress.

However, to import successfully, phpMyAdmin must be informed of the character set of the file to be imported. The default value is **utf8**. However, if we know that the import file was created with another character set, we should specify it here.

An **SQL compatibility mode** selector is available at import time. This mode should be adjusted to match the actual data that we are about to import, according to the type of the server where the data was previously exported.

To start the import, we click **Go**. The import procedure continues and we receive a message: **Import has been successfully finished, 2 queries executed**. We can browse our newly-created tables to confirm the success of the import operation.

The file could be imported for testing in a different database or even in a MySQL server.

Importing CSV files

In this section, we will examine how to import CSV files. There are two possible methods—**CSV** and **CSV using LOAD DATA**. The first method is implemented internally by phpMyAdmin and is the recommended one for its simplicity. With the second method, phpMyAdmin receives the file to be loaded, and passes it to MySQL. In theory, this method should be faster. However, it has more requirements due to MySQL itself (see the *Requirements* sub-section of the *CSV using LOAD DATA* section).

Differences between SQL and CSV formats

There are some differences between these two formats. The CSV file format contains data only, so we must already have an existing table in place. This table does not need to have the same structure as the original table (from which the data comes); the **Column names** dialog enables us to choose which columns are affected in the target table.

Because the table must exist prior to the import, the CSV import dialog is available only from the **Import** subpage in the Table view, and not in the Database view.

Exporting a test file

Before trying an import, let's generate an `author.csv` export file from the `author` table. We use the default values in the **CSV export** options. We can then **Empty** the `author` table — we should avoid dropping this table because we still need the table structure.

CSV

From the **author** table menu, we select **Import** and then **CSV**.

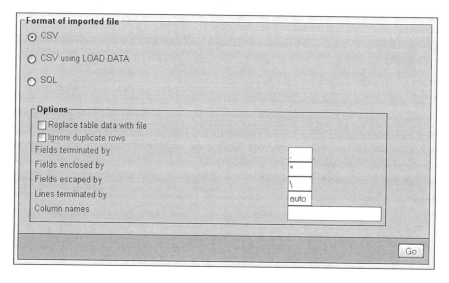

We can influence the behavior of the import in a number of ways. By default, importing does not modify existing data (based on primary or unique keys). However, the **Replace table data with file** option instructs phpMyAdmin to use `REPLACE` statement instead of `INSERT` statement, so that existing rows are replaced with the imported data.

Using **Ignore duplicate rows**, `INSERT IGNORE` statements are generated. These cause MySQL to ignore any duplicate key problems during insertion. A duplicate key from the import file does not replace existing data, and the procedure continues for the next line of CSV data.

We can then specify the character that terminates each field, the character that encloses data, and the character that escapes the enclosing character. Usually this is \. For example, for a double quote enclosing character, if the data field contains a double quote, it must be expressed as **"some data \" some other data"**.

For **Lines terminated by**, recent versions of phpMyAdmin offer the **auto** choice, which should be tried first as it detects the end-of-line character automatically. We can also specify manually which characters terminate the lines. The usual choice is **\n** for UNIX-based systems, **\r\n** for DOS or Windows systems, and **\r** for Mac-based system (up to Mac OS 9). If in doubt, we can use a hexadecimal file editor on our client computer (not part of phpMyAdmin) to examine the exact codes.

By default, phpMyAdmin expects a CSV file with the same number of fields and the same field order as the target table. But this can be changed by entering a comma-separated list of column names in **Column names**, respecting the source file format. For example, let's say our source file contains only the author ID and the author name information:

```
"1","John Smith"
"2","Maria Sunshine"
```

We'd have to put **id, name** in **Column names** to match the source file.

When we click **Go**, the import is executed and we get a confirmation. We might also see the actual INSERT queries generated if the total size of the file is not too big.

```
Import has been successfully finished, 2 queries executed.
INSERT INTO `author` VALUES ('1', 'John Smith', '+01 445 789-1234'
)# 1 row(s) affected.

INSERT INTO `author` VALUES ('2', 'Maria Sunshine', '333-3333'
)# 1 row(s) affected.
```

CSV using LOAD DATA

With this method, phpMyAdmin relies on the server's LOAD DATA INFILE or LOAD DATA LOCAL INFILE mechanisms to do the actual import, instead of processing the data internally. These statements are the fastest way for importing text in MySQL. They cause MySQL to start a read operation either from a file located on the MySQL server (LOAD DATA INFILE) or from another place (LOAD DATA LOCAL INFILE), which in this context, is always the web server's file system. If the MySQL server is located on a computer other than the web server, we won't be able to use the LOAD DATA INFILE mechanism.

Requirements

Relying on the MySQL server has some consequences. Using LOAD DATA INFILE requires that the logged-in user possess a global FILE privilege. Also, the file itself must be readable by the MySQL server's process.

Chapter 18 explains phpMyAdmin's interface, for system administrators to manage privileges.

Usage of the LOCAL modifier in LOAD DATA LOCAL INFILE must be allowed by the MySQL server and MySQL's client library used by PHP.

Both the LOAD methods are available from the phpMyAdmin LOAD interface, which tries to choose the best possible default option.

Using the LOAD DATA interface

We select **Import** from the **author** table menu. Choosing **CSV using LOAD DATA** brings up the following dialog:

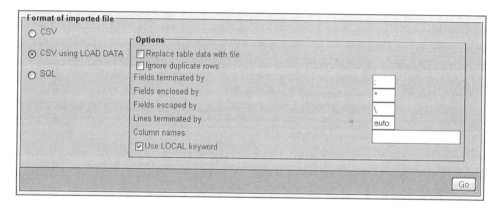

 The available options have already been covered in the *CSV* section.

In the familiar **Location of the text file** question, we choose our author.csv file.

Finally, we can choose the LOAD method, as discussed earlier, by selecting the **Use LOCAL keyword** option. We then click **Go**.

If all goes well, we can see the confirmation screen as follows:

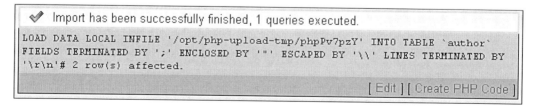

This screen shows the exact **LOAD DATA LOCAL INFILE** statement used. Here is what has happened:

- We chose **author.csv**.
- The contents of this file were transferred over HTTP and received by the web server.
- The PHP component inside the web server saved this file in a work directory (here **/opt/php-upload-tmp/**) and gave it a temporary name.
- phpMyAdmin, informed of the location of this working file, built a **LOAD DATA LOCAL INFILE** command, and sent it to MySQL. Note that just one query was executed, which loaded many rows.
- The MySQL server read and loaded the contents of the file into our target table. It then returned the number of affected rows (**2**), which phpMyAdmin displayed in the results page.

Web server upload directories

To get around cases where uploads are completely disabled by a web server's PHP configuration, or where upload limits are too small, phpMyAdmin can read upload files from a special directory located on the web server's file system. This mechanism is applicable for SQL and CSV imports.

We first specify the directory name of our choice in the `$cfg['UploadDir']` parameter, for example, `'./upload'`. We can also use the `%u` string, as described in Chapter 7, to represent the user's name.

Now, let's go back to the **Import** subpage. We get an error message:

`The directory you set for upload work cannot be reached.`

This error message is expected, as the directory does not exist. It is supposed to have been created inside the current `phpMyAdmin` installation directory. The message might also indicate that the directory exists, but can't be read by the web server. (In PHP safe mode, the owner of the directory and the owner of the phpMyAdmin-installed scripts must be the same.)

Using an SFTP or FTP client, we create the necessary directory, and can now upload a file there (for example **book.sql**) bypassing any PHP timeouts or upload maximum limits. Note that the file itself must have permissions that allow the web server to read it. In most cases, the easiest way is to allow everyone to read the file.

Refreshing the **Import** subpage brings up the following:

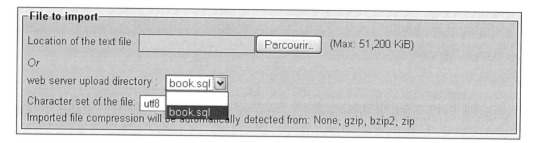

Clicking **Go** should execute the file.

Automatic decompression is also available for the files located in the upload directory. The file names should have extensions such as .bz2, .gz, .sql.bz2, or .sql.gz.

 Using the double extensions (.sql.bz2) is a better way to indicate that a .sql file was produced and then compressed, as we see all the steps used to generate this file.

Summary

This chapter covers:

- Various options in phpMyAdmin that allow us to import data
- The different mechanisms involved in importing SQL and CSV files
- The limits that we might hit when trying a transfer, and ways to bypass these limits

Chapter 9 will explain how to do single-table searches (covering search criteria specification) and how to search in the whole database.

9
Searching Data

In this chapter, we present mechanisms that can be used to find the data we are looking for, instead of just browsing tables page-by-page and sorting them. This chapter covers single-table searches besides entire database searches. Chapter 13 is a complement to this chapter and presents multi-table query with examples.

Daily usage of phpMyAdmin

For some users, the main use of phpMyAdmin is the **Search** mode, which is used for finding and updating data. For this, the phpMyAdmin team has made it possible to define which subpage is the starting page in Table view, with the $cfg['DefaultTabTable'] parameter. Setting it to 'tbl_select.php' defines the default subpage for search.

With this mode, application developers can look for data in ways not expected by the interface they are building—adjusting and sometimes repairing data.

Single-table searches

This section describes the **Search** subpage where a single-table search is available.

Entering the search subpage

The **Search** subpage can be accessed by clicking the **Search** link in the Table view. This has been done here for the book table:

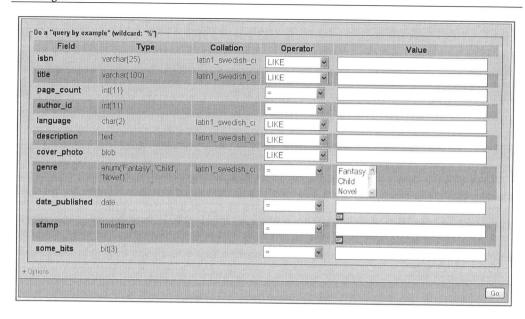

The most commonly used section of the **Search** interface (the query by example) is the one immediately displayed, whereas other dialogs are hidden in a slider that can be activated by the **Options** link (more on these dialogs later in this chapter).

Search criteria by field—query by example

The main use of the **Search** panel is to enter criteria for some fields so as to retrieve only the data we are interested in. This is called **query by example** because we give an example of what we are looking for. Our first retrieval will concern finding the book with ISBN **1-234567-89-0**. We simply enter this value in the **isbn** box and choose the **Operator** '='.

Clicking on **Go** gives these results (shown partially in the following screenshot).

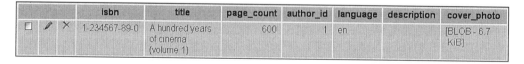

This is a standard results page. If the results ran in pages, we could navigate through them, and edit and delete data for the subset we have chosen during the process. Another feature of phpMyAdmin is that the fields used as the criteria are highlighted by changing the border color of the columns to better reflect their importance on the results page.

It isn't necessary to specify that the **isbn** column be displayed even though this is the column in which we search. We could have selected only the **title** column for display (see the *Selecting Fields to be Displayed* section) and chosen the **isbn** column as a criterion.

Searching for empty / non-empty values

In version 3.1.0, two handy operators have been added in the operator's list:

```
=  ' '
!=  ' '
```

Those are the ones to use when you want to search for an empty (= ' ') or not empty (!= ' ') value in some field. Normally, typing nothing in a field's **Value** means that this field does not participate in the search process. However, with one of these operators, this field is included in the generated search query.

Please do not confuse this method with searching for a NULL value, which is quite different. Indeed, a NULL value (refer to `http://en.wikipedia.org/wiki/Null_(SQL)` for a more complete explanation) is a special value that conveys that some information is missing in this column.

Print view

We see the **Print view** and **Print view (with full texts)** links on the results page. These links produce a more formal report of the results (without the navigation interface) directly to the printer. In our case, using **Print view** would produce the following:

SQL result

Host: my server
Database: marc_book
Generation Time: Dec 24, 2008 at 12:09 PM
Generated by: phpMyAdmin 3.1.1 / MySQL 5.0.67-standard
SQL query: SELECT * FROM `book` WHERE `isbn` = '1-234567-89-0' LIMIT 0, 30 ;
Rows: 1

isbn	title	page_count	author_id	language	description	cover_photo	genre	date_published	stamp	some_bits
1-234567-89-0	A hundred years of cinema (volume 1)	600	1	en		[BLOB - 6.7 KiB]	Fantasy	0000-00-00	2008-12-22 12:23:22	011

This report contains information about the server, database, time of generation, version of phpMyAdmin, version of MySQL, and generated SQL query. The other link, **Print view (with full texts)** would print the contents of the **TEXT** fields in their entirety.

Wildcard search

Let's assume we are looking for something less precise—all books with "cinema" in their title. First, we go back to the search page. For this type of search, we will use SQL's **LIKE** operator. This operator accepts wildcard characters—the % character (which matches any number of characters) and the underscore (_) character (which matches a single character). Thus we can use **%cinema%** to let phpMyAdmin find any substring that matches the word "cinema". If we left out both wildcard characters, we will get exact matches with only that single word.

This substring matching is easier to access, being part of the **Operator** drop-down list. We only have to enter the word **cinema** and use the operator **LIKE %...%** to perform that match. We should avoid using this form of the **LIKE** operator on big tables (thousands of rows), as MySQL does not use an index for data retrieval in this case, leading to wait time that could add up to half an hour (or more). This is why this operator is not the default one in the drop-down list, even though this method of search is commonly used on smaller tables.

Here is a screenshot showing how we ask for a search on **cinema** with the operator **LIKE %...%**:

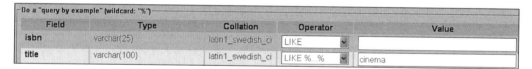

The LIKE operator can be used for other types of wildcard searches, for example History%, which would search for this word at the beginning of a title. This form of LIKE query also has the benefit of using an index, if MySQL finds one that speeds up data retrieval.

Using either of these methods of doing the query produces the following results:

			isbn	title	page_count	author_id	language	description
☐	✎	✕	1-234567-89-0	A hundred years of cinema (volume 1)	600	1	en	
☐	✎	✕	1-234567-90-0	A hundred years of cinema (volume 2)	602	1	en	

The % character (which matches any number of characters) and the underscore (_) character (which matches a single character) are the wildcard characters available here.

Case sensitivity

In the previous example, we could have replaced **cinema** with **CINEMA** and achieved similar results. The reason is that the collation of the `title` column is `latin1_swedish_ci`. Here, `ci` means that comparisons are done in a case-insensitive way. Please refer to `http://dev.mysql.com/doc/refman/5.1/en/case-sensitivity.html` for more details.

Combining criteria

We can use multiple criteria for the same query (for example, to find all the English books of more than 300 pages). There are more comparative choices in **Operator** because the **page_count** field is numeric, as shown in the following screenshot:

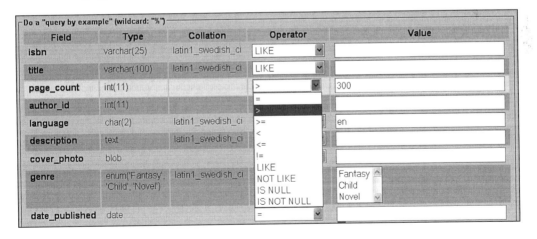

Search options

The **Options** slider reveals additional panels to further refine the search process.

Selecting the fields to be displayed

In the **Options** slider, a **Select fields** panel facilitates selection of the fields to be displayed in the results. All fields are selected by default, but we can control-click other fields to make the necessary selections. Mac users would use command-click to select/unselect the fields.

Here are the fields of interest in this example:

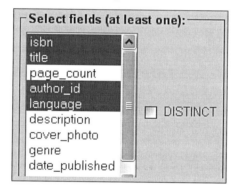

We can also specify the number of rows per page in the textbox next to the field selection. The **Add search conditions** box will be explained in the *Applying a WHERE clause* section, which will follow shortly.

Ordering the results

The **Display order** dialog permits the specification of an initial sorting order for the results to come. In this dialog, a drop-down menu contains all the table's columns; it's up to us to select the one on which we want to sort. By default, the sorting will be in **Ascending** order, but a choice of **Descending** order is also available.

It should be noted that on the results page, we can change the sort order using the techniques explained in Chapter 4.

Applying a WHERE clause

Sometimes, we may want to enter a search condition that is not offered in the **Function** list of the **query by example** section. The list cannot contain every possible variation in the language. Let's say we want to find all the English or French books using the IN clause. To do this, we can use the **Add search conditions** section.

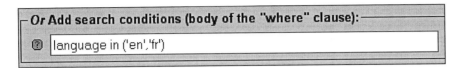

Or **Add search conditions (body of the "where" clause):**

⑦ language in ('en','fr')

> The complete search expression is generated by combining the search
> conditions, a logical AND, and the other criteria entered in the **query by**
> **example** lines.

We could have a more complex list of search conditions that would be entered in the
same textbox, possibly with brackets and operators such as AND or OR.

A **Documentation** link points to the MySQL manual, where we can see a huge choice
of available functions. (Each function is applicable to a specific field type.)

Obtaining distinct results

Sometimes, we may want to avoid getting the same results more than once. For
example, if we want to know in which cities we have clients, displaying each city
name once would be enough. Here, we want to know in which languages our books
are written. In the **Select Fields** dialog, we choose just the **language** field, and we
check **DISTINCT**, as shown in the following screenshot:

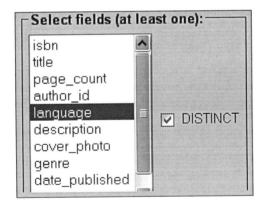

Clicking on **Go** produces the following image:

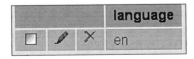

Using **DISTINCT**, we see each language only once. Without this option, the row containing **en** would have appeared three times.

Complete database search

In the previous examples, searching was limited to one table. This assumes knowledge of the exact table (and columns) where the necessary information might be stored.

When the data is hidden somewhere in the database, or when the same data can be presented in various columns (for example, a **title** column or a **description** column), it is easier to use the database search method.

We enter the **Search** page in the Database view for the `marc_book` database:

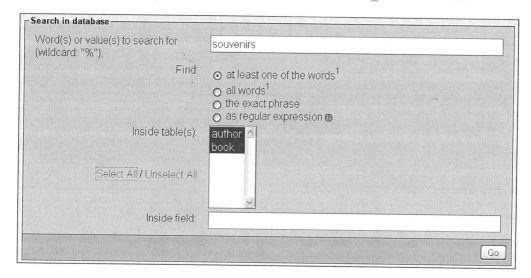

In the **Word(s) or value(s)** section, we enter what we want to find. The % wildcard character can prove useful here. We enter **souvenirs**.

In the **Find** section, we specify how to treat the values entered. We might need to find **at least one of the words** entered, **all words** (in no particular order), or **the exact phrase** (words in the same order, somewhere in a column). Another choice is to use a **regular expression**, which is a more complex way of doing pattern matching. We will keep the default value—**at least one of the words**.

We can choose the tables to restrict the search or select all the tables. As we only have two (small) tables, we select both.

As the search will be done on each row of every table selected, we might hit some time limits if the number of rows or tables is too big. Thus, this feature can be deactivated by setting $cfg['UseDbSearch'] to FALSE. (It is set to TRUE by default).

Clicking **Go** finds the following for us:

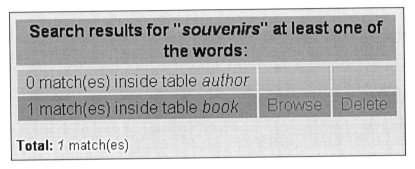

This is an overview of the number of matches and the relevant tables. We might get some matches in the tables in which we may not be interested. However, for the matches that look promising, we can **Browse** the results page, or we can **Delete** the unwanted rows.

Restricting search to a column

Sometimes, a particular column name is part of one (or many) tables, and we want to search only inside this column. For example, suppose that we are looking for "Marc", but this name could be also part of a book's title. So, we want to restrict the search to only the "name" column in all the chosen tables. This can be achieved by entering "name" in the **Inside field** choice.

Summary

In this chapter, we take an overview of single table searches with "query by example criteria" and additional criteria specification—selecting displayed values and ordering results. We also look at wildcard searches and full database search. The next chapter will explain how to perform the operations on tables—for example, changing a table's attributes, such as its storage engine. The subjects of repairing and optimizing tables are covered in this chapter as well.

10
Table and Database Operations

In the previous chapters, we dealt mostly with table fields. In this chapter, we will learn how to perform some operations that influence tables or databases as a whole. We will cover table attributes and how to modify them, and will also discuss multi-table operations.

Various links that enable table operations have been put together on the **Operations** subpage of the Table view. Here is an overview of this subpage:

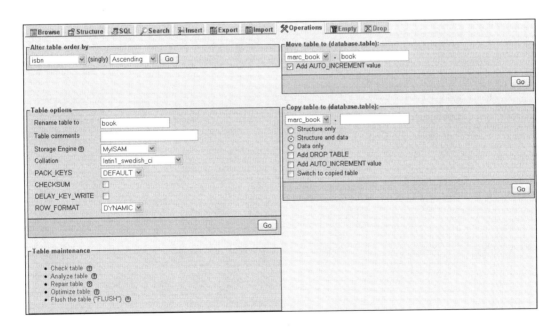

Table maintenance

During the lifetime of a table, it repeatedly gets modified; so, it continually grows and shrinks. Outages may occur on the server, leaving some tables in a damaged state.

Using the **Operations** subpage, we can perform various operations, which are listed next. However, not every operation is available for every table type.

- **Check table**: Scans all rows to verify that deleted links are correct. Also, a checksum is calculated to verify the integrity of the keys; we should get an **OK** message if everything is all right.

- **Analyze table**: Analyzes and stores the key distribution; this will be used on subsequent JOIN operations to determine the order in which the tables should be joined.

- **Repair table**: Repairs any corrupted data for tables in the MyISAM and ARCHIVE engines. Note that a table might be so corrupted that we cannot even go into Table view for it! In such a case, refer to the *Multi-Table Operations* section for the procedure to repair it.

- **Optimize table**: This is useful when the table contains overheads. After massive deletions of rows or length changes for VARCHAR fields, lost bytes remain in the table. phpMyAdmin warns us in various places (for example, in the Structure view) if it feels the table should be optimized. This operation is a kind of defragmentation for the table. In MySQL 4.x, this operation works only on tables in the MyISAM, Berkeley (DB), and InnoDB engines. In case of MySQL 5.x, the concerned tables are in the MyISAM, InnoDB, and ARCHIVE engines.

- **Flush table**: This must be done when there have been many connection errors and the MySQL server blocks further connections. Flushing will clear some internal caches and allow normal operations to resume.

- **Defragment table**: Random insertions or deletions in an InnoDB table fragment its index. The table should be periodically defragmented for faster data retrieval.

 The operations are based on the available underlying MySQL queries— phpMyAdmin only calls those queries.

Changing table attributes

Table attributes are the various properties of a table. This section discusses the settings for some of them.

Table storage engine

The first attribute we can change is called **Storage Engine**.

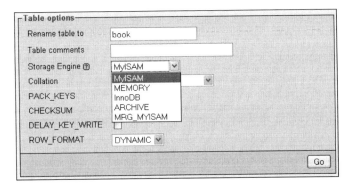

This controls the whole behavior of the table—its location (on-disk or in-memory), the index structure, and whether it supports transactions and foreign keys. The drop-down list varies depending on the storage engines supported by our MySQL server.

 Changing a table's storage engine may be a long operation if the number of rows is large.

Table comments

This allows us to enter comments for the table.

These comments will be shown at appropriate places—for example, in the navigation panel, next to the table name in the Table view, and in the export file. Here is what the navigation panel looks like when the $cfg['ShowTooltip']$ parameter is set to its default value of TRUE:

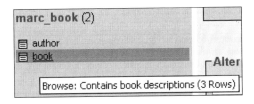

The default value (FALSE) of $cfg['ShowTooltipAliasDB'] and $cfg['ShowTooltipAliasTB'] produces the behavior we saw earlier—the true database and table names are displayed in the left panel and in the Database view for the **Structure** subpage. Comments appear when the mouse pointer is moved over a table name. If one of these parameters is set to TRUE, the corresponding item (database names for DB and table names for TB) will be shown as the tooltip instead of the names. This time, the mouseover shows the true name for the item. This is convenient when the real table names are not meaningful.

There is another possibility for $cfg['ShowTooltipAliasTB']—the 'nested' value. Here is what happens if we use this feature:

- The true table name is displayed in the left panel
- The table comment (for example project_) is interpreted as the project name and is displayed as it is (see the *Nested display of tables within a database* section in Chapter 3)

Table order

When we browse a table, or execute a statement such as SELECT * from book without specifying a sort order, MySQL uses the order in which the rows are physically stored. This table order can be changed with the **Alter table order by** dialog. We can choose any field and the table will be reordered once on this field. We choose **author_id** in the example, and after we click **Go**, the table gets sorted on this field.

Reordering is convenient if we know that we will be retrieving rows in this order most of the time. Moreover, if we use an ORDER BY clause later on, and the table is already physically sorted on this field, the performance should be higher.

This default ordering will last as long as there are no changes in the table (no insertions, deletions, or updates). This is why phpMyAdmin shows the **(singly)** warning.

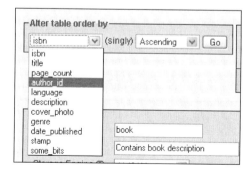

After the sort has been done on **author_id**, books for author **1** will be displayed first, followed by the books for author **2**, and so on (we are talking about a default browsing of the table without explicit sorting). We can also specify the sort order as **Ascending** or **Descending**.

If we insert another row, describing a new book from author **1**, and then click **Browse**, the book will not be displayed along with the other books for this author because the sort was done before the insertion.

Table collation

To better see the issues of collation change at various levels, let's first create a new author with a character **é** in his name:

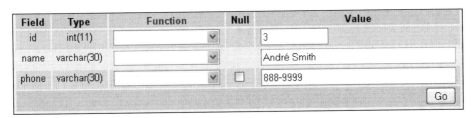

The name column currently has a `latin1_swedish_ci` collation, as can be seen via the **Structure** page. On the **Operations** page, if we change the collation for table author from `latin1_swedish_ci` to, say, `utf8_general_ci`, this generates:

```
ALTER TABLE `author` DEFAULT CHARACTER SET utf8 COLLATE
utf8_general_ci
```

Therefore, we only changed the default collation for future columns that will be added to this table.

In an effort to further test collation changes, we can go to **Structure** page and change the collation of author's **name** column to `utf8_general_ci` (by clicking the **Change** icon). Having done that, we browse the author table and still see correctly the **é** character, because MySQL updated the contents of this column on collation change.

Impact of switching connection collation

Changing the connection collation (from the **home**page collation dialog) can have unexpected effects. Let's switch it to `latin1_bin` and browse our `author` table again:

The data encoded in `UTF-8` in the database is now (wrongly) interpreted as being in `latin1`, introducing an inconsistency in the display. Therefore, we have to be careful with our collation changes, and you should revert the collation changes made in this section and the previous one.

Table options

Other attributes that influence the table's behavior may be specified using the **Table options** dialog:

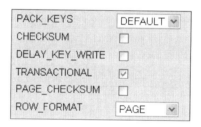

The options are:

- **PACK_KEYS**: Setting this attribute results in a smaller index. This can be read faster but takes more time to update. Available for the MyISAM storage engine.

- **CHECKSUM**: This makes MySQL compute a checksum for each row. This results in slower updates, but finding of corrupted tables becomes easier. Available for MyISAM only.

- **DELAY_KEY_WRITE**: This instructs MySQL not to write the index updates immediately, but to queue them for writing later. This improves performance. Available for MyISAM only.

- **ROW_FORMAT**: To the storage engines that support this feature (MyISAM, InnoDB, PBXT, and Maria), a choice of row format is presented. The default value being the current state of this table's row format.

- **TRANSACTIONAL, PAGE_CHECKSUM**: Applies to the Maria storage engine. Currently documented at `http://dev.mysql.com/doc/refman/5.1-maria/en/se-maria-tableoptions.html`.

- **auto-increment**: This changes the auto-increment value. It is shown only if the table's primary key has the auto-increment attribute.

Renaming, moving, and copying tables

The **Rename** operation is the easiest to understand — the table simply changes its name and stays in the same database.

The **Move** operation (shown in the following screen) can manipulate a table in two ways — change its name and also the database in which it is stored.

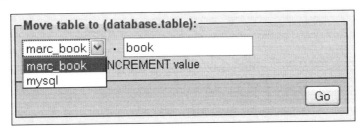

Moving a table is not directly supported by MySQL. So, phpMyAdmin has to create the table in the target database, copy the data, and then finally drop the source table.

The **Copy** operation leaves the original table intact and copies its structure or data (or both) to another table, possibly in another database. Here, the **book-copy** table will be an exact copy of the `book` source table. After the copy, we remain in the Table view for the `book` table, unless we select **Switch to copied table**.

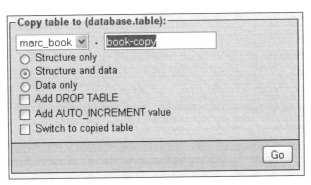

The **Structure only** copy is done to create a test table with the same structure.

Appending data to a table

The **Copy** dialog may also be used to append (add) data from one table to another. Both tables must have the same structure. This operation is achieved by entering the table to which we want to copy the data and choosing **Data only**.

For example, we would want to append data when book data, coming from various sources (various publishers), is stored in more than one table, and we want to aggregate all the data to one place. For MyISAM, a similar result can be obtained by using the Merge storage engine (which is a collection of identical MyISAM tables). However, if the table is InnoDB, we need to rely on phpMyAdmin's **Copy** feature.

Multi-table operations

In the Database view, there is a checkbox next to each table name and a drop-down menu under the table list. This enables us to quickly choose some tables and perform an operation on all those tables at once. Here, we select the **book-copy** and the **book** tables, and choose the **Check table** operation for the selected tables.

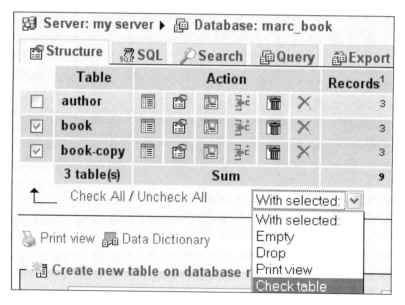

We could also quickly select or deselect all the checkboxes with **Check All / Uncheck All**.

Repairing an "in use" table

The multi-table mode is the only method (unless we know the exact SQL query to type) for repairing a corrupted table. Such tables may be shown with the **in use** flag in the database list. Users seeking help in the support forums for phpMyAdmin often receive this tip from experienced phpMyAdmin users.

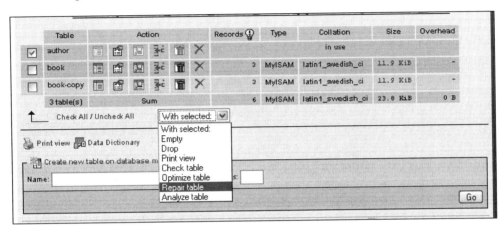

Database operations

The **Operations** tab in the Database view gives access to a panel that enables us to perform operations on a database taken as a whole.

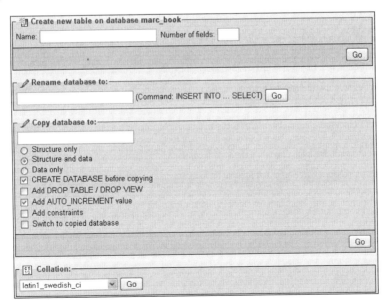

Renaming a database

A **Rename database to** dialog is available. Although this operation is not directly supported by MySQL, phpMyAdmin does it indirectly by creating a new database, renaming each table (thus sending it to the new database), and dropping the original database.

Copying a database

It is also possible to do a complete copy of a database, even if MySQL itself does not support this operation natively.

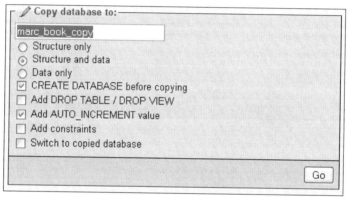

Summary

This chapter covers the operations we can perform on entire tables or databases. It also looks at table maintenance operations for table repair and optimization, changing various table attributes, table movements (including renaming and moving to another database), and multi-table operations. In the next chapter, we will begin to examine advanced features that rely on the linked-tables infrastructure, such as the relational system.

11
The Relational System

Welcome to the section of the book where we start to cover advanced features. The relational system allows users to work more closely with phpMyAdmin, as we will see in the following chapters. This chapter explains how to define inter-table relations. It also explains how to install the linked-tables infrastructure—a prerequisite for the advanced features.

Relational MySQL

When application developers use PHP and MySQL to build web interfaces or other data manipulation applications, they usually establish relations between tables using the underlying SQL queries. Examples of this would be: "get an invoice and all its items" and "get all books by an author".

In the first versions of phpMyAdmin, MySQL stored information about which table belonged to which database. However, the relational data structure (how tables relate to each other) was not stored into MySQL. Relations were temporarily made by the applications to generate meaningful results. In other words, the relations were in our head.

This was considered a shortcoming of MySQL by phpMyAdmin developers and users. Hence, the team started to build an infrastructure to support relations for MyISAM tables. The infrastructure evolved to support a growing array of special features. We can describe this infrastructure as **metadata**, that is, data about data.

phpMyAdmin 2.2.0 already had the **bookmarks** feature, that is, the ability to recall frequently used queries (described in Chapter 14), and version 2.3.0 generalized the metadata system. Subsequent versions were built on this facility. Examples of this would be: the 2.5.x family with its MIME-based **transformations** (as described in Chapter 16) and the 2.10.x family with a graphical relation builder called **Designer** (described in this chapter).

InnoDB and PBXT

InnoDB is a MySQL storage engine having its own webpage at
http://www.innodb.com. It is developed by Innobase Oy, a subsidiary of Oracle.
As the InnoDB sub-system must be activated by a system administrator, it may not
be available on every MySQL server.

The PrimeBase XT storage engine or PBXT (http://www.primebase.org) is
available for MySQL 5.1 and 6.0, and is developed by PrimeBase Technologies. The
minimum MySQL required version is 5.1, as this version supports the pluggable
storage engine API that is used by PBXT and other third-parties to offer alternative
storage engines. This transactional storage engine is newer than InnoDB. It is usually
installed after downloading it from their website and then going through a compile
step. For some operating systems, a precompiled binary is available—please visit the
aforementioned website for download and installation instructions.

When considering the relational aspect, here are the benefits of using the InnoDB
or PBXT storage engine for a table:

- They support referential integrity based on foreign keys, which are the
  keys in a foreign (or reference) table. By contrast, using only phpMyAdmin's
  internal relations (discussed later) brings no automatic referential
  integrity verification.

- The exported structure for InnoDB and PBXT tables contains the
  defined relations. Therefore, they are easily imported back for
  better cross-server interoperability.

The foreign key feature of these storage engines can effectively replace the part
of phpMyAdmin's infrastructure that deals with relations. We will see how
phpMyAdmin interfaces with the InnoDB and PBXT foreign key system.

> The other parts of phpMyAdmin's infrastructure (for example,
> bookmarks) have no equivalent in InnoDB, PBXT, or MySQL. Hence,
> they are still required to access the complete phpMyAdmin feature set.
> However, in MySQL 5.x, views are supported, and have similarities with
> phpMyAdmin's bookmarks.

Linked-tables infrastructure

The relational system's infrastructure is stored in tables that follow a predetermined
structure. The data in these tables is generated and maintained by phpMyAdmin on
the basis of our actions from the interface.

Goal of the infrastructure

Metadata tables contain, for all storage engines, information to support the special phpMyAdmin's features such as bookmarks and transformations. Moreover, for tables in a storage engine that does not support foreign keys, relations between tables are kept in this infrastructure.

Location of the infrastructure

There are two possible places to store these tables:

- A user's database—to facilitate every web developer owning a database to benefit from these features.
- A dedicated database called `pmadb` (phpMyAdmin database). In a multi-user installation (discussed later), this database may be accessible to a number of users while keeping the metadata private.

As this infrastructure does not exist by default, and because phpMyAdmin's developers want to promote it, the interface displays the following error message for every database when on the **Operations** subpage in the Database view:

```
The additional features for working with linked tables have been
deactivated. To find out why click here.
```

This message can be disabled with the following parameter (which, by default, is set to `FALSE`):

```
$cfg['PmaNoRelation_DisableWarning'] = TRUE;
```

 The message is the same regardless of the current database, as the infrastructure is shared for all our databases and tables (or all users on a multi-user installation).

Installing linked-tables infrastructure

The previous error message is displayed even if only a part of the infrastructure is lacking. Of course, on a fresh installation, all parts are lacking—our database has not yet heard of phpMyAdmin and needs to be outfitted with this infrastructure. Following the **here** link in the previous message brings up a panel explaining that the `pmadb`, and the tables that are supposed to be a part of it, are either missing or undefined.

It's important to realize that the relational system will work only if two conditions are met:

- Proper definitions are present in `config.inc.php`
- The corresponding tables (and maybe the database) are created

To create the necessary structure that matches our current version of phpMyAdmin, a command file called `create_tables.sql` is available in the `scripts` subdirectory of the phpMyAdmin installation directory. However, we should not blindly execute it before understanding the possible choices—multi-user installation or single-user installation.

Multi-user installation

In this setup, we will have a distinct database— pmadb— to store the metadata tables. Our control user will have specific rights to this database. Each user will work with his/her login name and password, which will be used to access his/her databases. However, whenever phpMyAdmin itself accesses pmadb to obtain some metadata, it will use the control user's privileges.

> Setting a multi-user installation is possible only for a MySQL system administrator who has the privileges of assigning rights to another user (here, the pma user). If you are not in this situation, please refer to the *Single-user installation* section.

We first ensure that the control user pma has been created, as explained in Chapter 2, and that its definition in `config.inc.php` is appropriate.

```
$cfg['Servers'][$i]['controluser'] = 'pma';
$cfg['Servers'][$i]['controlpass'] = 'bingo';
```

We then look in the `scripts` directory for `create_tables.sql`. There might be the other scripts available for different MySQL versions, so we should pick the one which looks the most appropriate. Next, we copy this script to our local workstation and edit it. We replace the following lines:

```
-- GRANT SELECT, INSERT, DELETE, UPDATE ON `phpmyadmin`.* TO
--     'pma'@localhost;
```

with these:

```
GRANT SELECT, INSERT, DELETE, UPDATE ON `phpmyadmin`.* TO
    'pma'@localhost;
```

We then execute this script by importing it (see Chapter 8). The net effect is to create the phpmyadmin database, assign proper rights to user pma, and populate the database with all the necessary tables.

Infrastructure and config.inc.php

It is now time to adjust all the relational-features related parameters in config.inc. php. This can be done easily with the setup script as seen in Chapter 1, or by pasting the appropriate lines from the config.sample.inc.php file. These database and table names are the ones that have just been created:

```
$cfg['Servers'][$i]['pmadb']           = 'phpmyadmin';
$cfg['Servers'][$i]['bookmarktable']   = 'pma_bookmark';
$cfg['Servers'][$i]['relation']        = 'pma_relation';
$cfg['Servers'][$i]['table_info']      = 'pma_table_info';
$cfg['Servers'][$i]['table_coords']    = 'pma_table_coords';
$cfg['Servers'][$i]['pdf_pages']       = 'pma_pdf_pages';
$cfg['Servers'][$i]['column_info']     = 'pma_column_info';
$cfg['Servers'][$i]['history']         = 'pma_history';
$cfg['Servers'][$i]['designer_coords'] = 'pma_designer_coords';
```

 As table names are case sensitive, we must use the same names as the tables created by the installation script. We are free to change the table names (see the right-hand part of the configuration directives listed), provided we change them accordingly in the database.

The pmadb and each table have a specific function as listed next:

- pmadb: Defines the database where all tables are located
- bookmarktable: Contains the bookmarks (explained in Chapter 14)
- relation: Defines inter-table relations, as used in many of the phpMyAdmin's features
- table_info: Contains the display field (explained later in this chapter)
- table_coords and pdf_pages: Contain the metadata necessary for drawing a schema of the relations in a PDF format (explained in Chapter 15)
- column_info: Used for column-commenting and MIME-based transformations (explained in Chapter 16)
- history: Contains SQL query history information (explained in Chapter 12)
- designer_coords: Holds the coordinates used by the Designer feature (explained later in this chapter)

Between each phpMyAdmin version, the infrastructure may be enhanced. (The changes are explained in `Documentation.html`.) This is why phpMyAdmin has various checks to ascertain the structure of the tables. If we know we are using the latest structure, `$cfg['Servers'][$i]['verbose_check']` can be set to FALSE to avoid checks, thereby slightly increasing phpMyAdmin's speed.

The installation is now complete. We will test the features in the coming sections and chapters. We can do a quick check by going back to the homepage; the warning message should be gone.

Single-user installation

Even if we are entitled to only one database by the system administrator, we can still use all the relational features of phpMyAdmin.

In this setup, we will use our normal database (let's assume its name is **marc_book**) to store the metadata tables, and will define our own login name (marc) as the control user in `config.inc.php`.

```
$cfg['Servers'][$i]['controluser']   = 'marc';
$cfg['Servers'][$i]['controlpass']   = 'bingo';
```

The next step is to modify a local copy of the `scripts/create_tables.sql` file to populate our database with all the needed tables. They will have the prefix `pma_` to make them easily recognizable. (See also the remark in the *Multi-user installation* section about other scripts that may be available in the `scripts` directory.)

If we are using `scripts/create_tables.sql`, the modification we need is to remove the following lines:

```
CREATE DATABASE IF NOT EXISTS `phpmyadmin`
  DEFAULT CHARACTER SET utf8 COLLATE utf8_bin;
USE phpmyadmin;
```

This is done because we won't be using a `phpmyadmin` database. Next, we should open our **marc_book** database in phpMyAdmin. We are now ready to execute the script. There are two ways of doing this:

- As we already have the script in our editor, we can just copy the lines and paste them in the query box of the **SQL** subpage.
- Another way is to use the import technique shown in Chapter 8. We select the `create_tables.sql` script that we just modified.

After the creation, the left panel shows us the special **pma_** tables along with our normal tables.

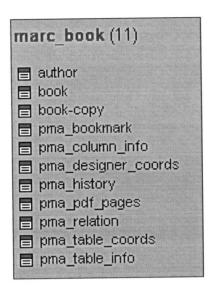

The last step is to adjust all the parameters in `config.inc.php` that relate to relational features. Please refer to the previous section, except for the database name in the `pmadb` parameter:

```
$cfg['Servers'][$i]['pmadb'] = 'marc_book';
```

Defining relations with the relation view

After the installing of the linked-tables infrastructure, there are now more options available in the Database view and the Table view. We will now examine a new link—**Relation view**—in the **Structure** subpage of the Table view.

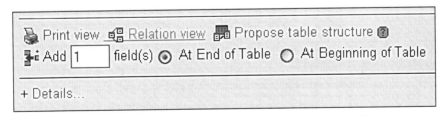

This view is used to:

- Define the relations of the current table with the other tables
- Choose the display field

Our goal here is to create a relation between the book table (which contains the author ID) and the author table (which describes each author by an ID). We start on the Table view for the book table, go to **Structure,** and click the **Relation view** link.

Internal relations

As the **book** table is in MyISAM format, we see the following screen (otherwise, the display would be different, as explained in the *Foreign Key Relations* section later):

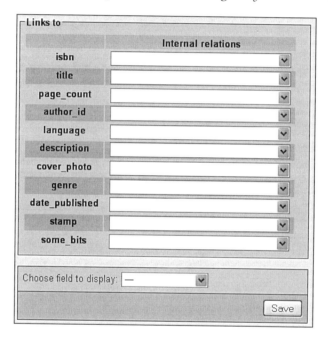

This screen allows us to create **Internal relations** (stored in the pma_relation table) because MySQL itself does not have any relational notion for MyISAM tables. The empty drop-down list next to each column indicates that there are no relations (links) to any foreign table.

Defining the relation

We can relate each field of the book table to a field in another table (or in the same table, because self-referencing relations are sometimes necessary). The interface finds both the unique and the non-unique keys in all the tables of the same database, and presents the keys in drop-down lists. (Creating internal relations to other databases from the interface is not currently supported.) The appropriate choice for the **author_id** field is to select the corresponding **author_id** field from the author table—also called **defining the foreign key**.

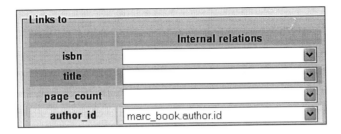

We then click **Save**, and the definition is saved in phpMyAdmin's infrastructure. To remove the relation, we just come back to the screen, select the empty choice, and click **Save**.

Defining the display field

The primary key of our `author` table is the `author_id`, which is a unique number that we made up for key purposes. The name field in our table—the `name`— represents the author's name. It would be interesting to see the author's name as a description of each row of the `book` table. This is the purpose of the display field. We should normally define a display field for each table that participates in a relation as a foreign table.

We will see how this information is displayed in the *Benefits of the Defined Relations* section. We now go to the **Relation view** for the `author` table (which is the foreign table in this case) and specify the display field. We choose **name** as the display field and click **Save**.

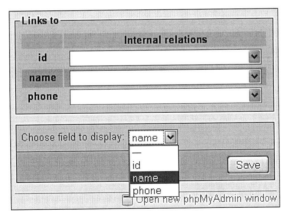

phpMyAdmin offers to define only one display field for a table, and this field is used in all the relations where this table is used as a foreign table.

The definition of this relation is now done. Although we did not relate any of the fields in the `author` table to another table, it can be done. For example, we could have a country code in this table and could create a relation to the country code of a country table.

We will discuss the benefits of having defined this relation in a later section. For now, we will see what happens if our tables are under the control of the InnoDB or PBXT storage engine.

Foreign key relations

The InnoDB and PBXT storage engines offer us a foreign key system.

 At your choice, the exercises in this section can be accomplished with either InnoDB or PBXT. InnoDB has been chosen in the text.

First, we will switch our **book** and **author** tables to the InnoDB storage engine. We can do this from the **Operations** subpage in the Table view. We start by doing this for the **author** table, as shown in the following screenshot:

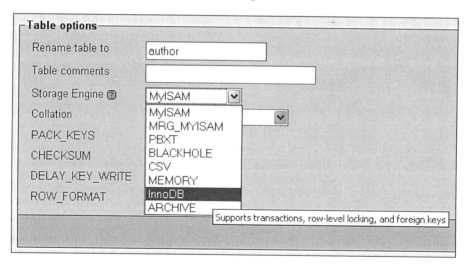

A problem arises when the storage engine of the **book** table is changed to InnoDB. We have a full-text index in this table, and the InnoDB engine currently does not support this kind of index:

```
ALTER TABLE `book` ENGINE = InnoDB;
MySQL said:
#1214 - The used table type doesn't support FULLTEXT indexes
```

To get rid of this error message, we go back to the **Structure** for the book table and remove the full-text index on the **description** field. While we are on this screen, let's also remove the combined index we created on **author_id** and **language**. We will do this because we want to see the consequences of a missing index later in this chapter. At this point, we are able to switch the book table to InnoDB.

The foreign key system in InnoDB maintains integrity between the related tables. Hence, we cannot add a non-existent author ID to the book table. In addition, actions are programmable when DELETE or UPDATE operations are performed on the master table (in our case, book).

Opening the book table on its **Structure** subpage and entering the **Relation view,** now displays a different page:

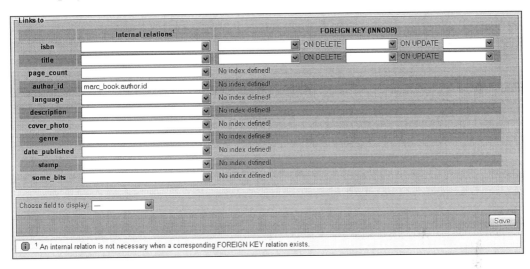

This page tells us:

- We have an internal relation defined for **author_id** to the author table.

- We don't yet have any InnoDB relations defined.

- We will be able to remove the internal relation, when the same relation has been defined in InnoDB. Indeed, phpMyAdmin advises us that: "**An internal relation is not necessary when a corresponding FOREIGN KEY relation exists**". So, it would be better to remove it.

- **ON DELETE** and **ON UPDATE** options are available for InnoDB relations.

In the possible choices for the related key, we see the keys defined in all the InnoDB tables of the same database. (Creating a cross-database relation is currently not supported in phpMyAdmin.) We even see the keys defined in the current table, as self-referring relations are possible. We now remove the internal relation for the **author_id** field and click **Save**. We would like to add an InnoDB-type relation for the **author_id** field, but we cannot. We see the **No index defined!** message on this line. This is because foreign key definitions in InnoDB or PBXT can be done only if both the fields are defined as indexes.

 Other conditions regarding constraints are explained in the MySQL manual. Please refer to http://dev.mysql.com/doc/refman/5.0/en/innodb-foreign-key-constraints.html.

Thus, we come back to the **Structure** page for the book table and add an ordinary (non-unique) index to the **author_id** field producing:

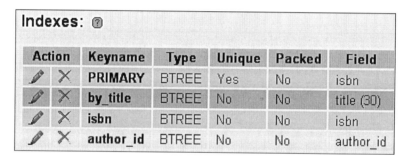

Action		Keyname	Type	Unique	Packed	Field
✎	✕	PRIMARY	BTREE	Yes	No	isbn
✎	✕	by_title	BTREE	No	No	title (30)
✎	✕	isbn	BTREE	No	No	isbn
✎	✕	author_id	BTREE	No	No	author_id

In the **Relation view**, we can try again to add the relation we wanted; it works this time!

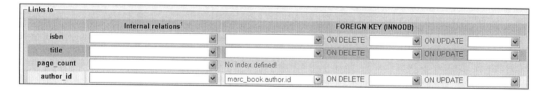

We can also set some actions with the **ON DELETE** and **ON UPDATE** options. For example, **ON DELETE CASCADE** would make MySQL automatically delete all the rows in the related (foreign) table when the corresponding row is deleted from the parent table. This would be useful, for example, when the parent table is invoices, and the foreign table is invoice-items.

If we have not done so already, we should define the display field for the `author` table, as explained in the *Internal phpMyAdmin Relations* section.

Foreign keys without linked-tables infrastructure

We see the **Relation View** link on the **Structure** page of a InnoDB or PBXT table, even though the linked-tables infrastructure is not installed. This brings us to a screen where we can define the foreign keys, in this case for the **book** table.

Note that, if we choose this, the display field for the linked table (`author` here) cannot be defined, as it belongs to phpMyAdmin's infrastructure. Thus, we would lose the benefit of seeing the associated description of the foreign key.

Defining relations with the Designer

The Ajax-based Designer feature appeared in phpMyAdmin 2.10. It offers a mouse-driven way of managing relations (both internal and foreign key-based), and defining the display field for each table. It can also act as:

- A menu to access the structure of existing tables and to access the table creation page.
- A PDF schema manager, if we want a PDF schema encompassing all our tables.

On the Designer workspace, we can work on the relations for all tables on the same panel. On the other hand, the Relation view shows the relations for only a single table at a time.

We access this feature from the Database view by clicking the **Designer** menu tab.

 If this menu tab does not appear, it's because we are yet to install the linked-tables infrastructure as described previously in this chapter—especially the `designer_coords` special table.

Interface overview

The Designer page contains the main workspace where the tables can be seen. This workspace will dynamically grow and shrink, depending on the position of our tables. A top menu contains icons whose description is revealed by hovering the mouse over them. Here is a summary of the goals for the top menu's icons:

- **Show/Hide left menu**: For left menu presence
- **Save position**: Saves the current state of the workspace to the infrastructure
- **Create table**: Quits the designer and enters a dialog to create a table
- **Create relation**: Puts the designer in a relation creating mode
- **Choose field to display**: Specifies which field represents a table
- **Reload**: Fetches information about the tables again
- **Help**: Brings an explanation about selecting the relations
- **Angular links/Direct links**: Specifies the shape of relation links
- **Snap to grid**: Influences the behavior of table movements, relative to an imaginary grid
- **Small/Big All**: Hides or displays the list of columns for every table
- **Toggle small/big**: Reverses the display mode of columns for every table, as this mode can be chosen by the table with its corner icon V or >
- **Import/Export**: Generates PDF
- **Move Menu**: The top menu can move to right and back again

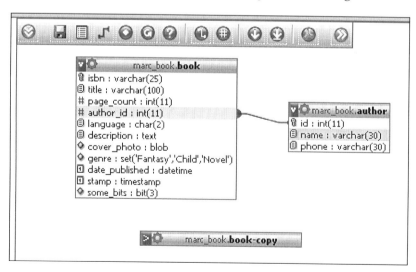

A side menu appears when clicking the **Show/Hide left menu** icon. Its purpose is to present the complete list of tables, to decide which table appears on the workspace, and to enable access to the **Structure** page of a specific table. In this example, we choose to remove the **book-copy** table from the workspace as shown here:

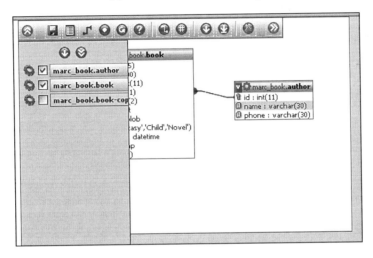

If we want this removal to be permanent, we click on the **Save position** top icon. This icon also saves the current position of our tables on the workspace.

Tables can be moved on the workspace by dragging their title bars, and the list of columns for a table can be made visible/invisible with the help of upper-left icon of each table. In this list of columns, small icons show us the data type (numeric, text, date), and also tell us whether this column is a key.

Defining relations

As we have already defined a relation with the Relation view, we'll first see how to remove it. The Designer does not permit a change in a relation. However, the Designer allows the relation to be removed and defined.

The question mark top icon displays a panel that explains where to click, in order to select a relation for subsequent deletion.

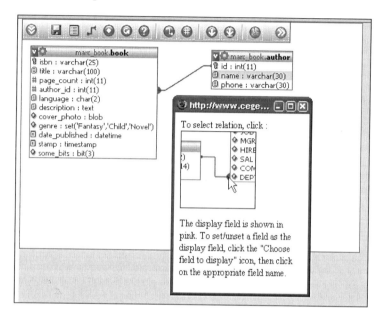

Let's click at the appropriate place to delete this relation. We get a confirmation panel on which we click **Delete**.

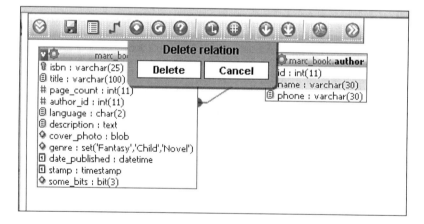

We can then proceed to recreate it. To do this, we start by clicking the **Create relation** icon. The cursor then takes the form of a short message saying **Select referenced key**. In our case, the referenced key is the **id** column of the **author** table; so we bring the cursor on this column and click it. A validation is done, ensuring that we chose a primary or unique key.

Next, having changed the cursor to **Select foreign key**, we bring it to the `author_id` column of the `book` table and click again. This confirms the creation of the relation. Currently, the interface does not permit the creation of compound keys (having more than one column).

Foreign key relations

The procedure to delete or define a relation between InnoDB or PBXT tables, is the same as that for internal relations. The only exception is that, at the time of creation, a different confirmation panel appears, enabling us to specify the ON DELETE and ON UPDATE actions.

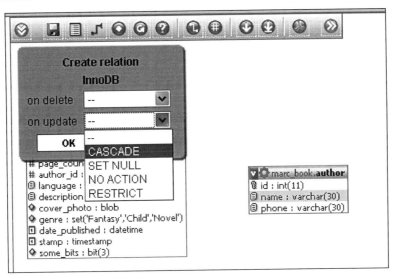

Defining the display field

On the workspace, we notice in the `author` table that the `name` column has a special background color. This indicates that this column serves as the display field. We can simply click the **Choose field to display** top icon, and drag the short message **Choose field to display** onto another column—for example, the `phone` column. This changes the display field to this column. If we were to drag the message to an existing display field column, we would have removed this column as a display field for the table.

Exporting for PDF schema

In Chapter 15, we'll see how to produce a PDF schema for a subset of our database. We can import the co-ordinates of tables from such a schema into the Designer's workspace, and conversely export them to the PDF schema. The **Import/export coordinates** top icon is available for that purpose.

Benefits of the defined relations

In this section, we will look at the benefits of the defined relations that we can currently test. Other benefits will be described in chapters 13 and 15. Additional benefits of the linked-tables infrastructure will appear in chapters 14 and 16.

These benefits are available for both internal and foreign key relations.

Foreign key information

Let's browse the book table by entering the **Search** subpage and choosing to display the first four columns. We see that the related key (**author_id**) is now a link. Moving the mouse pointer over any **author_id** value reveals the author's name (as defined by the display field of the author table).

←T→			isbn	title	page_count	author_id
☐	✎	✗	1-234567-22-0	Future souvenirs	200	2
☐	✎	✗	1-234567-89-0	A hundred years of cinema (volume 1)	600	1
☐	✎	✗	1-234567-90-0	A hundred years of cinema (volume 2)	602	1

Clicking on the **author_id** brings us to the relevant table — author — for this specific author:

←T→			id	name	phone
☐	✎	✗	1	John Smith	+01 445-789-1234

No

The drop-down list of foreign keys

Going back to the book table, in **Insert** mode (or in **Edit** mode), we now see a drop-down list of the possible keys for each field that has a defined relation. The list contains the keys and the description (display field) in both orders — key to the display field as well as display field to the key. This enables us to use the keyboard, and type the first letter of either the key or the display field.

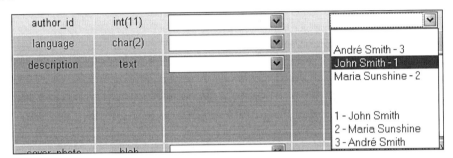

 Only the key (in this case **1**) will be stored in the book table. The display field is there only to assist us.

By default, this drop-down list will appear if there are a maximum of 100 rows in the foreign table. This is controlled by the following parameter:

```
$cfg['ForeignKeyMaxLimit'] = 100;
```

For foreign tables bigger than that, a distinct window appears — the foreign-table window (see the next section) that can be browsed.

We might prefer to see information differently in the drop-down list. Here, **John Smith** is the content and **1** is the ID. The default display is controlled by

```
$cfg['ForeignKeyDropdownOrder'] = array( 'content-id', 'id-content');
```

We can use one or both of the strings — content-id and id-content — in the defining array and in the order we prefer. Thus, defining $cfg['ForeignKeyDropdownOrder'] to array('id-content') would produce a list with only those choices:

```
1 - John Smith
2 - Maria Sunshine
3 - André Smith
```

The browseable foreign-table window

Our current `author` tables have very few entries. Thus, to illustrate this mechanism, we will set the `$cfg['ForeignKeyMaxLimit']` to an artificially low number, 1. Now in the **Insert** mode for the `book` table, we see a small table-shaped icon for **author_id**. This icon opens another window, which will present the values of the table `author` and a **Search** input field. On the left, the values are sorted by key value (here, the **author_id** column), and on the right, they are sorted by description.

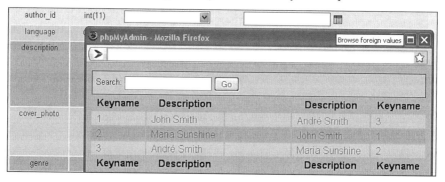

Choosing one of the values (by clicking either a key value or a description) closes this window and brings the value back to the **author_id** column.

Referential integrity checks

We discussed the **Operations** subpage and its **Table maintenance** section, in Chapter 10. For this exercise, we suppose that both the `book` and `author` tables are not under the control of the InnoDB or PBXT storage engine. If we have defined an internal relation for the `author` table, a new choice appears for the `book` table—**Check referential integrity**.

A link (**author_id -> author.id**) appears for each defined relation, and clicking it starts verification. For each row, the presence of the corresponding key in the foreign table is verified and errors, if any, are reported. If the resulting page reports zero rows, it is good news!

This operation exists because for tables under the storage engines that do not support foreign key natively, neither MySQL nor phpMyAdmin enforce referential integrity. It is perfectly possible, for example, to import data in the book table with invalid values for **author_id**.

Automatic updates of metadata

phpMyAdmin keeps the metadata for internal relations synchronized with every change that is made to the tables via phpMyAdmin. For example, renaming a column that is part of a relation would make phpMyAdmin rename this column in the metadata for the relation. This guarantees an internal relation continues to function, even after a column's name is changed. The same thing happens when a column or table is dropped.

 Metadata should be maintained manually in case a change in the structure is done from outside phpMyAdmin.

Column-commenting

Prior to MySQL 4.1, the MySQL structure itself did not support the addition of comments to a column. Nevertheless, thanks to phpMyAdmin's metadata—we could comment on columns. However, since MySQL 4.1, native column commenting has been supported. The good news is that for any MySQL version, column commenting in phpMyAdmin is always accessed via the **Structure** page by editing the structure of each field. In the following example, we need to comment three columns. Hence, we choose them and click the pencil icon near the **With selected** choice.

	Field	Type
☑	**isbn**	varchar(25)
☐	**title**	varchar(100)
☑	**page_count**	int(11)
☑	**author_id**	int(11)

To obtain the next panel, as seen here, we are working in vertical mode by setting `$cfg['DefaultPropDisplay']` to `'vertical'`. We enter the following comments:

- **isbn**: **book number**
- **page_count**: **approximate**
- **author_id**: **cf author table**

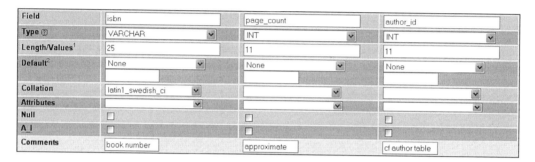

We then click **Save**.

These comments appear at various places—for example, in the export file (see Chapter 7) on the PDF relational schema (see Chapter 15), and in the browse mode.

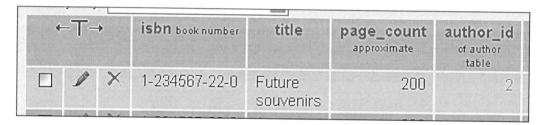

If we do not want the comments to appear in browse mode, we can set `$cfg['ShowBrowseComments']` to FALSE. (It is TRUE by default.)

Column comments also appear as a tool tip in the **Structure** page, and column names are underlined with dashes. To deactivate this behavior, we can set `$cfg['ShowPropertyComments']` to FALSE. (This one is also TRUE by default.)

Automatic migration

Whenever phpMyAdmin detects that column comments have been stored in its metadata, and that we are using MySQL 4.1.2 or a later version, it automatically migrates these column comments to the native MySQL column comments.

Summary

This chapter covers how to install the necessary infrastructure for keeping special metadata (data about tables), and how to define relations between both InnoDB and non-InnoDB tables. It also examines the modified behavior of phpMyAdmin (when relations are present) and foreign keys. Finally, it covers the Designer feature, column-commenting, and how to obtain information from the table. Chapter 12 will cover the means of entering SQL commands, which are useful when the phpMyAdmin's interface is not sufficient to accomplish what we need.

12

Entering SQL Commands

This chapter explains how we can enter our own SQL commands (queries) into phpMyAdmin, and how we can keep a history of those queries.

The SQL query box

phpMyAdmin allows us to accomplish many database operations via its graphical interface. However, there will be times when we have to rely on SQL query input to achieve complex operations. Here are some examples of complex queries:

```
SELECT department, AVG(salary) FROM employees GROUP BY department
HAVING years_experience > 10;
SELECT FROM_DAYS(TO_DAYS(CURDATE()) +30);
```

To enter such queries, the query box is available from a number of places within phpMyAdmin.

The Database view

We encounter our first query box when going to the **SQL** menu available in the Database view.

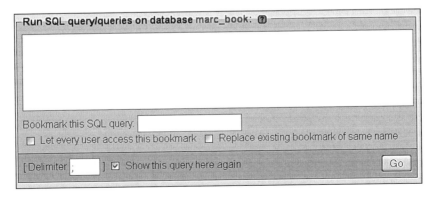

This box is simple—we type in some valid (hopefully) MySQL statement and click **Go**. Under the query text area, there are bookmark-related choices (explained later in Chapter 14). Usually, we don't have to change the standard SQL delimiter, which is a semicolon. However, there is a **Delimiter** dialog in case we need it (see chapter 17).

For a default query to appear in this box, we can set it with the `$cfg['DefaultQueryDatabase']` configuration directive, which is empty by default. We could put a query like SHOW TABLES FROM %d in this directive. The %d parameter in this query would be replaced by the current database name, resulting in SHOW TABLES FROM 'marc_book' in the query box.

The Table view

A slightly different box is available in the Table view from the **SQL** menu.

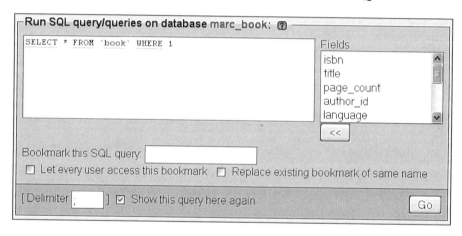

There is a **Fields** selector and an **Insert** button (**<<**) on the right. The box already has a default query as seen in the previous screenshot.

This default query is generated from the `$cfg['DefaultQueryTable']` configuration directive, which contains SELECT * FROM %t WHERE 1. Here, the %t is replaced by the current table name. Another placeholder available in `$cfg['DefaultQueryTable']` is %f. This placeholder would be replaced by the complete field list of this table, thus producing the following query:

```
SELECT `isbn`, `title`, `page_count`, `author_id`, `language`,
`description`, `cover_photo`, `genre`, `date_published`, `stamp`,
`some_bits` FROM 'book' WHERE 1.
```

WHERE 1 is a condition that is always true. Therefore, the query can be executed as it is. We can replace **1** with the condition we want, or we can type a completely different query.

The Fields selector

The **Fields** selector is a way to speed up query generation. By choosing a field and clicking on the arrows **<<**, this field name is copied at the current cursor position in the query box. Here, we select the **author_id** field, remove the digit **1**, and click **<<**. Then we add the condition = **2**.

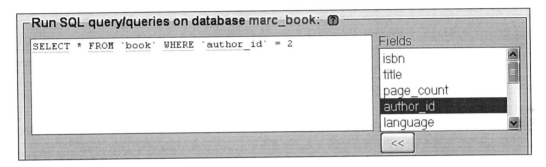

The **Show this query here again** option (checked by default) ensures that the query stays in the box after its execution if we are still on the same page. This can be seen more easily for a query like an UPDATE or DELETE, which affects a table, but does not produce a separate results page.

Clicking into the query box

We might want to change the behavior of a click inside the query box with the $cfg['TextareaAutoSelect'] configuration directive. Its default value is FALSE, which means that no automatic selection of the contents is done upon a click. Should you change this directive to TRUE, the first click inside this box will select all its contents. (This is a way to quickly copy the contents elsewhere or delete them from the box.) The next click would put the cursor at the click position.

The Query window

In Chapter 3, we discussed the purpose of this window, and the procedure for changing some parameters (like dimensions). This window can easily be opened from the left panel using the **SQL** icon or the **Query window** link, and is very convenient for entering a query and testing it.

The following screenshot shows the Query window that appears over the right panel:

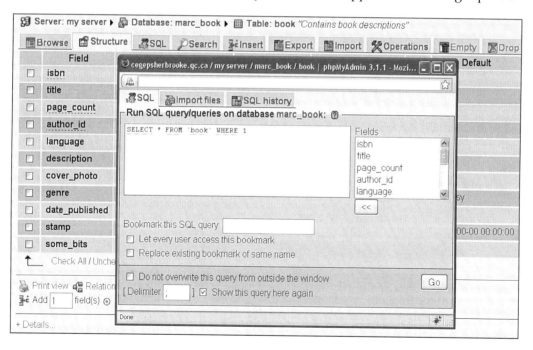

The window seen in the screenshot contains the same **Fields** selector and **<<** button as that used in a Table view context. This distinct Query window is a feature supported only on JavaScript-enabled browsers.

Query window options

The **SQL** tab is the default active tab in this window. This comes from the configuration directive $cfg['QueryWindowDefTab']$, which contains `sql` by default.

If we want another tab to be the default active tab, we can replace `sql` with `files` or `history`. Another value, `full`, shows the contents of all the three tabs at once.

In the Query window, we see a checkbox for the **Do not overwrite this query from outside the window** choice. Normally, this is not checked. The changes we make while generating queries are reflected in the Query window. This is called **synchronization**. For example, choosing a different database or table from the left or right panel would update the Query window accordingly. However, if we start to type a query directly in this window, the checkbox will get checked in order to protect its contents and remove synchronization. This way, the query composed here will be locked and protected.

Session based SQL history

This feature collects all the successful SQL queries we execute, as PHP session data, and modifies the Query window to make them available. This default type of history is temporary, as $cfg['QueryHistoryDB']$ is set to `FALSE` by default.

Database based SQL history (permanent)

As we installed the linked-tables infrastructure (see Chapter 11), a more powerful history mechanism is available. This mechanism is triggered by setting $cfg['QueryHistoryDB']$ to `TRUE`.

After we try some queries from one of the query boxes, a history is built, visible only from the Query window.

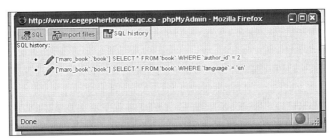

We see (in the reverse order) the last successful queries and the database on which they were made. Queries, typed only from the query box are kept in this history. Queries generated by phpMyAdmin (such as those generated by clicking on **Browse**) aren't kept here.

They are clickable for immediate execution, and the **Edit** icon is available to insert a recorded query into the query box for editing.

The number of queries that will be kept is controlled by `$cfg['QueryHistoryMax']`, which is set to 25 by default. This limit is not kept for performance reasons, but as a practical limit in order to achieve a visually unencumbered view. Extra queries are eliminated at login time in a process traditionally called **garbage collection**. The queries are stored in the table configured in `$cfg['Servers'][$i]['history']`.

Editing queries in the query window

On the results page of a successful query, a header containing the executed query appears as shown in the following screenshot:

Clicking **Edit** opens the Query window's **SQL** tab, with this query ready to be modified. This happens because of the following default setting for this parameter:

```
$cfg['EditInWindow']            = TRUE;
```

When it is set to FALSE, a click on **Edit** will not open the Query window; instead, the query will appear inside the query box of the **SQL** subpage.

Multi-statement queries

In PHP and MySQL programming, we can send only one query at a time using the `mysql_query()` function call. phpMyAdmin allows us to send many queries in one transmission, using a semicolon as a separator. Suppose we type the following query in the query box:

```
INSERT INTO author VALUES (100,'Paul Smith','111-2222');
INSERT INTO author VALUES (101,'Melanie Smith','222-3333');
UPDATE author SET phone='444-5555' WHERE name LIKE '%Smith%';
```

We will receive the following results screen:

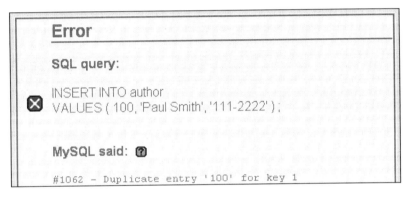

We see the number of affected rows through comments because `$cfg['VerboseMultiSubmit']` is set to TRUE.

Let's send the same list of queries again and watch the results:

It is normal to receive a **Duplicate entry** error that says, the value **100** exists already. We are seeing the results of the first **INSERT** statement; but what happens to the next one? Execution stops at the first error because `$cfg['IgnoreMultiSubmitErrors']` is set to FALSE telling phpMyAdmin not to ignore errors in multiple statements. If it is set to TRUE, the program successively tries all the statements, and we see two **Duplicate entry** errors.

This feature would not work as expected, if we tried more than one SELECT statement. We would see the results of only the last SELECT statement.

Pretty printing (syntax-highlighting)

By default, phpMyAdmin parses and highlights the various elements of any MySQL statement it processes. This is controlled by `$cfg['SQP']['fmtType']`, which is set to `'html'` by default. This mode uses a specific color for each different element (a reserved word, a variable, a comment, and so on) as described in the `$cfg['SQP']['fmtColor']` array located in the theme-specific `layout.inc.php` file.

In the previous examples, `fmtType` was set to `'text'` because this mode is more legible in a book. This mode inserts line breaks at logical points inside a MySQL statement, but there is no color involved. With `fmtType` set to `'html'`, phpMyAdmin would report the SQL statements with syntax highlighting. However, setting `fmtType` to `'none'` removes every kind of formatting, leaving our syntax intact.

 The multi-dimensional arrays used for holding some parameters in the configuration file reflect a programming style adopted by the phpMyAdmin development team. This ensures that parameter names are not very long.

The SQL Validator

Each time phpMyAdmin transmits a query, the MySQL server interprets it and provides feedback. The syntax of the query must follow MySQL rules, which are not the same as standard SQL. However, conforming to standard SQL ensures that our queries are usable on other SQL implementations.

A free external service, the Mimer SQL Validator, is available to us. It validates our query according to the Core SQL-99 rules and generates a report. The Validator is available directly from phpMyAdmin, and its homepage is located at `http://developer.mimer.com/validator/index.htm`.

 For statistical purposes, this service anonymously stores on its server, the queries it receives. When storing the queries, it replaces database, table, and column names with generic names. Strings and numbers that are part of the query, are replaced with generic values so as to protect the original information.

System requirements

This Validator is available as a SOAP service. Our PHP server must have XML, PCRE, and PEAR support. We need some PEAR modules too. The following command (executed on the server by the system administrator) installs the modules we need:

```
pear install Net_Socket Net_URL HTTP_Request Mail_Mime Net_DIME SOAP
```

If we have problems with this command due to some of the modules being in a beta state, we can execute the following command, which installs SOAP and other dependent modules:

```
pear -d preferred_state=beta install -a SOAP
```

Making the Validator available

Some parameters must be configured in `config.inc.php`. Setting `$cfg['SQLQuery']['Validate']` to TRUE enables the **Validate SQL** link.

We should also enable the Validator itself (as other validators might be available on future phpMyAdmin versions). This is done by setting `$cfg['SQLValidator']['use']` to TRUE.

The Validator is accessed with an anonymous Validator account by default, as configured using the following commands:

```
$cfg['SQLValidator']['username'] = '';
$cfg['SQLValidator']['password'] = '';
```

Instead, if the company has provided us with an account, we can use that account information here.

Validator results

There are two kinds of reports returned by the Validator—one if the query conforms to the standard, and the other if it does not conform.

Standard-conforming queries

We will try a simple query: `SELECT COUNT(*) FROM book`. As usual, we enter this query in the query box and send it. On the results page, we now see an additional link—**Validate SQL**.

Clicking on **Validate SQL** produces the following report:

```
Conforms to Core SQL-99
SQL queries stored anonymously for statistical purposes.
```

We have the option of clicking **Skip Validate SQL** to see our original query.

Non-standard-conforming queries

Let's try another query, which works correctly in MySQL: SELECT * FROM book WHERE language = 'en'. Sending it to the Validator produces the following report:

```
-SQL query:
SELECT * FROM book WHERE {error: 1}language = 'en'
{error: 2}LIMIT 0, 30

Errors:

    1.  syntax error: language
            expected: ( + - : ? <ascii identifier> <character set identifier>
                    <decimal literal> <delimited identifier> <float literal>
                    <hex string literal> <identifier> <integer literal>
                    <national string literal> <string literal> ANY ARRAY CASE CAST
                    CURRENT_DATE CURRENT_DEFAULT_TRANSFORM_GROUP CURRENT_PATH
                    CURRENT_ROLE CURRENT_TIME CURRENT_TIMESTAMP
                    CURRENT_TRANSFORM_GROUP_FOR_TYPE CURRENT_USER DATE DEREF EXISTS
                    FALSE GROUPING INTERVAL LOCALTIME LOCALTIMESTAMP MODULE NEW NOT
                    REPEAT ROW SESSION_USER SOME SYSTEM_USER TIME TIMESTAMP TREAT
                    TRUE UNIQUE UNKNOWN USER VALUE
            correction: <identifier>
    2.  syntax error: LIMIT 0 , 30 <end>
            expected: <end> * + - -> / ; [ || <string literal> AND AT COLLATE DAY
                    EXCEPT FOR GROUP HAVING HOUR INTERSECT MINUTE MONTH OR ORDER
                    SECOND UNION WINDOW YEAR . IS
            correction: <end>

SQL queries stored anonymously for statistical purposes.

    ☐ Profiling [ Edit ] [ Explain SQL ] [ Create PHP Code ] [ Refresh ] [ Skip Validate SQL ]
```

Each time the Validator finds a problem, it adds a message such as **{error: 1}** at the point of the error and adds a footnote in the report. This time, the **language** column name is non-standard. Hence, the Validator tells us that it was expecting an identifier at this point. Another non-standard error is reported about the use of a LIMIT clause, which was added to the query by phpMyAdmin.

Another case is that of the backquotes. If we just click on **Browse** for the book table, phpMyAdmin generates `SELECT * FROM `book``, enclosing the table name with backquotes. This is MySQL's way of protecting identifiers, which might contain special characters, such as spaces, international characters, or reserved words. However, sending this query to the Validator shows us that the backquotes do not conform to standard SQL. We may even get two errors, one for each backquote.

Summary

This chapter helps us understand the purpose of query boxes and shows us where to find them. It also gives us an overview of the Query window options, multi-statement queries, how to use the field selector, how to use the SQL Validator, and finally, how to get a history of the typed commands. The next chapter will show how to produce multi-table queries without typing, thanks to phpMyAdmin's query generator.

13

The Multi-Table Query Generator

The **Search** pages in the Database or Table view are intended for single-table lookups. This chapter covers the multi-table **Query by example** (**QBE**) feature available in the Database view.

Many phpMyAdmin users work in the Table view, table by table, and thus tend to overlook the multi-table query generator, which is a wonderful feature for fine-tuning queries. The query generator is useful not only in multi-table situations but also in single table situations. It enables us to specify multiple criteria for a column, a feature that the **Search** page in the Table view does not possess.

The examples in this chapter assume that a multi-user installation of the linked-tables infrastructure has been made (see Chapter 11), and that the book-copy table created during an exercise of Chapter 10 is still there in the marc_book database.

To open the page for this feature, we go to the Database view for a specific database (the query generator supports working on only one database at a time) and click on **Query**.

The screenshot overleaf shows the initial QBE page. It contains the following elements:

- Criteria columns
- An interface to add criteria rows
- An interface to add criteria columns
- A table selector

- The query area
- Buttons to update or to execute the query

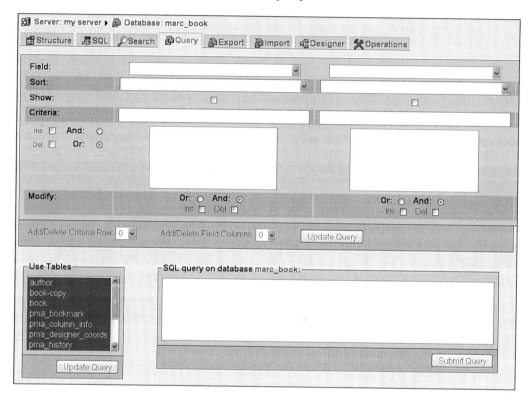

Choosing tables

The initial selection includes all tables. In this example, we assume that the linked-table infrastructure has been installed in the **marc_book** database. (See the section, *Single-user installation*, in Chapter 11.) Consequently, the **Field** selector contains a great number of fields. For our example, we will work only with the **author** and the **book** tables. Hence, we select only these from the **Use Tables** selector.

We then click on **Update Query**. This refreshes the screen and reduces the number of fields available in the **Field** selector. We can always change the selected tables later, using our browser's mechanism for multiple choices in drop-down menus (usually control-click).

Column criteria

Three criteria columns are provided by default. This section discusses the options we have for editing their criteria. These include options for selecting fields, sorting individual columns, entering conditions for individual columns, and so on.

Field selector: Single-column or all columns

The **Field** selector contains all the individual columns for the selected tables, plus a special choice ending with an asterisk (*) for each table, which means that all the fields are selected.

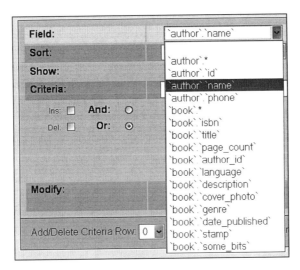

To display all the fields in the `author` table, we would choose `` `author`.* `` and check the **Show** checkbox, without entering anything in the **Sort** and the **Criteria** boxes. In our case, we select `` `author`.`name` ``, as we want to enter some criteria for the author's name.

Sorts

For each selected individual column, we can specify a sort (in **Ascending** or **Descending** order), or let this line remain intact (no sorting). If we choose more than one sorted column, the sorting will be carried out from left to right.

 When we ask for a column to be sorted, we normally check the **Show** checkbox. But this is not necessary, as we might want to do just the sorting operation without displaying this column.

Showing a column

We check the **Show** checkbox so that we can see the column in the results. Sometimes, we may just want to apply a criterion on a column, and not include it in the resulting page. Here, we add the phone column, ask for it to be sorted, and choose to show both the name and the phone number. We also ask for a sort on the name in the ascending order. The sort will be done first by name, and then by the phone number if the names are identical. This is because the name is in a column criterion to the left of the phone column, and thus has a higher priority.

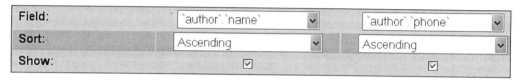

Field:	`author`.`name`	`author`.`phone`
Sort:	Ascending	Ascending
Show:	☑	☑

Updating the query

At any point, we can click the **Update Query** button to see the progress of our generated query. We have to click it at least once before executing the query. For now, let's click it and see the query generated in the query area. In the following examples, we will click **Update Query** after each modification.

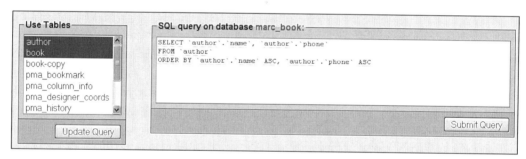

We have selected two tables, but have not yet chosen any column from the **book** table. Hence, this table is not mentioned in the generated query.

Criteria

In the **Criteria** box, we can enter a condition (respecting the SQL WHERE clause's syntax) for each of the corresponding columns. By default, we have two criteria rows. To find all the authors with **Smith** in their names, we use a **LIKE** criterion (LIKE '%SMITH%') and click **Update Query**.

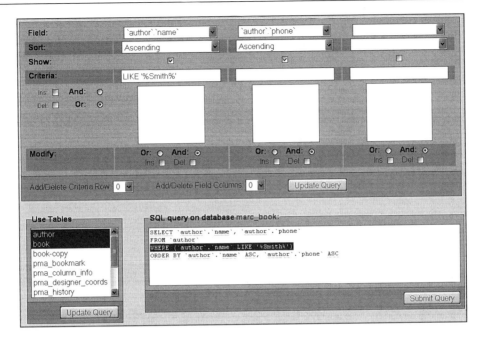

We have another line available to enter an additional criterion. Let's say we want to find the author **Maria Sunshine** as well. This time, we use an = condition. The two condition rows will be joined by the OR operator, selected by default from the left side of the interface.

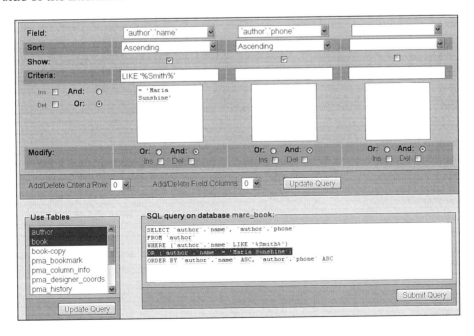

To demonstrate that the OR operator links both the criteria rows better, let's now add a condition, LIKE '%8%', on the phone number.

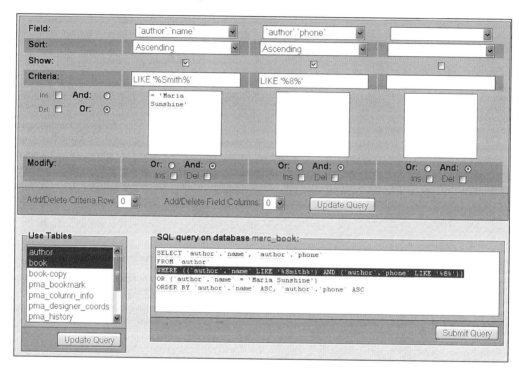

By examining the positioning of the AND and OR operators, we can see that the first row of the conditions is linked by the AND (because AND is chosen under the **name** column) operator, and the second row of conditions is linked to the rest by the OR operator. The condition we've just added (LIKE '%8%') is not meant to find anyone, since, we changed the phone number of all the authors with the name "Smith" to "444-5555" (in Chapter 12).

If we want another criterion on the same column, we just add a criteria row.

Adjusting the number of criteria rows

The number of criteria rows can be changed in two ways. First, we can select the **Ins** checkbox under **Criteria** to add one criteria row (after clicking on **Update Query**). As this checkbox can add only one criteria row at a time, we'll uncheck it and use the **Add/Delete Criteria Row** dialog instead. In this dialog, we choose to add two rows.

Another click on the **Update Query** button produces the following screen:

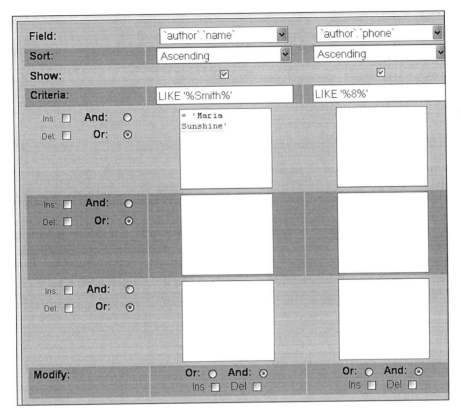

Now, you can see that there are two additional criteria rows (which are empty at the moment). We can also remove criteria rows. This can be done by choosing negative numbers in the **Add/Delete Criteria Row** dialog, or by ticking the **Del** checkbox beside the row(s) we want to remove. Let's remove the two rows we've just added. as we don't need them now. The **Update Query** button refreshes the page with the specified adjustment.

Adjusting the number of criteria columns

Using a similar mechanism, we can add or delete coloumns by checking the **INS** or **Del** checkboxes under each column, or the **Add/Delete Field Columns** dialog. We already had one unused column (not shown on the previous images to save space). Here, we have added one column using the **Ins** checkbox located under the unused column (this time, we will need it):

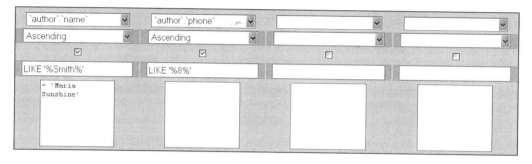

Automatic joins

phpMyAdmin can generate the joins between the tables in the query it builds. Let's now populate our two unused columns with the `title` and the `genre` fields from our **book** table, and see what happens when we update the query.

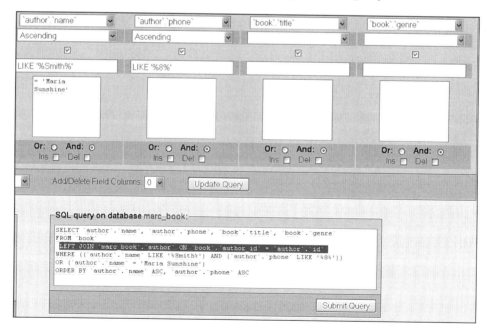

There are now two additional criteria columns that relate to the `book`.`title` and the `book`.`genre` columns respectively. phpMyAdmin used its knowledge of the relations defined between the tables to generate a LEFT JOIN clause (highlighted in the previous figure) on the **author_id** key field. A shortcoming of the current version is that only the internal relations, and not the InnoDB relations, are examined.

 There may be more than two tables involved in a join.

Executing the query

Clicking the **Submit Query** button sends the query for execution. In the following figure, you can see the complete generated query in the upper part and the resulting data row in the lower part:

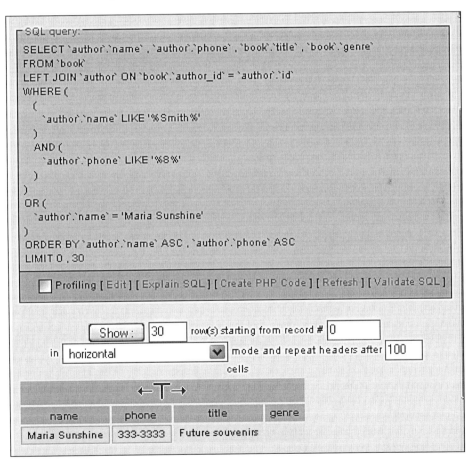

There is no easy way (except by using the browser's **Back** button) to come back to the query generation page once we have submitted the query. The next chapter discusses how to save the generated query for later execution.

Summary

This chapter covers various aspects including opening the query generator, choosing tables, entering column criteria, sorting and showing columns, and altering the number of criteria rows or columns. It also shows us how to use the AND and OR operators to define relations between the rows and columns, and how to use automatic joins between tables. Chapter 14 will show you how to keep permanent bookmarks of your queries.

14
Bookmarks

This chapter covers query bookmarks—one of the features of the linked-tables infrastructure. Being able to label queries, and recall them by label, can be a real time saver. Bookmarks are queries that are:

- Stored permanently
- Viewable
- Erasable
- Related to one database
- Recorded only as a consequence of a user's wish
- Labeled
- Private by default (only available to the user creating them), but possibly public

A bookmark can also have a variable part, as explained in the *Passing a parameter value to a bookmark* section later in this chapter.

There is no bookmark subpage to manage bookmarks. Instead, the various actions on bookmarks are available on specific pages, such as results pages or query box pages.

Comparing bookmark and query history features

In Chapter 12, we learned about the SQL history feature, which automatically stores queries (temporarily or permanently). There are similarities between queries stored in the history and bookmarks. After all, both features are intended to store queries for later execution. However, there are important differences, regarding the way they are stored and the action that triggers the recording of a query.

There is a configurable limit (see Chapter 12) on the number of queries stored in the permanent history; however, the number of bookmarks is not limited. Also, the history feature presents the queries in the reverse order of the time they were sent. However, the bookmarks are shown by label (not showing the query text directly). Finally, query storing in the history is automatic, whereas a query is saved as a bookmark via an explicit request from the user.

To summarize, the automatic query history is useful when we neither plan to recall a query, nor wish to remember which queries we typed. This contrasts with the bookmark facility where we intentionally ask the system to remember a query, even giving it a name (label). Therefore, we can do more with bookmarks than with the query history, but both features have their own importance.

Bookmark creation

There are two moments when it is possible to create a query — after a query is executed (in this case we don't need to plan ahead its creation) or before sending the query to the MySQL server for execution. Both these options are explored in the following sections.

Creating a bookmark after a successful query

Initial bookmark creation is made possible by the **Bookmark this SQL query** button. This button appears only after executing a query that generates a result (when at least one row is found); so this method for creating bookmarks only stores SELECT statements. For example, a complex query produced by the multi-table query generator (as seen in Chapter 13) could be stored as a bookmark this way, provided it finds some results.

Let's see an example. In the **Search** page for the book table, we select the fields that we want in the results, and enter the search values as shown in the following screenshot:

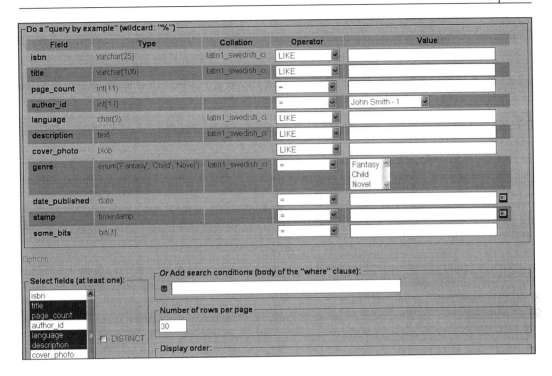

After clicking **Go**, we see that the results page shows a bookmark dialog. We enter only a label for this bookmark, and click **Bookmark this SQL query** to save this query as a bookmark. Bookmarks are saved in the table defined by `$cfg['Servers'][$i]['bookmarktable']`.

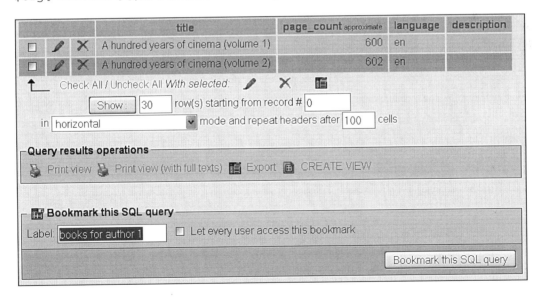

This bookmark dialog can be seen on any page that contains results. As a test, we could just click **Browse** for a table to get results, and then store this query as a bookmark. However, it does not make much sense to store (in a bookmark) a query that can easily be made with one click.

Storing a bookmark before sending a query

Sometimes, we may want to store a bookmark even if a query does not find any results. This may be the case if the matching data is not yet present, or if the query is not a SELECT statement. To achieve this, we have the **Bookmark this SQL query** dialog available in the **SQL** tab of the Database view, Table view, and the query window.

We now go to the **SQL** subpage of the **book** table, enter a query, and directly put the **books in French** bookmark label in the **Bookmark this SQL query** field. If this bookmark label has been used previously, a new bookmark with the same name will be created unless we select the **Replace existing bookmark of same name** checkbox. Bookmarks carry an internal identifying number, as well as a label chosen by the user.

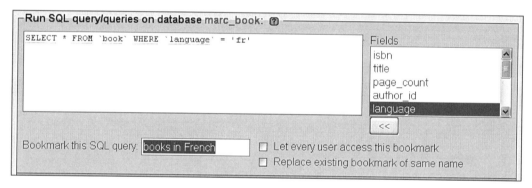

On clicking **Go**, the query is executed and stored as a bookmark. It does not matter if the query does not find anything. This is how we can generate bookmarks for non-SELECT queries such as UPDATE, DELETE, CREATE TABLE, and so on.

This technique can also be used for a SELECT statement that either returns results or does not return results.

Public bookmarks

All bookmarks we create are private by default. When a bookmark is created, the user name using which we are logged in, is stored with the bookmark. Let's suppose that we choose **Let every user access this bookmark** as shown in the following screenshot:

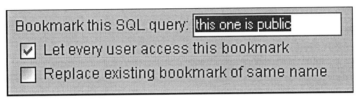

This would have the following effect:

- All users having access to the same database (the current one) will have access to the bookmark.

- A user's ability to see meaningful results from the bookmark depends on the privileges they have on the tables referenced in the bookmark.

- Users will be able to delete the bookmark.

The default initial query for a table

In the previous examples, we chose bookmark labels according to our preferences. However, by convention, if a bookmark has the same name as a table, it will be executed when **Browse** is clicked for this table. Thus, instead of seeing the normal **Browse** results of this table, we'll see the bookmark's results.

Suppose that we are interested in viewing (by default, in the **Browse** mode) the books with a page count lower than 300. We first generate the appropriate query, which can be done easily from the **Search** page, and then we use **book** as a label on the results page.

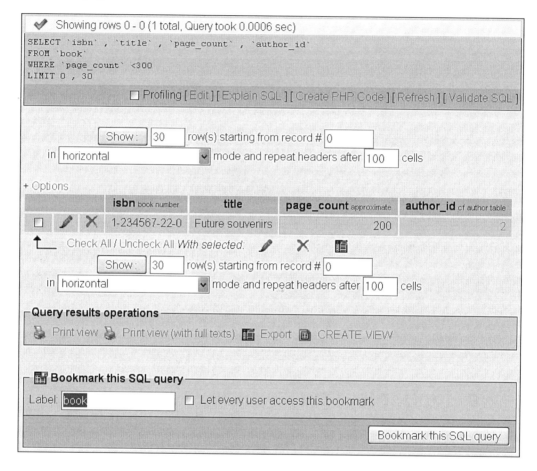

Multi-query bookmarks

A single bookmark can also store more than one query (separated by semicolon). This is mostly useful for non-SELECT queries. As an example, let's assume that we need to clean data about authors by removing an invalid area code from the phone numbers, on a regular basis. This operation would always be followed by a display of the author table.

To accomplish this goal, we store a bookmark (before sending it for execution) that contains these queries:

```
update author set phone = replace(phone,'(123)', '(456)');
select * from author;
```

In the bookmark, we could put many data modification statements such as INSERT, UPDATE, or DELETE, followed optionally by one SELECT statement. Stacking a lot of SELECT statements would not yield the intended result because we would only see the data fetched by the last SELECT statement.

Recalling from the bookmarks list

These bookmarks can now easily be found on the following pages:

- The Table view: **SQL** subpage of any table from **marc_book**
- The query window: The **SQL-History** tab
- While browsing the **pma_bookmark** table (see the *Executing Bookmarks from the pma_bookmark Table* section later)
- The Database view: **SQL** subpage of the **marc_book** database

Three choices are available when recalling a bookmark—**Submit**, **View only**, and **Delete** (**Submit** being the default).

Bookmark execution

Choosing the first bookmark and hitting **Go** executes the stored query and displays its results. The page resulting from a bookmark execution does not have another dialog to create a bookmark, as this would be superfluous.

 The results we get are not necessarily the same as when we created the bookmark. They reflect the current contents of the database. Only the query is stored as a bookmark.

Bookmark manipulation

Sometimes, we may just want to ascertain the contents of a bookmark. This is done by choosing a bookmark and selecting **View only**. Only the query will be displayed. We could then click **Edit** and rework its contents. By doing so, we would be editing a copy of the original bookmarked query. To keep this new edited query, we can save it as a bookmark. Again, this will create another bookmark even if we choose the same bookmark label, unless we explicitly ask for the original bookmark to be replaced.

A bookmark can be erased with the **Delete** option. There is no confirmation dialog to confirm the deletion of the bookmark. Deletion is followed only by a message stating: **The bookmark has been deleted**.

Bookmark parameters

If we look again at the first bookmark we created (finding all books for **author 1**), we realize that although it is useful, it is limited to finding the same author.

Special query syntax enables the passing of parameters to bookmarks. This syntax uses the fact that SQL comments enclosed within /* and */ are ignored by MySQL. If the /* [VARIABLE] */ construct exists somewhere in the query, it will be expanded at execution time with the value provided when recalling the bookmark.

Creating a parameterized bookmark

Let's say we want to find all the books for a given author when we don't know the author's name. We first enter the following query:

```
SELECT author.name, author.id, book.title
FROM book, author
WHERE book.author_id = author.id
/* AND author.name LIKE '%[VARIABLE]%' */
```

The part between the comments characters (/* */) will be expanded later, and the tags will be removed. We label this query as a bookmark named **find author by name** and click **Go**. The first execution of the query just stores the bookmark while retrieving all books by all the authors, as this time we haven't passed a parameter to the query.

In this example, we have two conditions in the WHERE clause, of which one contains the special syntax. If our only criterion in the WHERE clause needs a parameter, we can use a syntax such as WHERE 1 /* and author_id = [VARIABLE] */.

Passing a parameter value to a bookmark

To test the bookmark, we recall it as usual and enter a value in the **Variable** field.

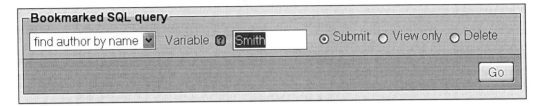

When we click **Go**, we see the expanded query and the author Smith's books.

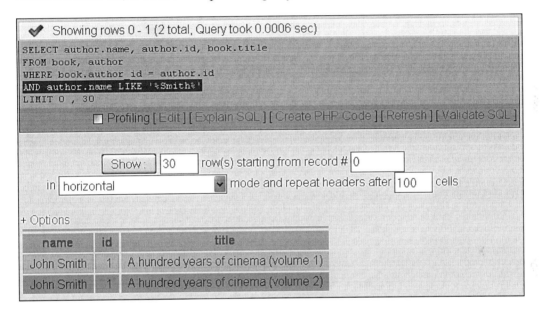

Executing bookmarks by browsing the pma_bookmark table

This feature is available only to users who can directly see the pma_bookmark table. This is the default name given when the linked-tables infrastructure is installed. In a multi-user installation, this table is usually located in a database invisible to unprivileged users. Browsing this table displays a new **Execute bookmarked query** button, which triggers the execution of the query:

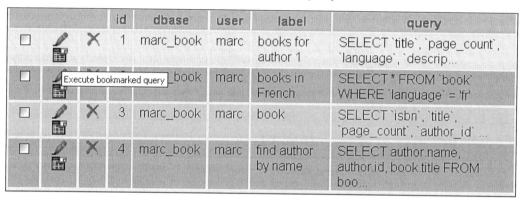

			id	dbase	user	label	query
☐	🖉	✗	1	marc_book	marc	books for author 1	SELECT `title`, `page_count`, `language`, `descrip...
☐				book	marc	books in French	SELECT * FROM `book` WHERE `language` = 'fr'
☐	🖉	✗	3	marc_book	marc	book	SELECT `isbn`, `title`, `page_count`, `author_id` ...
☐	🖉	✗	4	marc_book	marc	find author by name	SELECT author.name, author.id, book.title FROM boo...

We can now click the pencil icon to open the **Edit** page for a specific row to see the query's complete text.

Summary

In this chapter, we get an overview of how to record bookmarks (after or before sending a query), how to manipulate them, and how some bookmarks can be made public. The chapter also introduced us to the default initial query for **Browse** mode. It also covers passing parameters to bookmarks and executing bookmarks directly from the pma_bookmark table. The next chapter will explain how to produce documentation that explains the structure of your databases via the tools offered by phpMyAdmin.

15
System Documentation

Producing and maintaining good documentation about data structure is crucial for a project's success, especially when it's a team project. Indeed, being able to show the current data dictionary and proposed column changes to the other team members provides a valuable means of communication. Moreover, a graphical display of the inter-table relations quickly demonstrates the inner workings of the database. Fortunately, phpMyAdmin has features that take care of this.

Structure reports

From the **Structure** subpage of either the Database or the Table view, the **Print view** link is available to produce reports about our database's structure. Moreover, a **Data Dictionary** link in Database view produces a different report. These are detailed in the following sections. In the next major section, the visual relational schema in PDF is explained.

Using print view

When phpMyAdmin generates results, there is always a **Print view** link that can be used to generate a printable report of the data. The **Print view** feature can also be used to produce basic structure documentation. This is done in two steps. The first click on **Print view** puts a report on the screen, with a **Print** button at the end of the page. This **Print** button generates a report formatted for the printer.

The database print view

Clicking **Print view** on the **Structure** subpage for a database generates a list of tables. This list contains the number of records, storage engine, size, comments, the dates of creation, and the last update for each table.

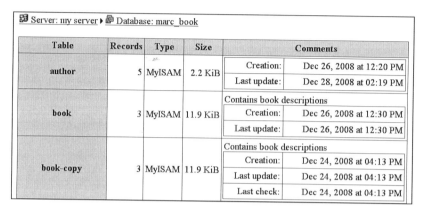

The selective database print view

Sometimes, we prefer to get a report only for certain tables. This can be done from the **Structure** subpage for a database by selecting the tables we want, and choosing **Print view** from the drop-down menu.

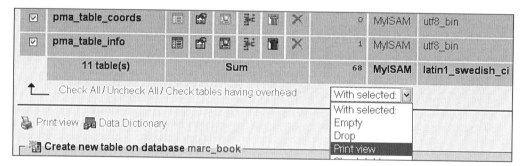

The table print view

There is also a **Print view** link on the **Structure** subpage for each table. Clicking this produces information about columns, indexes, space usage, and row statistics.

book

Table comments: Contains book descriptions

Field	Type	Null	Default	Links to	Comments	MIME
isbn	varchar(25)	No			book number	
title	varchar(100)	No				
page_count	int(11)	No			approximate	
author_id	int(11)	No		author -> id	cf author table	
language	char(2)	No	en			
description	text	No				
cover_photo	blob	No				
genre	enum('Fantasy', 'Child', 'Novel')	No	Fantasy			
date_published	date	No				
stamp	timestamp	No	0000-00-00 00:00:00			
some_bits	bit(3)	No				

Indexes: ⊚

Keyname	Type	Unique	Packed	Field	Cardinality	Collation	Null	Comment
PRIMARY	BTREE	Yes	No	isbn	3	A		
by_title	BTREE	No	No	title (30)	0	A		
isbn	BTREE	No	No	isbn	0	A		
author_id	BTREE	No	No	author_id	0	A		

The data dictionary

A more complete report about the tables and columns of a database is available from the **Structure** subpage of the Database view. We just have to click **Data dictionary** to get this report, which is partially shown here:

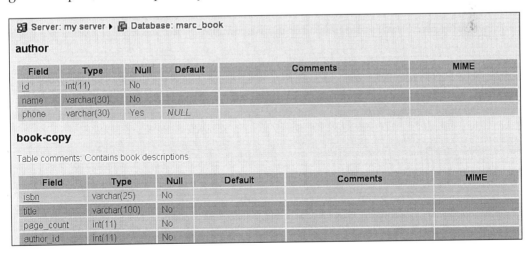

Field	Type	Null	Default	Comments	MIME

The **MIME** column is empty until we add MIME-related information to some columns (explained in Chapter 16).

Relational schema in PDF

In Chapter 11, we defined relations between the `book` and the `author` tables. These relations were used for various foreign key functions (for example, getting a list of possible values in **Insert** mode). We will now examine a feature that enables us to generate a custom-made relational schema for our tables in the popular PDF format. This feature requires that the linked-tables infrastructure be properly installed and configured, as explained in Chapter 11.

Adding a third table to our model

To get a more complete schema, we will now add another table, `country`, to our database. Here is its export file:

```
CREATE TABLE IF NOT EXISTS `country` (
   `code` char(2) NOT NULL,
   `description` varchar(50) NOT NULL,
   PRIMARY KEY  (`code`)
) ENGINE=MyISAM DEFAULT CHARSET=latin1;

INSERT INTO `country` (`code`, `description`) VALUES
('ca', 'Canada'),
('uk', 'United Kingdom');
```

We will now link this table to the `author` table. First, in the **Relation view** for the `country` table, we specify the field that we want to display.

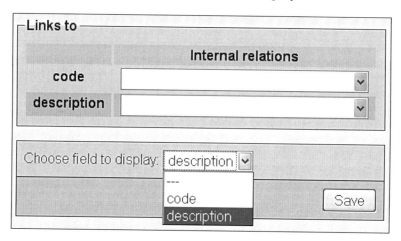

We then add a **country_code** column (same type and size as that of the code column of the country table) to the author table, and in the **Relation view**, we link it to the newly- created country table. We must remember to click **Save** for the relation to be recorded. For this example, it is not necessary to enter any country data for an author, as we are interested only in the relational schema.

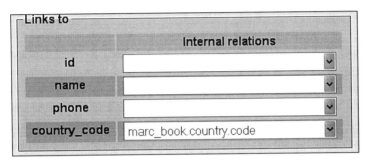

Editing PDF pages

Each relational schema is called a **page**. We can create or edit a page by clicking **Edit PDF pages** in the **Operations** subpage of the Database view.

Page planning

In phpMyAdmin version 3.1.x, a relational schema cannot span multiple databases. But even working with just one database, the number of tables might be large. Representing the various table relations in a clear way could be a challenge. This is why we may use many pages, each showing some tables and their relations.

We must also take into account the dimensions of the final output. Printing on letter-size paper gives us less space to show all our tables and still have a legible schema.

Creating a new page

As there are no existing pages, we need to create one. Again, as our most important table is book, we will also name this page, **book**.

We will choose which tables we wish to see in the relational schema. We could choose each table individually. However, for a good start, checking the appropriate **Automatic layout** checkbox is recommended. Doing this puts all the related tables from our database onto the list of tables to be included in the schema. It then generates appropriate coordinates so that the tables will appear in a spiral layout, starting from the center of the schema. These coordinates are expressed in millimeters, with (0, 0) being located at the upper left corner. We then click **Go**.

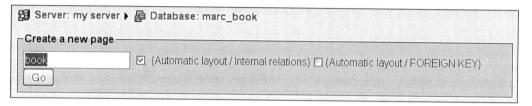

Editing a page

We now get a page with three different sections. The first one is the master menu, where we choose the page on which we want to work (from the drop-down menu). We can also delete the chosen page. We could also eventually create a second schema (page).

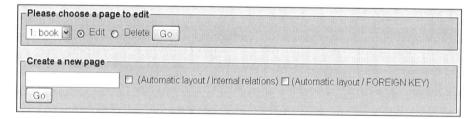

The next section is the table placement portion. We can now see the benefit of the **Automatic layout** feature—we already have our three tables selected, with the (X, Y) coordinates filled in. We can add a table (on the last line), delete a table (using the checkbox), and change the coordinates (which represent the position of the upper left corner of each table on the schema).

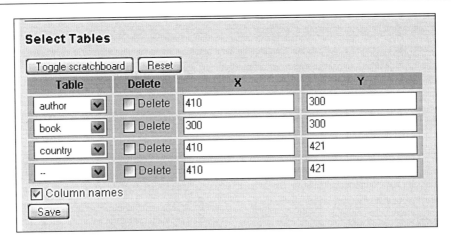

To help set exact coordinates, a visual editor is available for JavaScript-enabled browsers. To control the availability of this editor, the following parameter (which is set to TRUE by default) is available:

```
$cfg['WYSIWYG-PDF'] = TRUE;
```

The editor appears when the **Toggle scratchboard** button is clicked once. It will disappear when this button is clicked again. We can move tables on the scratchboard by using "drag and drop", and the coordinates will change accordingly. The appearance of the tables on the scratchboard provides a rough guide to the final PDF output. Some people prefer to see only the table names (without every column name) on the scratchboard. This can be done by unchecking the **Column names** checkbox and clicking **Save**.

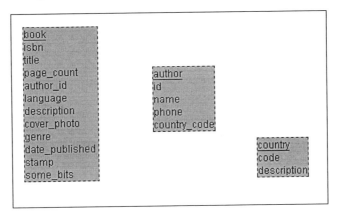

[When we are satisfied with the layout, we must click **Save**.]

Displaying a page

The last section of the screen is the PDF report generation dialog. Now that we have created a page, the **Display PDF schema** is also available from the **Operations** subpage of the Database view. We'll have a look at this dialog from the **Operations** page because the option set is more complete on this page.

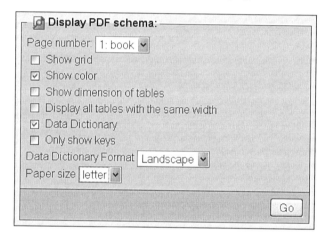

The available options are:

- **Show grid**: The schema will have a grid layer with the coordinates displayed.
- **Show color**: The links between tables, table names, and special columns (primary keys and display fields) will be in color.
- **Show dimensions of tables**: The visual dimension of each table in the table title (for example, **32x30**) will be displayed.
- **Display all tables with the same width**: All tables will be displayed using the same width. (Normally, the width adjusts itself according to the length of the table and the column names.)
- **Data Dictionary**: The data dictionary, which was covered earlier in this chapter, will be included at the beginning of the report.
- **Only show keys**: Do not show the columns on which there are no indexes defined.

- **Data Dictionary Format**: Here, we choose the printed orientation of the dictionary.

- **Paper size**: Changing this will influence the schema and the scratchboard dimensions.

In `config.inc.php`, the following parameters define the available paper sizes and the default choice:

```
$cfg['PDFPageSizes'] = array('A3', 'A4', 'A5', 'letter', 'legal');
$cfg['PDFDefaultPageSize']  = 'A4';
```

The following screenshot shows the last page of the generated report (the schema page) in the PDF format. The first four pages contain the data dictionary with an additional feature. On each page, the schema can be reached by clicking the table name, and in the schema, each page in the data dictionary can be reached by clicking the corresponding table.

Arrows point in the direction of the corresponding foreign table. If **Show color** has been selected, the primary keys are shown in gray and the display fields in black.

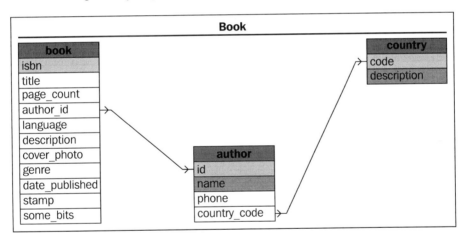

Here is another example generated from the same `book` table's PDF page definition. This time the grid is shown, but no colors.

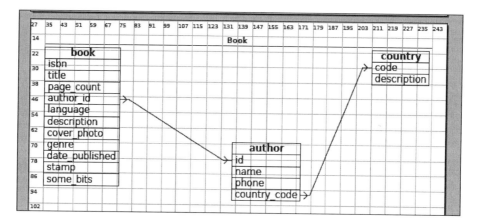

A note about fonts used

All the text we see in the PDF schema is drawn using a specific font. phpMyAdmin 3.1.x uses the **DejaVuSans** font (`http://dejavu.sourceforge.net`), which covers a wide range of characters.

For actual PDF generation, phpMyAdmin relies on the `tcpdf` library (`http://tcpdf.sourceforge.net`), which itself is an adaptation of the `fpdf` library (`http://www.fpdf.org`). These libraries have two ways of using fonts—embedded and not embedded. Embedded fonts produce a bigger PDF file because the whole font is included in the PDF. This is the default option chosen by phpMyAdmin because the library does not depend on the presence of a specific **TrueType** font in the client operating system.

The fonts are located in `libraries/tcpdf/font` under the main phpMyAdmin directory.

To use a different font file, we must first add it to the library (tools are present in the original `tcpdf` kit and a tutorial is available on the `http://www.fpdf.org` website) and then modify phpMyAdmin's `pdf_schema.php` source code.

Using the Designer for PDF layout

The Designer feature (available in the Database view) offers a more refined way of moving the tables on screen as the column links follow the table movements. Therefore, an interface exists between the tables' coordinates, as saved by the Designer, and the coordinates for the PDF schema. Let's enter the Designer and click the small PDF logo.

This brings us to a panel where we can choose the (existing) PDF schema name and the action we want to perform—in our case, to export the Designer coordinates to the PDF schema. We could also use the **Create a new page** dialog, entering a PDF page name and clicking **Go** to create an empty page. From here, we can subsequently export the coordinates saved from the Designer workspace.

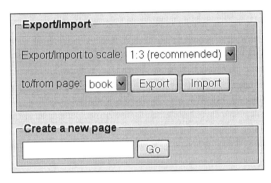

There is a difference in the span of tables managed by the **Designer** and by the **Edit PDF** feature. The **Designer** manipulates every table of a database, whereas the **Edit PDF** panel offers us a choice of tables enabling us to represent a subset of the relations in case there are many tables.

Summary

This chapter covers the documentation features offered by phpMyAdmin—the print view for a database or a table and the data dictionary for a complete column list. The chapter also covers PDF relational schemas. In particular, it focuses on how to create and modify a PDF schema page, and how to use the visual editor (scratchboard). The next chapter will explain how to apply transformations to data, in order to customize its format at view time.

16
MIME-Based Transformations

In this chapter, we will cover a powerful phpMyAdmin feature—its ability to transform a column's contents during a table **Browse**, based on certain specific rules called transformations. Normally, browsing a table shows only the original data that resides in it. However, MIME-based transformations permit alteration of the display format.

Display behavior in browse mode

Normally, the exact contents of each row are displayed, except that:

- The **TEXT** and **CHARACTER** fields might be truncated, according to $cfg['LimitChars'], depending on whether we have chosen to see **Full Texts** or not

- **BLOB** fields might be replaced by a message such as **[BLOB - 1.5 KB]**

We will use the term **cell** to indicate a specific column of a specific row. The cell containing the cover photograph for the "Future souvenirs" book (a **BLOB** column) is currently displayed as cryptic data such as **‰PNG\r\n\Z\n\0\0\0\rIHDR\0** or as a message stating the **BLOB** field's size. It would be interesting to see a thumbnail (shown in the second screenshot under the *Clickable thumbnail* section) of the picture directly in phpMyAdmin and possibly the full-size picture itself. This will be made possible with proper transformation.

Display options

In **Browse** mode, the **Options** link reveals a slider that contains, among other choices, a **Hide Browser transformation** checkbox. We can use it whenever we want to switch between seeing the real data of a cell and its transformed version.

Enabling transformations

We define **transformation** as a mechanism by which all the cells related to a column are transformed at browse time, using the metadata defined for this column. Only the cells visible on the results page are transformed. The transformation logic itself is coded in PHP scripts, stored in `libraries/transformations`, and is called using a plug-in architecture.

To enable this feature, we must set `$cfg['BrowseMIME']` to `TRUE` in `config.inc.php`. The linked-tables infrastructure must be in place (see Chapter 11) because the metadata necessary for the transformations is not available in the official MySQL table structure. It is an addition made especially for phpMyAdmin.

 In the documentation section on phpMyAdmin's homesite, there is a link pointing to additional information for developers who would like to learn the internal structure of the plug-ins in order to code their own transformations.

The MIME column's settings

If we go to the Table view of the **Structure** page for the `book` table and click the **Change** link for the **cover_photo**, we see three additional attributes for the fields (provided the transformations feature is enabled):

- **MIME type**
- **Browser transformation**
- **Transformation options**

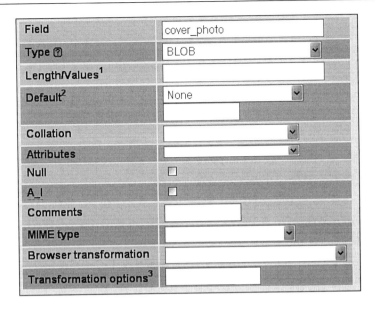

For a specific field, it is possible to indicate only one type of transformation. Here, the field is a **BLOB** field. Hence, it can hold any kind of data. In order for phpMyAdmin to interpret and act correctly on the data, the transformation system must be informed of the data format and the intended results. Accordingly, we have to ensure that we upload data that always follows the same file format.

We will first learn the purpose of those attributes and then try some possibilities in the *Examples of transformation* section.

MIME types

The MIME specification (http://en.wikipedia.org/wiki/MIME) has been chosen as a metadata attribute to categorize the kind of data a column holds. **Multipurpose Internet Mail Extensions (MIME)**, originally designed to extend mail, are now used to describe content types for other protocols as well. In the context of phpMyAdmin, the current possible values are:

- **image/jpeg**
- **image/png**
- **text/plain**
- **application/octetstream**

The **text/plain** type can be chosen for a column containing any kind of text (for example, XHTML or XML text). In the *Examples of Transformations* section, you'll see which MIME type you are required to choose to achieve a specific effect.

Browser transformations

This is where we set the exact transformation to be done. More than one transformation may be supported per MIME type. For example, for the **image/jpeg** MIME type, we have two transformations available—**image/jpeg: inline** for a clickable thumbnail of the image and **image/jpeg: link** to display just a link.

As we can see in the following image, moving the mouse over each choice in the drop-down menu provides a short explanation of the corresponding transformation. A more complete transformation explanation and the possible options are available on clicking the **transformation descriptions** link.

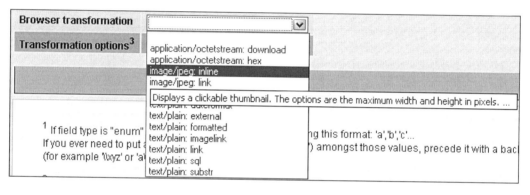

Transformation options

In the *Examples of transformations* section, we will see that some transformations accept options. For example, a transformation that generates an image will need the width and height in pixels. A comma is used to separate the values in the options list, and some options may need to be enclosed within quotes.

Some options have a default value, and we must be careful to respect the documented order for options. For example, if there are two options, and we only want to specify a value for the second option, we can use empty quotes as a placeholder for the first option to let the system use its default value.

Requirements for image generation

Normal thumbnail generation requires that some components exist on the web server, and that a parameter in `config.inc.php` be correctly configured.

The GD2 library

phpMyAdmin uses some internal functions to create the thumbnails. These functions need the GD2 library to be present on our PHP server.

phpMyAdmin can detect the presence of the correct GD2 library, but this detection takes some time. It also takes place not once per session, but almost every time an action is taken in phpMyAdmin.

Setting the `$cfg['GD2Available']` parameter in `config.inc.php` to its default value `'auto'` indicates that the detection of the library's presence and version is needed.

If we know that the GD2 library is available, setting `$cfg['GD2Available']` to `yes` will make execution quicker. If the GD2 library is not available, you are recommended to set this parameter to `no`.

To find out which GD2 library we have on the server, we can go to phpMyAdmin's homepage and click **Show PHP information**. If this link is not present, we have to set the `$cfg['ShowPhpInfo']` parameter to `true`. We then look for a section titled **gd** and verify which version is identified.

gd	
GD Support	enabled
GD Version	bundled (2.0.28 compatible)
GIF Read Support	enabled
GIF Create Support	enabled
JPG Support	enabled
PNG Support	enabled
WBMP Support	enabled
XBM Support	enabled

The JPEG and PNG libraries

Our PHP server needs to have support for the JPEG and PNG images if we or our users want to generate thumbnails for those types of images. For more details, please refer to `http://php.net/manual/en/ref.image.php`.

Memory limits

On some PHP servers, the default value in `php.ini` for `memory_limit` is 8 MB. This is too low for correct image manipulation because the GD functions used to produce the final images need some working memory. For example, in one test, a value of 11 MB in `memory_limit` was needed to generate the thumbnail from a 300 KB JPEG image.

Examples of transformations

We will now discuss a few transformation examples.

Clickable thumbnail (.jpeg or .png)

We will start by changing our **cover_photo** field type from **BLOB** to **MEDIUMBLOB** to ensure that we can upload photographs, which that are bigger than 65 KB in size. We then enter the following attributes:

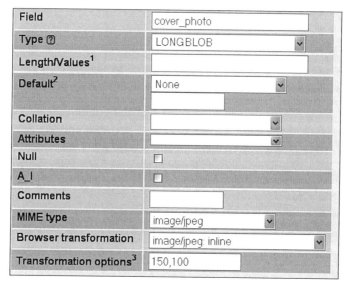

Field	cover_photo
Type ⑦	LONGBLOB
Length/Values[1]	
Default[2]	None
Collation	
Attributes	
Null	☐
A_I	☐
Comments	
MIME type	image/jpeg
Browser transformation	image/jpeg: inline
Transformation options[3]	150,100

Here, the options are presented in the form of width and height. If we omit the options, the default values are 100 and 100. The thumbnail generation code preserves the original aspect ratio of the image. Therefore, the values entered are the maximum width and height of the generated image. We then upload a .jpeg file in a cell (using instructions from Chapter 6). As a result, we get the following in **Browse** mode for this table:

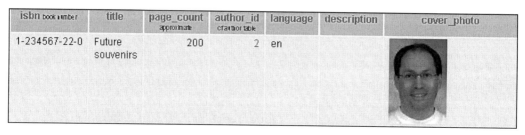

isbn book number	title	page_count approximate	author_id cf author table	language	description	cover_photo
1-234567-22-0	Future souvenirs	200	2	en		

This thumbnail can be clicked to reveal the full-size photograph.

The thumbnail is not stored anywhere in MySQL, but generated each time we go into **Browse** mode for this set of rows. On a double Xeon 3.2GHz server, we commonly experience a generation rate of six JPEG images per second.

For a .png file, we have to use **image/png** as the MIME type and **image/png: inline** as the transformation.

Links to an image

To get a link without thumbnails, we use the **image/jpeg: link** transformation. There are no transformation options. This link can be used to view the photograph (by left-clicking on the link) and then possibly download it (by right-clicking on the photograph itself).

isbn book number	title	page_count approximate	author_id citation table	language	description	cover_photo	genre
1-234567-22-0	Future souvenirs	200	2	en		[BLOB]	

Date formatting

We have a field named **date_published** in our book table; let's change its type to **DATETIME**. Then, we set its MIME type to **text/plain** and the browser transformation to **text/plain: dateformat**. The next step is to edit the row for the "Future souvenirs" book, and enter **2003-01-01 14:56:00** in the **date_published** field. When we browse the table, we now see the field has been formatted. Moving the mouse over the field reveals the unformatted original contents.

date_published	
Jan 01, 2003 at 02:56 PM	20
Nov 30, 1999	2003-01-01 14:56:00

This transformation accepts two options. The first is the number of hours that will be added to the original value, which is zero by default. Adding the number of hours can be useful if we store all times based on **Universal Coordinated Time (UTC)**, but want to display them for a specific zone (UTC+5). The second option is the time format we want to use, made from any PHP `strftime` parameters. So, if we put this in the transformation options—**'0','Year: %Y'**—we will get:

date_published	stamp
Year: 2003	2006-07-22 09:51:50
Year: 19[2003-01-01 14:56:00]00-00 00:00:00
Year: 1999	0000-00-00 00:00:00

Links from text

Suppose that we have put a complete URL—`http://domain.com/abc.pdf`—in the **description** field in our `book` table. The text of the link will be displayed while browsing the table, but we would not be able to click it. We'll now see the use of the **text/plain** MIME type in such a situation.

text/plain: link

If we use a **text/plain** MIME type and a **text/plain: link** browser transformation in the scenario just mentioned, we will still see the text for the link, and it will be clickable.

isbn book number	title	page_count approximate	author_id cf author table	language	description
1-234567-22-0	Future souvenirs	200	2	en	http://domain.com/abc.pdf
1-234567-89-0	A hundred years of cinema (volume 1)	600	1	en	

If all the documents that we want to point to are located at a common URL prefix, we can put this prefix (for example, `http://domain.com/`) in the first transformation option, within the enclosing quotes. Then, we would only need to put the last part of the URL (`abc.pdf`) in each cell.

A second transformation option is available for setting a title. This would be displayed in the **Browse** mode instead of the URL contents, but a click would nonetheless bring us to the intended URL.

 If we use only the second transformation option, we have to put quotes where the first option is to be entered. It could be done as: `'', 'this is the title'`

text/plain: imagelink

This transformation is similar to the previous one, except that in the cell, we place a URL that points to an image. This image will be fetched and displayed in the cell along with the link text. The image could be anywhere on the Web, including our local server.

Here we have the following three options available:

- The common URL prefix (like the one for `text/plain: link`)
- The width of the image in pixels (default: 100)
- The height (default: 50)

For our test URL, you should enter these options:

```
'', '100', '123'
```

If the text for the link is too long, the transformation does not occur. By default, the **Partial Texts** display option is selected.

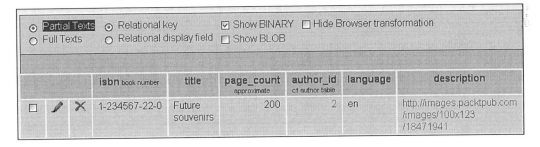

In this case, we can switch to **Full Texts** to reveal the complete link. We can then see the complete image.

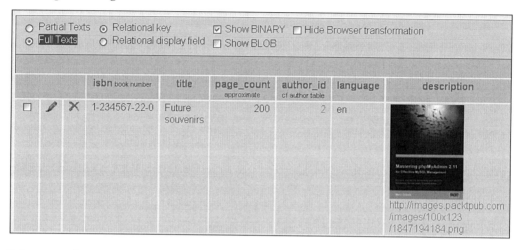

Other transformations, such as `image/jpeg: inline` and `image/png: inline`, specify the exact MIME type of the image. In these cases, phpMyAdmin uses GD2 library functions for the thumbnail generation. However, the link contained in a `text/plain: imagelink` transformation may refer to any browser-supported image type. Therefore, phpMyAdmin just displays a resized image with an HTML `img` tag and its `width` and `height` attributes, according to the size options defined in the transformation. To see the original image, we can click either the link or the thumbnail.

Preserving the original formatting

Normally, when displaying text, phpMyAdmin helps you get rid of special characters. For example, if we entered **This book is good** in the description field for one book, we would normally see **This book is good** when browsing the table. However, if we used the transformation **text/plain: formatted** for this field, we would get the following while browsing:

			isbn book number	title	page_count approximate	author_id cf author table	language	description
☐	✏	✕	1-234567-22-0	Future souvenirs	200	2	en	This book is **good**

In this example, the results are correct. However, other HTML entered in the data field could produce surprising results (including invalid HTML pages). For example, because phpMyAdmin presents results using HTML tables, a non-escaped `</table>` tag in the data field would ruin the output.

Displaying parts of a text

The text/plain: substr transformation is available for displaying only a portion of the text. Here are the options:

- First: where to start in the text (default: 0)
- Second: how many characters (default: all the remaining text)
- Third: what to display as a suffix to show that truncation has occurred; the default is to display ellipses (...)

Remember that $cfg['LimitChars'] is doing a character truncation for every non-numeric field. Hence, text/plain: substr is a mechanism for fine-tuning this field-by-field.

Download link

Let's say we want to store a small audio comment about each book inside MySQL. We add a new field to the book table, with the name **audio_contents**, and type **MEDIUMBLOB**. We set its **MIME type** to **application/octetstream** and choose the **application/octetstream: download** transformation. In the **Transformation options**, we insert **'comment.wav'**.

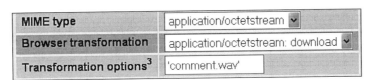

This MIME type and extension will inform our browser about the incoming data, and the browser should open the appropriate player. To insert a comment, we first record it in a .wav format, and then upload the contents of the file into the **audio_contents** field for one of the books. When browsing our table, we can see a link **comment.wav** for our audio comment.

Chapter 17 describes the BLOB streaming technique, which is more appropriate for bigger chunks of data (for example, using phpMyAdmin to watch a movie stored in MySQL!).

Hexadecimal representation

Characters are stored in MySQL (computers in general) as numeric data, and converted into something meaningful for the screen or printer. Users sometimes cut and paste data from one application to phpMyAdmin, leading to unexpected results if the characters are not directly supported by MySQL. I remember a case that involved special quotation marks entered in a Microsoft Word document and pasted to phpMyAdmin. It helps to be able to see the exact hexadecimal codes, and this can be done by using the `application/octetstream: hex` transformation.

In the following example, this transformation will be applied to the **title** field of our `book` table. When browsing the row containing the **Future souvenirs** title, we can see:

As we know which character set this column is encoded with, we can compare its contents with a chart describing each character. For instance, `http://en.wikipedia.org/wiki/Latin1` describes the latin1 character set.

SQL pretty printing

The term **pretty printing** (`http://en.wikipedia.org/wiki/Pretty_printing`) refers to a way of "beautifying" source code. Let's say we are using a table to store the text of a course about SQL. In one column, we might have put sample SQL statements. With the `text/plain: sql` transformation, these SQL statements will be displayed in color, with syntax highlighting, when the table is browsed.

IP address

An IP (v4) address can be encoded into a long integer (for example, via the PHP `iptolong()` function), and stored into a MySQL `UNSIGNED INT` column. To convert it back to the familiar dotted string (for example, `127.0.0.1`), you can use the `text/plain: longToIpv4` transformation.

External applications

The transformations that have been described previously are implemented directly from within phpMyAdmin. However, some transformations are better executed via existing external applications.

The text/plain: external transformation enables us to send a cell's data to another application that will be started on the web server, capture this application's output, and display it in the cell's position.

This feature is supported only on a Linux or UNIX server (under Microsoft Windows, output and error redirection cannot be easily captured by the PHP process). Furthermore, PHP should not be running in safe mode. Hence, the feature may not be available on hosted servers.

For security reasons, the exact path and name of the application cannot be set from within phpMyAdmin as a transformation option. The application names are set directly inside one of the phpMyAdmin scripts.

First, in the phpMyAdmin installation directory, we edit the text_plain__external. inc.php file in libraries/transformations/, and find the following section:

```
$allowed_programs = array();
//$allowed_programs[0] = '/usr/local/bin/tidy';
//$allowed_programs[1] = '/usr/local/bin/validate';
```

No external application is configured by default, and we have to explicitly add our own.

> The names of the transformation scripts are constructed using the following format—the MIME type, a double underscore, and then a part indicating which transformation takes place.

Every program that is allowed, along with its complete path, must be described here, with an index number starting from 0. Then we save the modifications to this script and put it back on the server if needed. The remaining setup is completed from the panel where we chose the options for the other browser transformations.

Of course, we will now choose **text/plain: external** in the transformations menu.

As the first option, we place the application number (for example, 0 would be for the tidy application). The second option holds the parameters we need to pass to this application. If we want phpMyAdmin to apply the htmlspecialchars() function to the results, we put **1** as the third parameter—done by default. We could put a **0** there to avoid protecting the output with htmlspecialchars().

If we want to avoid reformatting the cell's lines, we put **1** as the fourth parameter. This will use the NOWRAP modifier, and is done by default.

External application example: In-cell sort

This example shows how to sort the text contents of one cell. We start by modifying the `text_plain__external.inc.php` script, as mentioned in the above section, to add the `sort` program:

```
$allowed_programs[0] = '/bin/sort';
```

Note that our new program bears the index number `0`.

We then add a **TEXT** field and **keywords** to our book table. Finally, we fill in the MIME-related information, entering **'0','-r'** as the transformation options.

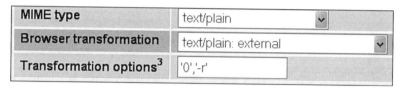

The **'0'** here refers to the index number for `sort`, and the **'-r'** is a parameter for `sort`, which makes the program sort in the reverse order.

Next, we **Edit** the row for the book "A hundred years of cinema (volume 1)", entering some keywords in no particular order (as seen in the following screenshot) and hitting **Go** in order to save the changes.

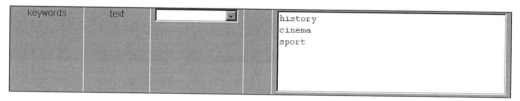

To test the effects of the external program, we browse our table and see the sorted in-cell keywords.

date_published	stamp	keywords
Year: 2003	2006-07-22 10:20:10	
Year: 1999	2006-07-22 10:58:39	sport history cinema

Notice that the keywords are displayed in reverse sorted order.

Summary

In this chapter, we learn how to improve the browsing experience by transforming data using various methods. The chapter also gives an overview of the thumbnail and full-size images of the `.jpeg` and `.png` **BLOB** fields, how to generate links, format dates, display only parts of texts, and how to execute external programs to reformat cell contents. Chapter 17 will cover phpMyAdmin's support for the MySQL features that are new in versions 5.0 and 5.1.

17
MySQL 5.0 and 5.1 Support

MySQL 5.0 introduced a number of new features. The announcement of these features calmed down a number of developers and industry observers who were claiming that MySQL was an inferior product as compared to some competitors' products, which already had these features. Views, stored procedures, triggers, a standard INFORMATION_SCHEMA, and (more recently) a profiling mechanism are now present in the MySQL spectrum.

Among the new features of MySQL 5.1, the ones that relate to a web interface (for example, partitioning and events) are supported in phpMyAdmin.

Views

MySQL 5.0 introduced support for the named, and updatable views. A view is a derived table (consider it a virtual table) whose definition is stored in the database. A SELECT statement done on one or more tables (or even on views), is stored as a view and can also be queried.

Views can be used to:

- Limit the visibility of columns (for example, do not show the salary)
- Limit the visibility of rows (for example, do not show data for specific world regions)
- Hide a changed table structure (so that legacy applications can continue to work)

As a view, by itself, has some permissions attached to it, it is easier to GRANT permissions on the view as a whole, rather than define cumbersome, column-specific privileges on the underlying tables.

To activate the support for views on a server after an upgrade from a pre-5.0 version, the administrator has to execute the `mysql_fix_privileges_tables` script, as described in the MySQL manual.

> Each user must have the appropriate SHOW_VIEW or CREATE_VIEW privilege to be able to see or manipulate views. These privileges exist at the global (server), database, and table levels.

phpMyAdmin supports two ways of creating a view. We'll explain the manual method first, and then go on with a more visual way.

Manually creating a view

To create a view manually, we use the query box to enter the appropriate statement. Let's input the following lines and click **Go**:

```
CREATE VIEW book_author AS
SELECT book.isbn, book.title, author.name FROM book
LEFT JOIN author ON author.id = book.author_id
```

> Creating a view implies that the user has privileges on the tables involved, or at least a privilege such as, SELECT or UPDATE on all the columns mentioned in the view.

At this point, the view has been created, and the left panel is updated to reflect this fact. If we refresh our browser's page and then access the `marc_book` database, we will see:

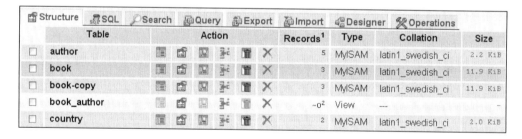

In the left panel, there is a different icon next to the **book_author** view indicating it's not a regular table. In the right panel, we see the information on newly-created view. The number of records for the view currently indicates 0 (more on this in the *Performance Hint* section later in this chapter), and **View** is indicated in the **Type** column. There is no collation or size associated with a view.

This creation step was completed manually. Other operations on views are handled by the phpMyAdmin interface.

Right panel and views

As a view has certain similarities with a table, its name is available in the navigation panel, along with the names of the ordinary tables. On clicking the view name, a panel similar to the one seen for tables is displayed, but with fewer menu tabs than seen in a normal table. Indeed, some operations do not make sense on a view—for example, **Import**. This is because a view does not actually contain data. However, other actions, such as **Browse**, are perfectly acceptable.

Let's browse this view:

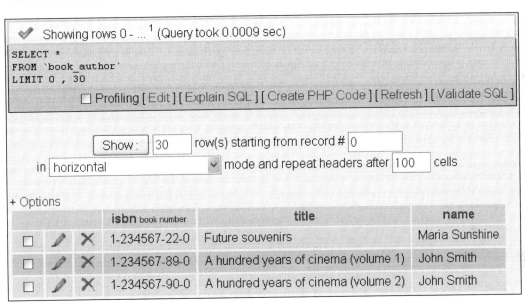

We notice that, in the generated SQL query, we do not see our original CREATE VIEW statement. The reason is that we are selecting from the view using a SELECT statement, hiding the fact that we are pulling data from a view. However, exporting the view's structure would show how MySQL internally stored our view.

```
CREATE ALGORITHM=UNDEFINED DEFINER='marc'@'%' SQL SECURITY DEFINER
VIEW `book_author` AS
select `book`.`isbn` AS 'isbn',
`book`.`title` AS 'title',
`author`.`name` AS 'name'
from (`book` left join `author` on((`book`.`author_id` = `author`.
`id`)));
```

The right panel's menu may look similar to that of a table. However, when necessary, phpMyAdmin generates the appropriate syntax for handling views. For example, a click on **Drop** would produce:

Do you really want to: DROP VIEW 'book_author'

At this point, we can confirm (or not) this view's deletion.

 To perform actions on existing views, a user needs to have the appropriate privilege at the view level, but not necessarily any privilege on the tables involved in this view. This is how we can achieve column and table hiding.

Creating a view from results

Creating a complex view may require typing the complete statement into a query box. Another possibility is to take advantage of phpMyAdmin's **Search** (at the table level) or **Query** (at the database level) features to build a rather complex query, execute it, and then easily create a view from the results. We'll see how this is done.

We mentioned that a view can be used to limit the visibility of columns (and in fact, of tables). Let's say that the number of pages in a book is highly classified information. We open the book table, click **Search**, and choose a subset of the columns:

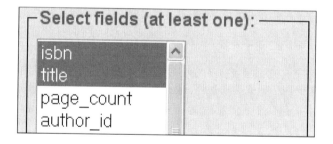

Clicking **Go** produces a results page, where we see a **CREATE VIEW** link in the **Query results operations** section. We use this link to access the view creation panel, which already has the underlying query in the **AS** box. We need to choose a name for this view (here **book_public_info**), and we can optionally set different column names for it (here **number, title**). The other options can influence the view's behavior, and have been explained in the MySQL manual (http://dev.mysql.com/doc/refman/5.1/en/create-view.html).

A click on **Go** generates the view we asked for.

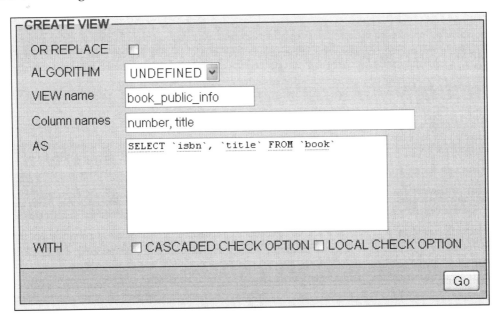

The CHECK OPTION clause influences the behavior of the updateable views (this is explained in the MySQL manual at the page cited previously).

Renaming a view

phpMyAdmin does not support renaming a view directly from the interface. However, since MySQL 5.0.14, the RENAME TABLE statement has been allowed to be used (from a phpMyAdmin's query box) as long as we are renaming inside the same database. For example, RENAME TABLE book_public_info2 TO book_public_info2.

Performance hint

phpMyAdmin has a configuration parameter, $cfg['MaxExactCountViews'], that controls the rows counting phase of phpMyAdmin. Sometimes, a view comprises many huge tables and browsing it would make a large number of virtual rows appear. Therefore, the default value of 0 for this parameter ensures that no row counting happens for views. In this case, we'll see rather strange results when browsing a view: **Showing rows 0 - -1 (0 total, Query took 0.0006 sec)**. But this is more acceptable than slowing down a server.

Nonetheless, if we prefer to see a more exact row count for views, we can put a larger value in this parameter which acts as an upper limit for the rows counting phase.

Routines—stored procedures and functions

It took a while before phpMyAdmin started to include support for these features. The reason is that stored procedures and functions are blocks of code (like a subprogram) that are kept as part of the database, and phpMyAdmin, being a web interface, is more oriented towards operations that are done quickly using a mouse.

Nonetheless, phpMyAdmin has a few features that permit a developer to create such routines, save them, recall them to make some modifications, and then delete them.

Procedures are accessed by a CALL statement to which we can pass parameters. On the other hand, functions are accessed from SQL statements (for example, SELECT), similar to other MySQL internal functions returning a value.

> The CREATE ROUTINE and ALTER ROUTINE privileges are needed to be able to create, see, and delete a stored procedure or function. The EXECUTE privilege is needed to run the routine, although the privilege is normally granted automatically to its creator.

Creating a stored procedure

We'll create a procedure to change the page count for a specific book, by adding a specific number of pages. The book's ISBN and the number of pages to be added, will be the input parameters to this procedure.

Changing the delimiter

The standard SQL delimiter is the semicolon, and this character will be used inside our procedure to delimit SQL statements. However, the CREATE PROCEDURE statement is by itself an SQL statement; hence, we must come up with a way to indicate to the MySQL parser where this statement ends. The query box has a **Delimiter** input box, which contains a semicolon by default. Therefore, we change it to another string, which, by convention, is a double slash //.

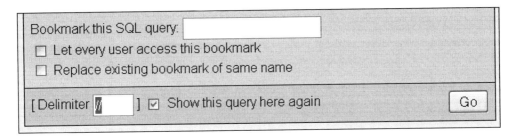

Entering the procedure

We then enter the procedure's code in the main query box:

```
CREATE PROCEDURE `add_page`(IN param_isbn VARCHAR(25), IN param_pages
INT, OUT param_message VARCHAR(100))
BEGIN
  IF param_pages > 100 THEN
    SET param_message = 'the number of pages is too big';
  ELSE
    UPDATE book SET page_count = page_count + param_pages WHERE
isbn=param_isbn;
    SET param_message = 'success';
  END IF;
END
//
```

On clicking **Go**, we get a success message if the syntax is correct. If it is not, well, it's time to revise our typing abilities or debug our syntax. Unfortunately, MySQL does not come with a procedure debugger.

Testing the procedure

Again, in the query box, we test our procedure by entering the following statements. Here, we are using an SQL variable, @message, which will receive the contents of the OUT parameter param_message:

```
call add_page('1-234567-22-0', 4, @message);
SELECT @message;
```

We can then verify whether the page count for this book has increased. We also need to test the problematic case:

```
call add_page('1-234567-22-0', 101, @message);
SELECT @message;
```

This procedure is now available for calling from PHP, using the mysqli extension.

Manipulation

A procedure is stored inside a database, and is not tied to a specific table. Therefore, the interface to manipulate procedures and functions can be found at the database level, on the **Structure** page, under the **Routines** slider.

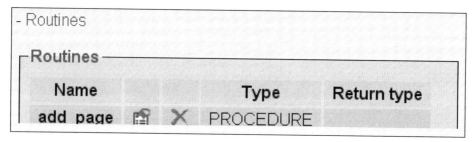

The first icon brings this procedure's text into a query box for editing. The second icon would be used to delete this procedure. When editing the procedure, we notice that the text has been somewhat modified.

```
DROP PROCEDURE `add_page`//
CREATE DEFINER=`marc`@`%` PROCEDURE `add_page`(IN param_isbn
VARCHAR(25), IN param_pages INT, OUT param_message VARCHAR(100))
BEGIN
  IF param_pages > 100 THEN
    SET param_message = 'the number of pages is too big';
  ELSE
    UPDATE book SET page_count = page_count + param_pages WHERE
isbn=param_isbn;
    SET param_message = 'success';
  END IF;
END
```

First, a DROP PROCEDURE appears. This is normal since MySQL does not offer a statement that would permit a change to the body of a procedure. Therefore, we have to delete a procedure every time we want to change it. It's true that the ALTER PROCEDURE statement exists, but it can only change the procedure's characteristics — for example, adding a comment. Then, a DEFINER clause is shown. It was generated at the creation time, and indicates who created this procedure.

At this point, we make any changes we need to the code and hit **Go** to save this procedure.

It might be tempting to open the book table on its **Structure** page and look for a list of procedures that manipulate this table, such as our add_page() procedure. However, all procedures are stored at the database level, and there is no direct link between the code itself (UPDATE book) and the place where the procedure is stored.

Manually creating a function

Functions are similar to stored procedures. However, a function may return just one value, whereas a stored procedure can have more than one OUT parameter. On the other hand, using a stored function from within a SELECT statement may seem more natural because it avoids the need for an intermediate SQL variable to hold the value of an OUT parameter.

What is the goal of functions? As an example, a function can be used to calculate the total cost of an order, including tax and shipping. Putting this logic inside the database, instead of at the application level, helps document the application-database interface. It also avoids duplicating business logic in every application that needs to deal with this logic.

We should not confuse MySQL 5.0 functions with UDF (User-Defined Functions), which existed prior to MySQL 5.0. A UDF constitutes code written in C or C++, compiled into a shared object, and referenced with a CREATE FUNCTION statement and the SONAME keyword.

phpMyAdmin's treatment of functions is in many ways similar to what we have covered in procedures:

- A query box to input a function
- The use of a delimiter
- A mechanism to manipulate a function that is already defined

Let's define a function that retrieves the country name, based on its code. I prefer to use a param_ prefix to clearly identify the parameters inside the function's definition, and a var_ prefix for local variables. We'll use our trusty SQL query box to input the function's code, again indicating to this box to use // as the delimiter.

```
CREATE FUNCTION get_country_name(param_country_code CHAR(2))
 RETURNS VARCHAR(50)
BEGIN
  DECLARE var_country_name VARCHAR(50) DEFAULT 'not found';
  SELECT description
```

```
      INTO var_country_name
      FROM country
      WHERE code = param_country_code;
   RETURN var_country_name;
END
//
```

We should note that our newly created function can be seen on the database's Structure page, along with its friend, the add_page procedure:

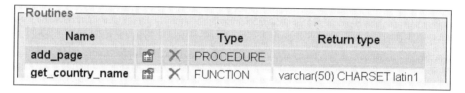

Testing the function

On testing this function:

```
SELECT CONCAT('ca->', get_country_name('ca'), ', zz->',
get_country_name('zz')) as test;
```

We get this result:

```
ca->Canada, zz->not found
```

Exporting stored procedures and functions

When exporting a database, procedures and functions do not appear (by default) in an SQL export. A checkbox, **Add CREATE PROCEDURE / FUNCTION / EVENT**, exists in the **Structure** dialog of the **Export** page, to include those in the SQL export file. If we try it, we obtain:

```
DELIMITER $$
--
-- Procedures
--
CREATE DEFINER=`marc`@`%` PROCEDURE `add_page`(IN param_isbn
VARCHAR(25), IN param_pages INT, OUT param_message VARCHAR(100))
BEGIN
 IF param_pages > 100 THEN
   SET param_message = 'the number of pages is too big';
 ELSE
   UPDATE book SET page_count = page_count + param_pages WHERE
isbn=param_isbn;
   SET param_message = 'success';
```

```
  END IF;
END$$

--
-- Functions
--
CREATE DEFINER=`marc`@`%` FUNCTION `get_country_name`
(param_country_code CHAR(2)) RETURNS varchar(50) CHARSET latin1
BEGIN
  DECLARE var_country_name VARCHAR(50) DEFAULT 'not found';
  SELECT description into var_country_name FROM country WHERE code =
param_country_code;
  RETURN var_country_name;
END$$

DELIMITER ;
```

Triggers

Triggers are code that we associate with a table to be executed when certain actions occur — for example, after a new INSERT in the table book. The action does not need to happen from within phpMyAdmin.

Contrary to routines that are related to an entire database and visible on the database's **Structure** page, triggers for each table are accessed from *this specific table's* **Structure** page.

 Prior to MySQL 5.1.6, we needed the SUPER privilege to create and delete triggers. In version 5.1.6, a TRIGGER table-level privilege was added to the privilege system. Hence, a user no longer needs the powerful SUPER privilege for these tasks.

In order to perform the following exercise, we'll need a new INT column — total_page_count — in our author table.

The idea here is that every time a new book is created, its page count will be added to the author's total page count. I know that some people may advocate that it would be better not to keep a separate column for the total here, instead compute the total every time we need it. In fact, a design decision must be made when dealing with this situation in the real world. Do we need to retrieve the total page count very quickly, for example, for web purposes? And what is the response time to compute this value from a production table with thousands of rows? Anyway, since I need it as an example, the design decision is easy to make here.

Let's not forget that following its addition to the table's structure, the `total_page_count` column should initially be seeded with the correct total. (However, this is not the purpose of our trigger.)

Manually creating a trigger

The current phpMyAdmin version does not have an interface for trigger creation. Therefore, we input the trigger definition in a query box, taking special care of entering `//` in the delimiter box:

```
CREATE TRIGGER after_book_insert AFTER INSERT ON book
FOR EACH ROW
BEGIN
 UPDATE author
  SET total_page_count = total_page_count + NEW.page_count
  WHERE id = NEW.author_id;
END
```

Afterwards, the **Structure** page for our book table reveals under the **Details** slider a new **Triggers** section that can be used the same way as routines, to edit or delete a trigger:

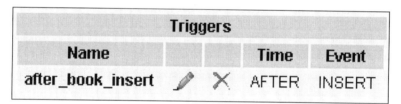

Testing the trigger

Contrary to testing stored procedures or functions, there is neither a `CALL` sequence nor a function inside a `SELECT` statement to execute the trigger. Any time the defined operation (a book `INSERT`) happens, the code will execute (in our case, after the insertion). Therefore, we just have to insert a new book to see that the `author.total_page_count` column is updated.

Of course, a completely automatic management of this column would involve creating `AFTER UPDATE` and `AFTER DELETE` triggers on the book table.

Information_schema

In the SQL:2003 standard, access to the data dictionary (or database metadata) is provided by a structure called `information_schema`. As this is part of the standard, and already exists in other database systems, the decision to implement this feature into MySQL was a very good one.

 MySQL has added some information that is not part of the standard—for example, `INFORMATION_SCHEMA.COLUMNS.COLUMN_TYPE`. Beware of the fact that if you plan to use this information in a software project, it has to remain portable to other SQL implementations.

A phpMyAdmin user sees the `information_schema` as a normal database containing views that describe many aspects of the structure of the databases hosted on this server. Here is a subset of what can be seen (and in fact, the only possible operation on this database is `SELECT`).

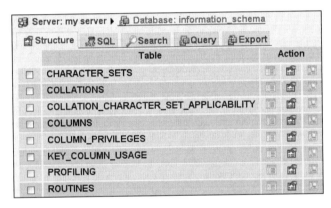

Internally, phpMyAdmin calls the `information_schema` for some of its operations instead of the corresponding SHOW statements to retrieve metadata. However, phpMyAdmin developers have noticed—and this was confirmed by other developers at the 2007 MySQL Users Conference—that some SELECT operations involving a `WHERE` clause on `information_schema` are really slow (many minutes of wait time) when the server hosts hundreds of databases or tables. Therefore, in the current state of MySQL, caution must be exercised about using this feature in our programming projects.

The `$cfg['Servers'][$i]['hide_db']` parameter can be used to hide this "database" to users who might be confused by the sudden apparition of a database they know nothing about. It will probably depend on their level of expertise in MySQL. On a multi-user installation of phpMyAdmin, we cannot please everyone about this parameter's value.

Profiling

Profiling support has been added in the MySQL versions 5.0.37 and 5.1.28. We have previously seen the **Profiling** checkbox appear in query results.

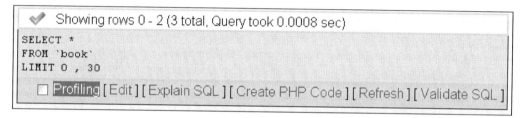

When this box is checked, phpMyAdmin will analyze every query (including the current one), and a report about the execution time of each MySQL internal operation is displayed.

Profiling

Status	Time
starting	0.000015
checking query cache for query	0.000042
checking permissions	0.000005
Opening tables	0.000296
System lock	0.000005
Table lock	0.000035
init	0.000025
optimizing	0.000006
statistics	0.000013
preparing	0.000012
executing	0.000003
Sending data	0.000174
end	0.000004
end	0.000002
query end	0.000002
storing result in query cache	0.000004
freeing items	0.000005
closing tables	0.000026
logging slow query	0.000002
cleaning up	0.000003

Although the profiling system can report additional information about operations (such as, the CPU time, and even the internal server's function names), phpMyAdmin currently displays only the name of the operation and its duration.

Partitioning

User-defined partitioning (`http://dev.mysql.com/doc/refman/5.1/en/partitioning.html`) is offered in MySQL 5.1. Using this feature in phpMyAdmin requires knowledge of its syntax because there are many partition types. Also, for each partition type, the number of partitions and the values associated with each partition are too random to be easily represented on a web interface.

Table creation

Let's try it by creating a table named `test` with one field. On the table creation panel, if connected to a MySQL 5.1 server, phpMyAdmin shows a **PARTITION definition** dialog:

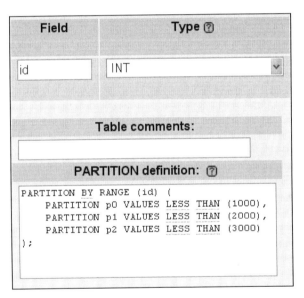

Here, we type in a **PARTITION BY RANGE** clause, which will create partitions on the `id` column.

Operations

On a table on which a partition has been defined, the **Operations** subpage displays a **Partition maintenance** dialog where we can:

- Choose a partition and then ask for an action such as **Rebuild** on it
- Remove all the partitioning

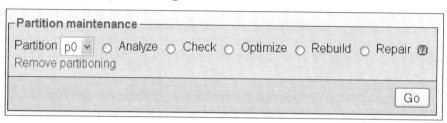

Exporting

Finally, exporting this `test` table in SQL mode produces statements with embedded comments that a MySQL 5.1 server would recognize and interpret to recreate the same partitions.

```
CREATE TABLE `test` (
  `id` int(11) NOT NULL
) ENGINE=MyISAM DEFAULT CHARSET=latin1
/*!50100 PARTITION BY RANGE (id)
(PARTITION p0 VALUES LESS THAN (1000) ENGINE = MyISAM,
 PARTITION p1 VALUES LESS THAN (2000) ENGINE = MyISAM,
 PARTITION p2 VALUES LESS THAN (3000) ENGINE = MyISAM) */;
```

Event scheduler

The Event Scheduler (`http://dev.mysql.com/doc/refman/5.1/en/events.html`), another new feature of MySQL 5.1, permits the creation of tasks that will run automatically according to a schedule. The schedule is quite flexible and permits, for example, a statement to be run every ten seconds, starting from midnight, May 18, 2011. These can be one-time events or recurring ones.

Activating the scheduler

We should first verify whether the scheduler is active on our server. If not, we need to activate it. Otherwise, nothing will happen! We start by typing this statement in the query box:

```
SHOW VARIABLES LIKE 'event%';
```

Next, we look for a variable named `event_scheduler`. If this variable is set to `OFF`, we need to ask the system administrator (or someone with the `SUPER` privilege) to execute the following statement:

```
SET GLOBAL event_scheduler = ON;
```

Granting EVENT permission

Every user who wants to create or drop an event needs the `EVENT` privilege, either globally, or on the database on which he/she plans to add the event. Please refer to Chapter 18 for details about granting such privileges.

Creating an event

The current 3.1.x phpMyAdmin version does not have a web interface on which we could choose the various parts of the `CREATE EVENT` statement. Therefore, the only method left is to use the SQL query box to enter the statement and to know its syntax! Here, we'll use a totally fictitious example:

```
CREATE EVENT add_page_count
    ON SCHEDULE
      EVERY 1 MINUTE
    DO
      UPDATE author set total_page_count = total_page_count + 1 WHERE
id = 1;
```

You can now get some amusement by browsing the `author` table once in a while, and see the counter incrementing for author 1.

Event manipulation

Events are related to one database, which is why you see an **Events** slider on the **Structure** page for the `marc_book` database. Activating it reveals this panel:

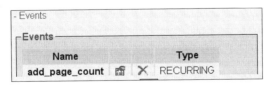

Indeed, this is a recurring event. We can use the first icon to edit the event (which will have the effect of deleting and recreating the event), and the X icon to remove it.

Exporting

It is possible to generate event-related statements at the end of an SQL database export by putting a check mark next to the **Add CREATE PROCEDURE / FUNCTION / EVENT** option. Please remember that some events may have an ending moment; Hence, they may have vanished between the time you create them and the time you attempt an export!

BLOB streaming

Starting with version 3.1.0, phpMyAdmin supports the Scalable BLOB streaming infrastructure for MySQL. The `http://blobstreaming.org` website explains the goals of this project. Please note that some of its documentation relates to command-line utilities which have few or no use in the context of a web interface such as phpMyAdmin. You should be familiar with BLOB streaming terms, such as repository and field references, before reading further.

In this section, we will use this technology to upload a movie and watch it after streaming from within phpMyAdmin.

System requirements

The chosen method of implementation in phpMyAdmin relies on all of these components:

- MySQL 5.1
- PBXT (PrimeBase XT storage engine)
- PBMS (PrimeBase Media Streaming)

PBXT is a streaming enabled storage engine. Although other non-streaming enabled storage engines are supported via PBMS UDFs, this mechanism is not implemented in phpMyAdmin.

The presence of the required components can be verified from the phpMyAdmin's homepage, by clicking the **Engines** link and looking for these lines:

```
PBXT / High performance, multi-versioning transactional engine
PBMS / The Media Stream engine for MySQL
```

In case these lines are not present, please follow the instructions on `http://www.primebase.org` to install PBXT, or on the BLOB Streaming website to install PBMS.

You won't see PBMS in the storage engine choices of the **Operations** subpage for a table. PBMS is not a storage engine that can be associated with the structure of a table.

Configuration

Some PBMS system variables have an impact on BLOB streaming behaviour, and can be defined in `config.inc.php`. More details about them on `http://blobstreaming.org/documentation/#sysvar`. The recommended values to be put in your server's definition are:

```
$cfg['Servers'][$i]['bs_garbage_threshold'] = 50;
$cfg['Servers'][$i]['bs_repository_threshold'] = '32M';
$cfg['Servers'][$i]['bs_temp_blob_timeout'] = 600;
$cfg['Servers'][$i]['bs_temp_log_threshold'] = '32M';
```

Implementation limitations in phpMyAdmin

In the current 3.1.1 version of phpMyAdmin, a few limitations exist, with respect to using BLOB streaming. The first limitation has to do with the MySQL server. On a server which has just started, the `pbms_field_references` global MySQL variable may be set to `off`. As field references are used extensively for BLOB referencing, phpMyAdmin tries to set the parameter to `on`, and this can be done only by a user possessing the SUPER privilege. Therefore, such a user must log in once via phpMyAdmin to set this parameter to the appropriate value, and this will have to be repeated on each restart of the MySQL server.

The second limitation is related to the upload mechanism used to send data to the BLOB repository. The data has to travel first from your workstation to the web server, and then from the web server to the MySQL server. The first travel occurs via a normal HTTP upload. Please refer to Chapter 8, *Importing Structure and Data*, in the *Limits for the transfer* section, for more details on the requirements for uploading. To avoid being hindered by this limit, you can use the web server upload directory (also described in Chapter 8).

 An important note about the host name is due here: In `config.inc.php`, your server name in `$cfg['Servers'][$i]['host']` should be a **FQDN (fully-qualified domain name)**. It should not something like "localhost"; otherwise, the links used to retrieve streaming data will not work.

Creating the PBMS system tables

If all the requirements have been met, we can go to the `marc_book` database in the **Operations** subpage. We should see a **BLOB Repository** dialog, a **Status: Disabled** message, and an **Enable** button. We now have to click **Enable** to create the PBMS system tables inside this database. There are two system tables required by PBMS (`pbms_repository` and `pbms_reference`), and another one (`pbms_custom_content_type`) for phpMyadmin's internal needs.

After creation, we'll see **Status: Enabled** on the same page, but not the newly created system tables. Usually, these tables are kept invisible from within phpMyAdmin because a user should not play with them directly.

We also see a **Disable** button. Clicking on it shows a warning:

```
You are about to DISABLE a BLOB Repository! Are you sure you want to
disable all BLOB references for database marc_book?
```

Confirming this warning message would make PBMS forget all the BLOB references in this database, which would eventually delete all BLOB streaming data previously referenced from this database (if no other reference exists for it from *another* database).

Table preparation

For this exercise, we'll use the `book.cover_photo` column, and `LONGBLOB` to hold the BLOB reference (remember that the stream data itself is located in the BLOB repository, and the `LONGBLOB` column is only there to contain the reference). We ensure that the book table is under the `PBXT` storage engine, and if it's not the case, we just need to go to **Operations** for this table and change the engine, as explained in Chapter 10.

 Using a `LONGBLOB` for `BLOB` reference is currently a PBXT requirement.

Uploading to BLOB repository

We are finally ready to try our first upload to the repository. In the `book` table, we access the **Insert** panel (or we edit an existing row). Note the new **Upload to BLOB repository** option in the dialog for the `cover_photo` column:

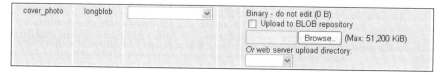

One might ask why this new option is shown. After all, don't we want to upload to the BLOB repository? Maybe! But as this LONGBLOB column may also hold regular data, two possibilities exist:

- Clicking the **Upload to BLOB repository** option, and then browsing for a file or picking one in the web server upload directory. This will send the file to the repository for streaming later.
- Not clicking the option, thereby sending the data directory to this column (not for streaming later).

Obviously, we pick the first choice and upload our favorite movie (we can try a short one first). If the upload works well, we'll see a query similar to this:

```
UPDATE `marc_book`.`book`
SET `cover_photo` = '~*marc_book/~1-150-15591197-0*3907219'
WHERE `book`.`isbn` = '1-234567-22-0' LIMIT 1;
```

Here, cover_photo was updated with the BLOB reference, a number generated by the PBMS storage engine.

Streaming the data from repository

When browsing our table and looking at the row for which we made an upload into the BLOB repository, we see, under the cover_photo column, depending on the data format, one of these messages:

- View image
- Play audio
- View video
- Download file

Clicking on the displayed message starts streaming directly from the server's port 8080 to our browser, sending the appropriate MIME type to inform the browser about which format to expect.

We also see the MIME type of the uploaded data (here **video/mp4**).

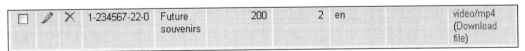

Changing repository data

In case the MIME type for the uploaded data was not interpreted correctly, it's possible to modify it by clicking this link and typing in the correct type. Note that this feature is a work in progress in version 3.1.1.

Finally, when editing this row, we'll see a **Remove BLOB Repository Reference** option. Putting a check mark on this option and saving the row tells the PBMS engine to forget about this reference, eventually eliminating the BLOB data from the repository.

Summary

MySQL 5.0's new features helped the product comply with standards. Even though phpMyAdmin has limited support for these features (especially lacking a syntax-oriented editor), it has a basic set of features to work with views, routines, triggers and `information_schema`, and to display profiling information. phpMyAdmin also supports MySQL 5.1 partitions and events, the PBXT storage engine, and BLOB streaming. The next chapter covers administration of a MySQL server, focusing on the management of user accounts and privileges.

18
MySQL Server Administration

This chapter will discuss how a system administrator can use the phpMyAdmin server management features for day-to-day user account maintenance, server verification, and server protection. Non-administrators can also obtain server information from phpMyAdmin.

Server administration is mostly done via the Server view, which is accessed via the menu tabs available on phpMyAdmin's homepage.

User and privileges management

The **Privileges** subpage (visible only if we are logged in as a privileged user) contains dialogs to manage MySQL user accounts. It also contains dialogs to manage privileges on global, database, and table levels. This subpage is hierarchical. For example, when editing a user's privileges, we can see the global privileges as well as the database-specific privileges. We can then go deeper to see the table-specific privileges for this database-user combination.

The user overview

The first page displayed when we enter the **Privileges** subpage is called **User overview**. This shows all user accounts and a summary of their global privileges, as shown in the next screenshot:

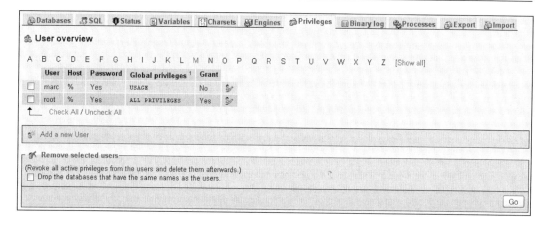

From this page, we can:

- Edit a user's privileges with the **Edit** link on a user's line
- Use the checkboxes to remove users with the **Remove selected users** dialog
- Access the page where the **Add a new User** dialog is available

The displayed users' list has columns with the following characteristics:

- **User**: The user account we are defining.
- **Host**: The machine name, or IP address, from which this user account will be connecting to the MySQL server. A % value here indicates all hosts.
- **Password**: Contains **Yes** if a password is defined and **No** if it isn't. The password itself cannot be seen from phpMyAdmin's interface, or by directly looking at the `mysql.user` table, as it is obfuscated with a one-way hashing algorithm.
- **Global privileges**: Listed for each user.
- **Grant**: Contains **Yes** if the user can grant his/her privileges to others.

Privileges reload

At the bottom of **User Overview**, this message is displayed:

```
Note: phpMyAdmin gets the users' privileges directly from MySQL's
privilege tables. The content of these tables may differ from the
privileges the server uses, if they have been changed manually. In
this case, you should reload the privileges before you continue.
```

Here, **reload the privileges** is clickable. The effective privileges (the ones against which the server bases its access decisions) are the privileges that are located in the server's memory. Privilege modifications, to be made from the **User overview** page, are made both in memory and on disk, in the mysql database. Modifications made directly to the mysql database do not have immediate effect. The **reload the privileges** operation reads the privileges from the database and makes them effective in memory.

Adding a user

The **Add a new User** link brings a dialog for user account creation. First, we see the panel where we'll describe the account itself.

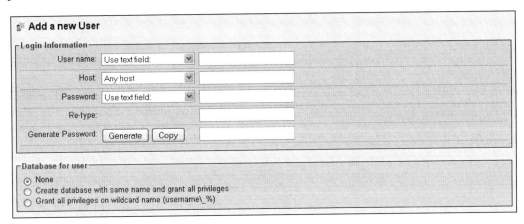

The second part of the **Add a new User** dialog is where we'll specify this user's global privileges, which apply to the server as a whole (see the *Global privileges* section).

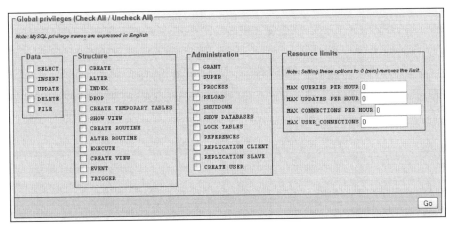

User name

The **User name** menu offers two choices. We can choose **Use text field** and input a user name in the box, or we can choose **Any user** to create an anonymous user (the blank user). Let's choose **Use text field** and enter **bill**.

Host

By default, this menu is set to **Any host** with % as the host value. The **Local** choice means "localhost". The **Use host table** choice (which creates a blank value in the host field) means to look in the mysql.hosts table for database-specific privileges. Choosing **Use text field** allows us to input the exact host value we want. Let's choose **Local**.

Password

Even though it's possible to create a user without a password (with the **No password** choice), it's best to have a password. We have to enter it twice (as we cannot see what is entered) to confirm the intended password. Let's input **bingo**.

Some administrators prefer to improve security by having phpMyAdmin generate a password itself. In the **Generate Password** dialog, a click on **Generate** puts a random password (in clear) on screen. At this point, we should note the password so that we can pass it on to the user. Then a click on **Copy** puts this password in the **Password** and **Re-Type** fields.

Database creation and rights

A frequent convention is to assign a user, the rights to a database, having the same name as this user. To accomplish this, the **Database for user** section offers the checkbox **Create database with same name and grant all privileges;**. Clicking this checkbox automates the process by creating both the database and the corresponding rights. Please note that, with this method, each user would be limited to one database (user bill, database bill).

Another possibility is to allow users to create databases that have the same prefix as their usernames. Therefore, the other choice **Grant all privileges on wildcard name (username_%)** performs this function by assigning a wildcard privilege. With this in place, user bill could create the databases bill_test, bill_2, bill_payroll, and so on; phpMyAdmin does not pre-create the databases in this case.

Global privileges

Global privileges determine the user's access to all databases. Hence, these are sometimes known as "superuser privileges". A normal user should not have any of these privileges unless there is a good reason.

Of course, if we are really creating a superuser, we will select every global privilege that he/she needs. These privileges are further divided into **Data**, **Structure**, and **Administration** groups.

In our example, **bill** will not have any global privileges.

Resource limits

We can limit the resources used by this user on this server (for example, the maximum queries per hour). Zero means no limit. We will not impose any resources limits on **bill**.

The following screenshot shows the status of the screen, just before hitting **Go** to create this user's definition (with the fields that are left being set to default):

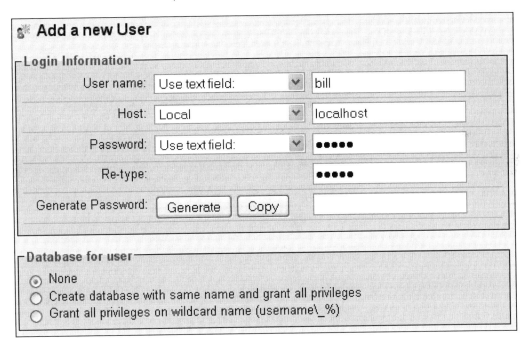

Editing a user

The page used to edit a user appears after a user's creation, or whenever we click **Edit** for a user in the **User overview** page. There are four sections on this page, each with its own **Go** button. Hence, each section is operated independently and has a distinct purpose.

Edit privileges

The section for editing the user's privileges has the same look as the **Add a new User** dialog, and is used to view and to change global privileges.

Database-specific privileges

In this section, we define the databases to which our user has access, and his/her exact privileges.

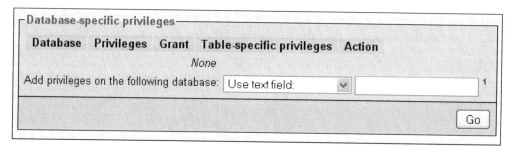

As shown in the above screenshot, we see **None** because we haven't defined any privileges yet. There are two ways of defining database privileges. First, we can choose one of the existing databases from the drop-down menu.

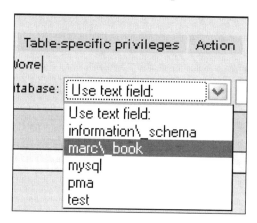

This assigns privileges only for the chosen database. We can also choose **Use text field** and enter a database name. We could insert a non-existent database name, so that this user can create it later (provided we give him/her the CREATE privilege in the next panel). We can also use special characters, such as the underscore and the percent sign for wildcards.

For example, entering **bill** here would enable him to create a **bill** database, and entering **bill%** would enable him to create a database with any name that starts with **bill**. For our example, we will enter **bill**.

The next screen is used to set **bill**'s privileges on the **bill** database and create table-specific privileges.

To learn more about the meaning of a specific privilege, we can move the mouse over a privilege name (which is always in English), and an explanation about this privilege appears in the current language. We give **SELECT, INSERT, UPDATE, DELETE, CREATE, ALTER, INDEX**, and **DROP** privileges to **bill** on this database. We then click **Go**.

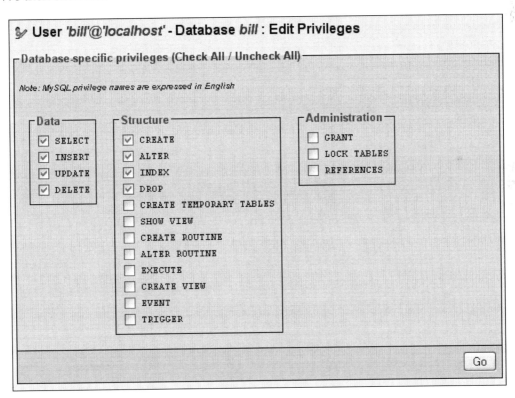

After the privileges have been assigned, the interface stays at the same place, so that we can refine these privileges further. We cannot assign table-specific privileges for the moment, as the database yet does not exist.

The way to go back to **bill**'s general privileges page is to click the **'bill'@'localhost'** title.

This brings us back to the familiar page, except for a change in one section.

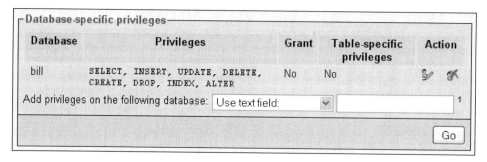

We see the existing privileges on the **bill** database for user **bill** (which we can **Edit** or **Revoke**), and we can add privileges for **bill** on another database. We also see that **bill** has no table-specific privilege on the **bill** database.

Changing the password

This dialog is part of the **Edit user** page, and we can use it either to change **bill's** password or to remove it. Removing the password will enable **bill** to login without a password.

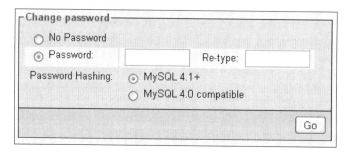

Changing login information or copying a user

This dialog can be used to change the user's login information, or to copy his/her login information to a new user. For example, suppose that Bill calls and tells us that he prefers the login name **billy** instead of **bill**. We just have to add a **y** to the user name, choose **Local** as the host, and select **delete the old one from the user tables**.

After this operation, **bill** no longer exists in the `mysql` database. Also, all his privileges, including the privileges on the **bill** database, will have been transferred to the new user — **billy**. But **bill**'s user definition will still exist in memory, and hence it is still effective. If we had chosen the **delete the old one from the user tables and reload the privileges afterwards** option instead, **bill**'s user definition would immediately have ceased to be valid.

Alternatively, we could have created another user based on **bill**, by making use of the **keep the old one** choice. We can transfer the password to the new user by choosing **Do not change the password**, or change it by entering a new password twice. The **revoke all active privileges…** option immediately terminates the effective current privileges for this user if he/she is logged in.

Removing a user

This is done from the **User overview** section of the **Privileges** page. We select the user to be removed. Then (in **Removing selected users**) we can choose **Drop**, to remove any databases that have the same name as the users we are deleting. A click on **Go** effectively removes the selected users.

Database information

The **Databases** subpage is intended to quickly get privileges information for each database. Optionally, it can also be used to obtain global statistics on these databases, without having to click on each database in the navigation panel. When we enter the **Databases** subpage, we see the list of existing databases.

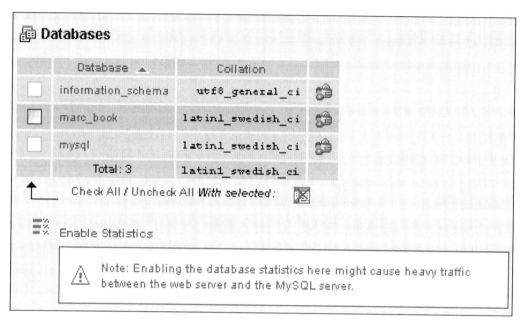

We also see an **Enable Statistics** link. By default, statistics are not enabled because computing the size of data and indexes for all the tables in all the databases may cost valuable MySQL server resources.

Enabling statistics

If we click this **Enable Statistics** link, a modified page appears. For each database, we get the default collation for tables in this database, along with the number of tables and the total number of rows for all tables. Next, information about the space used by the data portion of the tables is given, followed by the space taken by all indexes and total space for all tables. Finally, the space that could be reclaimed by optimizing some tables in this database is presented under **Overhead**.

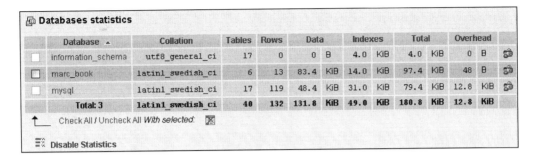

Sorting statistics

By default, the list is sorted by database name in ascending order. If we need to find the database with the most tables or the database that takes the most space, a simple click on the **Tables** or **Total** column header sorts them accordingly. A second click reverses the sort order.

Checking the database privileges

Clicking the **Check Privileges** icon displays all the privileges on a specific database. A user's global privilege might be shown here, as it gives him/her access to this database as well. We can also see the privileges specific to this database. An **Edit** link takes us to another page that is used to edit the user's privileges.

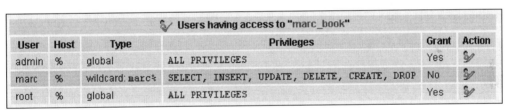

Dropping selected databases

This is an operation that should not be taken lightly. To drop one or more databases, we put check marks next to the names of the databases to be dropped, and click on the red X next to **With selected**. We then get a confirmation screen.

Server information

The **Status**, **Variables**, and **Processes** menu tabs are available to get information about the MySQL server, or to act upon specific processes.

Server status verification

These statistics reflect the MySQL server's total activity, including (but not limited to) the activity generated by queries sent from phpMyAdmin.

The general status page

Clicking the **Status** link produces runtime information about the server. The page has several sections. First, we get information about the elapsed running time and the startup time. Then we get the total and average values, for traffic and connections (where the ø means average).

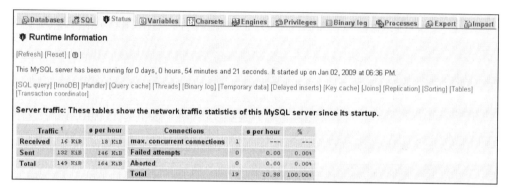

Next, the statistics about the queries are displayed (shown in part here). The average number of queries per hour, minute, and second give a good indication of the server load.

This is followed by statistics about each MySQL command, the absolute number of times, hour average, and the number of times as a percentage of the total.

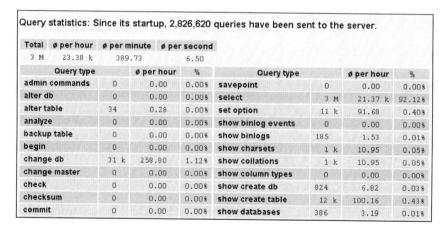

Depending on the MySQL version, many other sections containing server information are displayed.

InnoDB status

On servers supporting InnoDB, a link appears at the end of the **InnoDB section**. When this link is clicked, information about the InnoDB subsystem is displayed, including information about the last InnoDB error that occurred.

```
🐞 InnoDB Status


=====================================
040709 15:27:16 INNODB MONITOR OUTPUT
=====================================
Per second averages calculated from the last 2 seconds
----------
SEMAPHORES
----------
OS WAIT ARRAY INFO: reservation count 3, signal count 3
Mutex spin waits 0, rounds 0, OS waits 0
RW-shared spins 6, OS waits 3; RW-excl spins 0, OS waits 0
------------
TRANSACTIONS
------------
Trx id counter 0 7424
Purge done for trx's n:o < 0 6989 undo n:o < 0 0
Total number of lock structs in row lock hash table 0
LIST OF TRANSACTIONS FOR EACH SESSION:
---TRANSACTION 0 0, not started, process no 17315, OS thread id 1158499248
MySQL thread id 115, query id 2522 localhost root
SHOW INNODB STATUS
--------
FILE I/O
--------
I/O thread 0 state: waiting for i/o request (insert buffer thread)
I/O thread 1 state: waiting for i/o request (log thread)
I/O thread 2 state: waiting for i/o request (read thread)
I/O thread 3 state: waiting for i/o request (write thread)
Pending normal aio reads: 0, aio writes: 0,
 ibuf aio reads: 0, log i/o's: 0, sync i/o's: 0
Pending flushes (fsync) log: 0; buffer pool: 0
48 OS file reads, 4 OS file writes, 4 OS fsyncs
0.00 reads/s, 0 avg bytes/read, 0.00 writes/s, 0.00 fsyncs/s
```

Server variables

The **Variables** subpage displays various settings of the MySQL server, which can be defined in, say, the my.cnf MySQL configuration file. These values can't be changed from within phpMyAdmin.

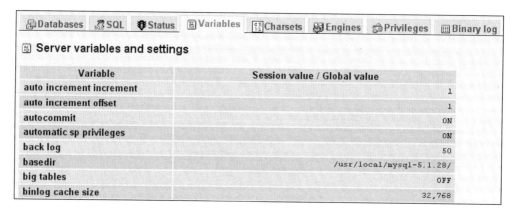

Server processes

The **Processes** subpage is available to superusers and normal users. A normal user would see only the processes belonging to him/her, whereas a superuser sees all the processes.

This page lists all active processes on the server. There is a **Kill** link that allows us to terminate a specific process.

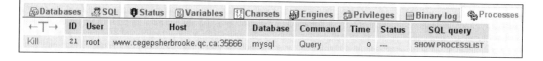

This example has only one running process—the one created by the SHOW PROCESSLIST command itself. This process is not killable because it is no longer running when we get to see the page. We would normally see more processes running on a server.

Storage engines

Information about the various storage engines is available on a two-level format. First, the **Engines** tab displays an overview of the possible engines for the current MySQL version. The names of the engines that are enabled on this server are clickable.

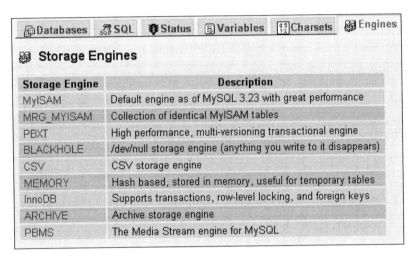

A click on one engine name brings a detailed panel about its settings. Moving the mouse over the numbers in superscript reveals even more information about a particular setting.

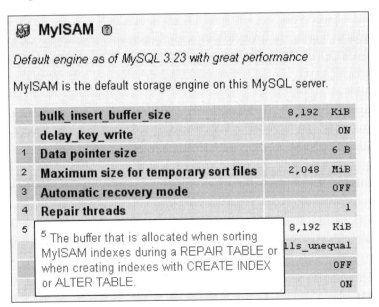

Available character sets and collations

The **Charsets** menu tab on the homepage opens the Server view for the **Charsets** subpage, which lists the character sets and collations supported by the MySQL server. The default collation for each character set is shown with a different background color (using the row-marking color defined in `$cfg['BrowseMarkerColor']`).

The binary log

If MySQL's binary log is active on our server, the menu in the Server view changes so that a **Binary log** tab appears. This tab gives access to an interface through the SHOW BINLOG EVENTS command. This command produces the list of SQL statements that have updated data on our servers. This list could be huge, and currently phpMyAdmin does not limit its display with a pagination technique. Hence, we could hit the browser's memory limits, which depend on the particular browser we are using.

In the following screen, we choose the binary log that we want to examine (unless the server has only one binary log), and the statements are then displayed.

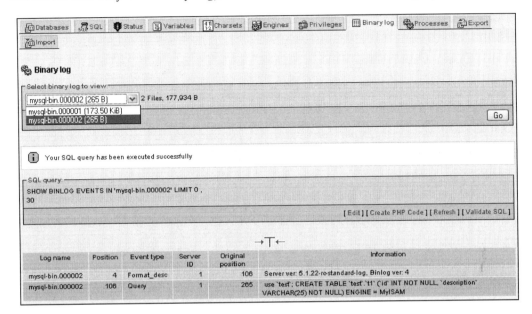

Summary

This chapter covers various features available to system administrators, such as user account management, privileges management, database privileges checks, and server status verification. Appropriate knowledge of the MySQL privileges system is crucial to maintain a MySQL server adequately, and this chapter proposes exercises centered around the notion of a user and his/her privileges. Next is the Appendix A, which tells the history of the phpMyAdmin project.

A
History of phpMyAdmin

This appendix details the birth and evolution of phpMyAdmin over its ten-year history. A one-person hobby project back in 1998, this software has grown, in terms of both the features and the number of people involved. As a testimony to this growth, the earliest source kit I could find (for version 1.1.0) occupied 9 KB, compared to version 3.1.2's size of 3.4 MB.

Early events

The first internal version (0.9.0) was programmed by Tobias Ratschiller from Switzerland, and bears the date September 09, 1998. He then released version 1.0.1 on October 26, 1998. The early versions were offered on Tobias's site `http://www.phpwizard.net` (this site is no longer associated with him). Tobias wrote in the accompanying notes:

"This work is based on Peter Kuppelwieser's MySQL-Webadmin. It was his idea to create a web-based interface to MySQL using PHP3. Although I have not used any of his source-code, there are some concepts I've borrowed from him. phpMyAdmin was created because Peter told me he wasn't going to further develop his (great) tool."

Compared to today's version (ten years after the original), the first version was somewhat limited in features. Neverthless it could be used to create databases and tables, edit their structures, and enter and retrieve data. In the figure that follows, you can see that the left panel was already in place to list database names (not table names yet), and the right panel was the workspace to manage a database or table. This is how the interface for databases looked like in version 1.3.0:

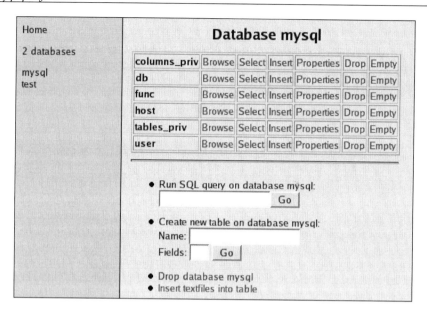

To work on a table, you had the following screen:

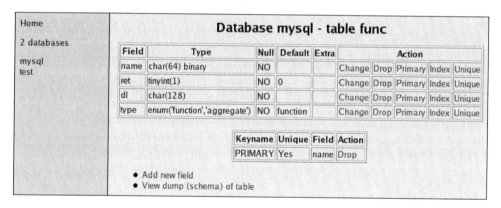

I was using phpMyAdmin version 1.2.0 (released November 29, 1998), and was immediately hooked to the idea of being able to use a web application to maintain a remote database. However, students at Collège de Sherbrooke, where I work in Québec, Canada, are French speaking folks. Therefore, I contacted Tobias and offered to transform his source code by outsourcing all messages in a message file. He accepted the offer, and I created both the English and French message files. Then, on December 27, 1998, Tobias released version 1.3.1, the first multi-language version. (Meanwhile, he had managed to create the German message file.)

In 1999, and the first half of 2000, Tobias improved the navigation system, added features, and merged more language files. His project site maintained a discussion forum allowing new ideas to come along and patches to be discussed. Version 2.1.0 was released on August 06, 2000, which was the last version released by Tobias, who had no more time to devote to this project.

Project re-launch

However, user base had already multiplied, and they were asking for more of the product. Patches were floating on the Internet, with no way of coordinating them. A security alert (and fix) had been published by a third-party, but no new version was being released. Finally, on March 31, 2001, Olivier Müller registered the phpMyAdmin project on `SourceForge.net`, and released a 2.2.0 pre-launch version. It was then called the *unofficial* version. This restart of the project attracted some developers, who now had the SourceForge infrastructure (CVS server, forums, bug trackers, and mailing lists) to help speed up the development. I personally re-joined the project in May 2001, and started fixing and improving the code, as my co-developers were doing.

We became *official* on May 28, 2001, as Tobias accepted our version as the new official one. I remember those months of very intense development effort, with daily improvements and bug fixes, along with new documentation sections. This effort culminated on August 31, 2001, with the release of version 2.2.0.

Here's an excerpt from the announcement file for 2.2.0:

"After five months, five beta releases, and four release candidate versions, the phpMyAdmin developers are pleased to announce the availability of phpMyAdmin 2.2.0. [...] on March 31, 2001. Olivier Müller (Switzerland), supported by Marc Delisle (Québec), Loïc Chapeaux (France), and a team of eight other developers re-started the phpMyAdmin project on `SourceForge.net`, with the authorization of the original package maintainer. Now, after five months of patches, bug fixes, new features, and testing, the version 2.2.0 is finally ready."

This version had security fixes and seven new languages (with dynamic language detection). The code had been reworked to be CSS2 and XHTML 1.0 compliant, and to follow the PEAR coding guidelines. The bookmarks feature appeared in this version, and this came from a separate add-on called "phpMyBookmark".

During the following year, the development continued, with the release of seven minor versions. The last version of the 2.2.x series is 2.2.7-pl1, which is also the last to have been fully tested under PHP 3. We registered `phpmyadmin.net` as the official domain name for the project on April 03, 2002—the date is worth being noted.

Distributors

The list of distributors for phpMyAdmin would be too long and complex to gather, but here are a few pointers. First, the Downloads page of MySQL's website had a "contrib" section in which phpMyAdmin was mentioned very early after its birth. Also, many, if not all, Linux distributors included phpMyAdmin in their kit. Finally, a number of package builders prepare kits for various platforms. I'll just mention the renowned XAMPP kit from Apache Friends, available at `http://www.xampp.org`. Back in mid-2002, the Apache Friends group was already busy integrating Apache, PHP, MySQL, and phpMyAdmin.

Evolution

On August 11, 2002, version 2.3.0 was released. There had been so many new features that the pages were becoming too long. So, this version was the "great split version", creating subpages to group together related features, and thereby enhancing the Database and Table views.

The team started a schedule of releasing a new minor version (2.3.1, 2.3.2 ...) every two months. Version 2.4.0, released on February 23, 2003, included a new server/user management facility. Then came version 2.5.0, on May 11, 2003, to mark the new MIME-type cell transformation system.

Version 2.6.0—released on September 27, 2004—added support for the new `mysqli` extension available in PHP 5 for better performance and improved security. The interface for this version has been redesigned, including new icons and a theme manager. All these features are explained in this book. On April 16, 2005, version 2.6.2 was born, adding basic support for MySQL's views.

In June 2005, the first meeting of phpMyAdmin's development team took place in Karlsruhe, Germany, during LinuxTag 2005. Six members of the team from Switzerland, Germany, Czech Republic, and Canada were present, displaying phpMyAdmin and discussing its features with the event's attendees. We also celebrated PHP's and MySQL's 10th anniversary on the same occasion, along with the respective fathers of these products—Rasmus Lerdorf and Michael "Monty" Widenius. A few weeks before that, at the MySQL Users Conference in Santa Clara, a presentation was titled "PHP 5 + MySQL 5 = A Perfect 10". Indeed, we were aware of what this anniversary meant in terms of the product's maturity.

Version 2.7.0 was released on December 04, 2005. With this version, we ended support for older configuration files—those prior to phpMyAdmin 2.3.0. Also, in 2.7.0, a new plug-in-based import module made its debut.

Version 2.8.0 was made available on March 06, 2006. It included a new web-based setup mechanism. With 2.8.0, the team started a new numbering scheme for version releases. The 2.8 family contains fixes for only those features that are already present in 2.8.0. Here are some examples of the versions, which were expected to follow 2.8.0:

- 2.8.0.1, for anything urgent like a security fix
- 2.8.1, containing normal fixes for the 2.8 family
- 2.9.0, with new features

Version 2.9.0, released on September 20, 2006, added many small improvements such as a font size selector, new export formats, and the possibility of using an external authentication method. Version 2.10.0, released on February 27, 2007, had its main attraction as the Designer—a new graphical Ajax-based relation manager. Version 2.11.0, released on August 21, 2007, offered support for creating views. It also offered support for managing procedures, functions, and triggers.

GoPHP5 and the 3.x branch

phpMyAdmin finally accepted an invitation to become an initial member of the GoPHP5 initiative (see `http://GoPHP5.org`). This initiative promotes the adoption of PHP 5 among web hosts. This means that the new feature releases of phpMyAdmin, after February 05, 2008, require a server that can at least run PHP 5.2.

To better indicate the new PHP requirements, the team switched the major version number to 3. At the same time, it was decided to stop supporting MySQL prior to version 5.0 in the 3.x branch.

Version 3.0 was released on September 27, 2008, with support for MySQL 5.1 features, such as partitioning and the event scheduler. This version also had a new start page and made use of JavaScript effects. Then, on November 11, 2008, version 3.1 incorporated a new setup script and support for BLOB streaming—the work of two students from Google Summer of Code 2008. This version also added support for Swekey hardware authentication.

phpMyAdmin continues to be popular. The cumulative downloads, since April 2001, have reached an impressive count of more than seventeen million in January 2009, at the time of writing this book.

Awards

phpMyAdmin has won some awards, as can be seen in the "Awards" section of the project's homepage. First, it was awarded "Project of the Month" for December 2002, by the administrators of SourceForge. In the interview-style document that we prepared to put on the SourceForge POTM page, I wrote that I was impressed by the download rate of our product, which was three per minute at that time. (Since then, we have reached ten per minute on peak days.)

phpMyAdmin received 75% of the votes from the readers of both the German PHP Magazine and its international version, in the category "Best PHP Application/Tool" for 2003. This award was officially presented to two members of the team at the International PHP Conference, held at Frankfurt in November 2003. The German PHP Magazine hosted the readers' choice again in 2005 and 2006, which phpMyAdmin won in both the years.

`SourceForge.net` hosted its "Community Choice Awards" for the first time in 2006, and phpMyAdmin won in two categories—Databases and System Administration. I represented the team at LinuxWorld, Boston, in April for the Awards presentation. The project also won "Best PHP Application of the Year" at the fifth Annual OS/2 World Awards. At the end of 2006, our project won a Silver Trophy at the third "Trophées du Libre" contest; I went to France to receive the trophy.

In 2007, at the `SourceForge.net` "Community Choice Awards", phpMyAdmin was nominated in the "Best Tool or Utility for Developers" category, and won the "Best Tool or Utility for SysAdmins" Award.

At the beginning of 2008, MySQL AB was acquired by Sun Microsystems for an amount of $1billion. I assume this gave `SourceForge.net` the idea to propose a new award category: "Most Likely to Be the Next $1B Acquisition". However, as envisaged, phpMyAdmin won this award too, along with "Best Tool or Utility for SysAdmins". phpMyAdmin was also a finalist for "Best Tool or Utility for Developers".

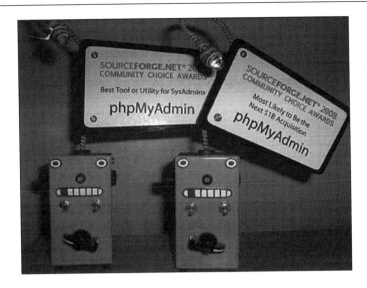

PhpMyAdmin also won the InfoWorld's "Best of open source platforms and middleware (MySQL administration)" prize for year 2008.

Summary

This appendix covers phpMyAdmin's history—from its roots back in 1998, through the project re-launch in 2001, and its subsequent evolution. It details each major version, explains the role of phpMyAdmin in the GoPHP5 initiative, and presents the list of awards collected by this software product. The next appendix explains how to troubleshoot phpMyAdmin, by examining some of its error messages and proposing solutions.

Troubleshooting and Support

B

This appendix proposes guidelines for solving some common problems, and gives hints on how to avoid them. It also explains how to interact with the development team for support, bug reports, and contributions.

System requirements

A section at the beginning of the `Documentation.html` file (which is included with the downloaded kit), discusses system requirements for the particular phpMyAdmin version we are using. It is crucial that these requirements be met, and that the environment be properly configured so that problems are avoided.

Some problems, such as phpMyAdmin bugs, are in fact caused by the server environment. Sometimes, the web server is not configured to interpret `.php` files correctly, or the PHP component inside the web server does not run with the `mysql` or `mysqli` extensions. MySQL accounts may be badly configured. This can happen on home servers as well as on hosted servers.

When we suspect that something is wrong, we can try a simple PHP script, `test.php`, which contains the following to check if the PHP component answers correctly.

```
<?php
echo 'hello';
?>
```

We should see the **hello** message. If this works, we can try another script:

```
<?php
phpinfo();
?>
```

This script displays information about the PHP component, including the available extensions. We should at least see a section about MySQL (proving that the `mysql` extension is available), which gives information about the MySQL **Client API version**.

We can also try other PHP scripts that make a connection to MySQL, to see if the problem is more general than just phpMyAdmin not working. As a general rule, we should be running the latest stable versions of every component.

Base configuration

We should always double-check the way we made the installation, including proper permissions and ownerships. Typos may occur while modifying `config.inc.php`.

Solving common errors

To help solve a problem, we should first pinpoint the origin of the error message. Here are the various components that can generate an error message:

- MySQL server: These messages are relayed by phpMyAdmin, which displays **MySQL said** followed by the message
- PHP component of the web server: For example, **Parser error**
- Web server: The error can be seen from the browser, or in the web server's log files.
- Web browser: For example, JavaScript errors

The *Error Messages* and *Other Problems* sections are mostly based on various messages found on phpMyAdmin's help forum and in the FAQ section of `Documentation.html`.

Error messages

This section refers to explicit error messages, as displayed by phpMyAdmin.

Cannot load MySQL extension

To connect to a MySQL server, PHP needs the `mysql` extension (`mysqli` extension is recommended for MySQL 4.1+), which is a set of MySQL functions. This extension may be compiled as a part of the PHP server. Or it may need to be loaded dynamically, in which case, phpMyAdmin may have tried to load it and failed. This error implies that no other PHP script can make connections to a MySQL server.

The required extension is contained in a file that can be named `mysql.so` or `mysqli.so` on Linux or UNIX, or `mysql.dll` (maybe `mysqli.dll`) on Windows. If our PHP server comes from a software package, we can find and install another software package—probably called `php-mysql` or `php-mysqli`. (The name is distribution dependent.) Otherwise, we can compile our own PHP server with the appropriate extension, as explained in the PHP documentation.

#2003 - Can't connect to MySQL server

This message indicates that the MySQL server is not running, or cannot be reached from the web server. It can also be a socket (Linux/UNIX) or a named pipe (Windows) configuration problem.

Socket problem (Linux/UNIX)

The socket configured in `php.ini` (an example of which is given below) does not correspond to the socket of the running MySQL server.

```
mysql.default_socket = /tmp/mysql.sock
```

As a result, PHP cannot reach MySQL. We can change it to:

```
mysql.default_socket = /var/lib/mysql/mysql.sock
```

However, to be sure, we must find the exact location of this socket.

Named pipe problem (Windows)

This is a problem similar to that indicated above, but on Windows. It can be solved by adjusting `mysql.default_socket` with the correct named pipe used to connect locally to a MySQL server. For example:

```
mysql.default_socket = MySQL
```

MySQL said: Access denied

This error can be solved when we understand the relevant login parameters.

When using http authentication

We cannot use the web server security mechanism based on a `.htaccess` file and the `http` authentication in `config.inc.php` together. As a workaround, use `cookie` as the authentication type instead of `http`.

When using http, cookie, or config authentication

The host parameter in `config.inc.php` must match the host defined in the user access privileges. Sometimes, a system administrator may create an account authorizing user `bill` and host `localhost`. If we try to use `127.0.0.1` host in `config.inc.php`, it will be rejected by MySQL even though it points to the same machine. The same problem can occur if we try the real name of the machine (`mysql.domain.com`) and the definition has been made for `localhost`.

Access denied ... "using password: NO"

If the message ends with **using password: NO**, it means that we are not transmitting a password, and MySQL is rejecting this login attempt. The password value may not have been set in `config.inc.php`.

Access denied ... "using password: YES"

A password is transmitted, but the host/username/password combination has been rejected by MySQL.

Warning: cannot add header information

This problem is caused by some characters (such as blank lines or spaces) being present in `config.inc.php`—either before the `<?php` tag at the beginning, or after the `?>` tag at the end. We should remove these with an editor that supports `.php` files (as discussed in Chapter 1).

MySQL said: Error 127, Table Must Be Repaired

In the left panel, we click on the database name. In the right panel, we select the name of the table for which there is an error (using the relevant checkbox). We then choose **Repair** from the lower drop-down list. More details are available in Chapter 10.

BLOB column used in key specification without a key length

MySQL requires that an index set on a **BLOB** column be limited in size. The simple index creation technique available when creating a column, does not permit the size to be specified. Therefore, we need to create the column without an index. We then come back to the **Structure** page, and use the **Create an index** dialog to choose the **BLOB** column and set a size for the index.

IIS: No Input File Specified

This is a permission problem. **Internet Information Server (IIS)** must be able to read our scripts. As the server is running under the user `IUSR_machinename`, we have to follow the steps mentioned next:

1. Right-click on the folder where we installed phpMyAdmin.
2. Choose **Properties.**
3. Click on **Add** under the **Security** tab, and select the `IUSR_machinename` user from the list.
4. Ensure that this user has read permission to the directory.

A "404: page not found" error when modifying a row

This happens when the `$cfg['PmaAbsoluteUri']` parameter in `config.inc.php` is not set properly. Chapter 1 explains how to take care of this parameter.

Other problems

Here, we cover solutions to problems that do not show up on screen as a specific error message.

Blank page or weird characters

By default, phpMyAdmin uses output buffering and compression techniques to speed up the transmission of results to the browser. These techniques can interfere with other components of the web server, causing display troubles. We can set `$cfg['OBGzip']` to FALSE in `config.inc.php`. This should solve the problem.

Not being able to create a database

No privileges appears next to the **Create database** dialog on the homepage, if phpMyAdmin detects that the account used to log in does not have the permissions to create a database. This situation occurs frequently on hosted servers, where the system administrator prefers to create one database for each customer.

If we are not on a hosted server, this message simply reflects the fact that we have neither the global **CREATE** privilege nor any **CREATE** privilege on a wildcard database specification.

Problems importing large files or uploading large BLOB files

Usually, these problems indicate that we have hit a limit during the transfer. Chapter 8 explains these limits and the recommended course of action. As a last resort, we might have to split our large text files. (Search the Internet for **file splitters**.)

MySQL root password lost

The MySQL manual explains the general solution at
`http://www.mysql.com/doc/en/Resetting_permissions.html`.

The solution involves stopping the MySQL server and restarting it with the special option `skip-grant-tables` (which basically starts the server without security). The way to stop and restart the server depends on the server platform used. We can then connect to the server from phpMyAdmin as a superuser (like root) and any password. The next step is to change the root's password (see Chapter 18). We can then stop the MySQL server and restart it using normal procedures. (Security will become active again.)

Duplicate field names when creating a table

Here is a curious symptom. When we try to create a table containing, for example, one field named `FIELD1` of type `VARCHAR(15)`, it looks like phpMyAdmin has sent a command to create two identical fields named `FIELD1`. The problem is not caused by phpMyAdmin, but by the environment. In this case, the Apache web server seems well-configured to run PHP scripts when in fact it is not. However, this bug appears only for some scripts.

The problem occurs when two different (and conflicting) sets of directives are used in the Apache configuration file. The first set of directives are:

```
SetOutputFilter PHP
SetInputFilter PHP
```

and the second one:

```
AddType application/x-httpd-php .php
```

These sets of directives may be in two different Apache configuration files, and hence, difficult to notice. The recommended way is to use AddType. Using this, we just need to put comments on the other lines (as shown in the following snippet) and restart Apache.

```
#SetOutputFilter PHP
#SetInputFilter PHP
```

Authentication window displayed more than once

This problem occurs when we try to start phpMyAdmin with a URL other than the one set in $cfg['PmaAbsoluteUri']. For example, a server may have more than one name, or we may try to use the IP address instead of the name.

Column size changed by phpMyAdmin

For a more efficient column definition, MySQL itself sometimes decides to change the column type and size. This happens mostly with **CHAR** and **VARCHAR**.

Seeing many databases that are not ours

This problem occurs mostly after an upgrade to MySQL 4. The automatic server upgrade procedure gives the global privileges **CREATE TEMPORARY TABLES**, **SHOW DATABASES**, and **LOCK TABLES** to all users. These privileges also enable users to see the names of all the databases (but not their tables) until we upgrade the GRANT tables privilege as described in the MySQL manual. If the users do not need these privileges, we can revoke the privileges. The users will then see only those databases to which they have access rights.

Not being able to store a value greater than 127

This is normal if we have defined a column of type TINYINT, as 127 is the maximum value for this column type. Similar problems may arise with other numeric column types. Changing the type to INT expands the available range of values.

Seeking support

The starting point for support is the homepage, http://www.phpmyadmin.net, which has sections on documentation and support. There, you will find links to the discussion forums and to various trackers, such as:

- Bug tracker
- Feature requests tracker

- Translations tracker
- Patches tracker
- Support tracker

FAQs

The `Documentation.html` file, which is part of the product, contains a lengthy FAQ section with numbered questions and answers. It is recommended to peruse this FAQ section as the first source for help.

Help forums

The development team recommends that you first use the product's forums to search for the problem encountered, and then start a new forum discussion before opening a bug report.

Creating a SourceForge account

Creating a (free) SourceForge user account, and using it for posting on forums, is highly recommended. This enables better tracking of questions and answers.

Choosing the thread title

It is important to choose the summary title carefully when you start a new forum thread. Titles like "Help me!", "Help a newbie!", "Problem", or "phpMyAdmin error!" are difficult to deal with, as the answers are threaded to these titles and further reference becomes problematic. Better titles would be: "Import with UploadDir", "User can't but root can login", or "Server not responding".

Reading the answers

As people will read, and almost always answer your question(s), giving feedback in the forum about the answers can really help the person who answered, and others who have the same problem.

Support tracker

This is another place to ask for support. Also, if we have submitted a bug report, which is in fact a support request, the report will be moved to the support tracker. With your SourceForge user account, you will be notified of this tracker change.

Bug tracker

In this tracker, we see bugs that have not yet been fixed, along with the bugs that have been fixed for the next version. (This is to avoid getting duplicate bug reports.)

Environment description

As developers will try to reproduce the problem mentioned, it helps to describe your environment. This description can be short, but should contain the following items:

- phpMyAdmin version (the team, however, expects that it is the current stable version)
- Web server name and version
- PHP version
- MySQL version
- Browser name and version

Usually, it isn't necessary to specify the operating system on which the server or the client is running, unless we notice that the bug pertains to only one OS. For example, FAQ 5.1 describes a problem where the user could not create a table having more than fourteen fields. This happens only under Windows 98.

Bug description

We should give a precise description of what happens (including any error message, the expected results, and the effective results we get). Reports are easily managed if they describe only one problem per bug report (unless the problems are clearly linked).

Sometimes, it might help to attach a short export file to the bug report, to help developers reproduce the problem. Screenshots are welcome.

Contributing to the project

Since 1998, hundreds of people have contributed translations, code for new features, suggestions, and bug fixes.

The code base

The development team maintains an evolving code base from which they periodically issue releases. A paragraph on the download homepage section describes how to use Subversion to get the latest version in development. (This can also be done by downloading the Subversion snapshot.) A contribution (translation update, patch, new feature, and so on) will be considered with a higher priority if it refers to the latest code base, and not to an outdated phpMyAdmin version.

Translation updates

Taking a look at the project's current list of 55 languages, you will notice that they are not equally well maintained. The details about translations are available at `http://www.phpmyadmin.net/home_page/translations.php`. You can try to email the official translator for a particular language to propose corrections or translations of recently added messages. If this person does not answer, you can send your modifications to the translation tracker, inside a compressed (`.zip`) file.

Patches

The development team can manage patches more easily if they are submitted in the form of a `context diff` against the current code base, with an explanation of the solved problem or the new feature achieved. Contributors are officially credited in `Documentation.html`, or at least in `ChangeLog`.

Future phpMyAdmin versions

Here are the points that the development team is considering for the next versions:

- Improved support of MySQL's new features
- User preferences in permanent storage
- Internal code improvements

Summary

This appendix covers how to prevent problems with a properly configured server, along with where and how to ask for help. The appendix also explains some common errors and suggests solutions. Moreover, the *Contributing to the Project* section covers how one can contribute to help improve phpMyAdmin.

Index

A

ALTER ROUTINE privileges 262
authentication, phpMyAdmin
  about 29
  authentication types 29
  control user 29
  cookie authentication 31, 32
  HTTP authentication 30
  HTTP authentication, limitations 30
  logging out feature 30
  password storage, cookie authentication 31

B

Binary Large Objects. *See* **BLOB fields**
Bit field 110
BLOB fields
  about 104, 105
  binary content 105, 106
BLOB streaming
  configuring 275
  data, streaming from repository 277
  implementation limitations,
      in phpMyAdmin 275
  PBMS system tools, creating 276
  repository data, changing 278
  repository, uploading 276, 277
  system requirements 274
  system requirements, MySQL 5.1 274
  system requirements, PBMS 274
  system requirements, PBXT
      (PrimeBase XT storage engine) 274
  table, preparing 276
bookmarks
  and query history features,
      comparing 219, 220
  creating 220
  executing 225
  features 219
  from pma_bookmark table, executing 228
  initial query 223
  manipulating 226
  multi-query bookmarks 224
  parameterized bookmark, creating 226
  parameters 226
  parameter value, passing to bookmark 227
  public bookmarks 223
  public bookmarks, effects 223
  recalling 225
  recalling, choices 225
  storing 222
browse mode
  about 78
  color-marking rows 84
  column length, display options 85
  column length, limiting 85
  customizing 86
  data, sorting 83, 84
  distinct values, browsing 85
  headwords 84
bug tracker, phpMyAdmin
  about 313
  bug description 313
  environment description 313

C

cell 241
character set 50
collation

about 50
MySQL version 4.1.x 50
column-commenting
about 193
automatic migration 194
column criteria, multi-table query generator
columns in result, displaying 212
criteria box 212
criteria columns, adjusting 216
criteria rows, adjusting 214
criteria rows, removing 215
editing 211
field selector 211
LIKE criteria 212, 213
query, updating 212
sorting 211
config.inc.php file, phpMyAdmin
about 14
creating, manually 22
editing on Windows client 22
permissions 14
configuration parameters
$cfg['AllowArbitraryServer'] 35
$cfg['AllowUserDropDatabase'] 99
$cfg['BgcolorOne'] 86
$cfg['BgcolorTwo'] 86
$cfg['blowfish_secret'] 31
$cfg['Border'] 86
$cfg['BrowseMarkerColor'] 84
$cfg['BrowseMarkerEnable'] 84
$cfg['BrowseMIME'] 242
$cfg['BrowsePointerColor'] 84
$cfg['CharEditing'] 77
$cfg['CharTextareaRows'] 78
$cfg['Confirm'] 95
$cfg['CtrlArrowsMoving'] 91
$cfg['DisplayServerList'] 60
$cfg['DefaultConnectionCollation'] 53
$cfg['DefaultDisplay'] 80
$cfg['DefaultLang'] 51
$cfg['DefaultPropDisplay'] 102
$cfg['DefaultQueryDatabase'] 198
$cfg['DefaultQueryTable'] 198
$cfg['DefaultTabDatabase'] 64
$cfg['DefaultTabServer'] 66
$cfg['DefaultTabTable'] 65
$cfg['EditInWindow'] 202

$cfg['ErrorIconic'] 45
$cfg['Error_Handler'] ['display'] 37
$cfg['ExecTimeLimit'] 144
$cfg['FilterLanguages'] 52
$cfg['ForeignKeyDropdownOrder'] 191
$cfg['ForeignKeyMaxLimit'] 191
$cfg['GD2Available'] 245
$cfg['HeaderFlipType'] 81
$cfg['IgnoreMultiSubmitErrors'] 203
$cfg['Import'] 143
$cfg['InsertRows'] 76
$cfg['Lang'] 52
$cfg['LeftBgColor'] 54
$cfg['LeftDisplayLogo'] 54
$cfg['LeftDisplayServers'] 60
$cfg['LeftFrameDBTree'] 56
$cfg['LeftFrameLight'] 55
$cfg['LeftFrameTableLevel'] 58
$cfg['LeftFrameTableSeparator'] 58
$cfg['LeftPointerColor'] 54
$cfg['LeftPointerEnable'] 54
$cfg['LeftWidth'] 54
$cfg['LightTabs'] 66
$cfg['LimitChars'] 85, 251
$cfg['LoginCookieRecall'] 32
$cfg['MainPageIconic'] 53
$cfg[MaxExactCount] 64
$cfg['MaxRows'] 82
$cfg['MemoryLimit'] 145
$cfg['ModifyDeleteAtLeft'] 89
$cfg['ModifyDeleteAtRight'] 89
$cfg['MySQLManualBase'] 4
$cfg['MySQLManualType'] 4
$cfg['NaturalOrder'] 46
$cfg['NavigationBarIconic'] 82
$cfg['OBGzip'] 309
$cfg['Order'] 83
$cfg['PDFDefaultPageSize'] 237
$cfg['PersistentConnections'] 25
$cfg['PmaAbsoluteUri'] 23, 309, 311
$cfg['PmaNoRelation_
    DisableWarning'] 175
$cfg['PropertiesIconic'] 89
$cfg['QueryFrame'] 66
$cfg['QueryHistoryDB'] 201
$cfg['QueryHistoryMax'] 202

$cfg['QueryWindowDefTab'] 201
$cfg['QueryWindowHeight'] 67
$cfg['QueryWindowWidth'] 67
$cfg['RecodingEngine'] 128
$cfg['RepeatCells'] 86
$cfg['ReplaceHelpImg'] 47
$cfg[RestrictColumnTypes] 92
$cfg['RestrictFunctions'] 92
$cfg['RightBgColor'] 62
$cfg['RightBgImage'] 62
$cfg['ServerDefault'] 34
$cfg['Servers'][$i] 34
$cfg['Servers'][$i]['AllowDeny']['order'] 38
$cfg['Servers'][$i]['AllowDeny']['rules'] 38
$cfg['Servers'][$i]['AllowRoot'] 39
$cfg['Servers'][$i]['auth_type'] 30
$cfg['Servers'][$i]['bookmarktable'] 221
$cfg['Servers'][$i]['connect_type'] 25
$cfg['Servers'][$i]['controlpass'] 178
$cfg['Servers'][$i]['controluser'] 30
$cfg['Servers'][$i]['extension'] 24
$cfg['Servers'][$i]['hide_db'] 40
$cfg['Servers'][$i]['history'] 202
$cfg['Servers'][$i]['host'] 24
$cfg['Servers'][$i]['only_db'] 39
$cfg['Servers'][$i]['password'] 28
$cfg['Servers'][$i]['port'] 24
$cfg['Servers'][$i]['socket'] 24
$cfg['Servers'][$i]['user'] 28
$cfg['Servers'][$i]['verbose'] 24
$cfg['Servers'][$i]['verbose_check'] 178
$cfg['ShowAll'] 82
$cfg['ShowBrowseComments'] 194
$cfg['ShowChgPassword'] 63
$cfg['ShowFunctionFields'] 93
$cfg['ShowFunctionFields'] 92
$cfg['ShowPhpInfo'] 63
$cfg['ShowPropertyComments'] 194
$cfg['ShowSQL'] 71
$cfg['ShowStats'] 63
$cfg['ShowTooltipAliasDB'] 166
$cfg['ShowTooltipAliasTB'] 166
$cfg['SQLQuery']['Edit'] 79
$cfg['SQLQuery']['Explain'] 79
$cfg['SQLQuery']['Refresh'] 79
$cfg['SQLQuery']['ShowAsPHP'] 79
$cfg['SQLQuery']['Validate'] 205

$cfg['SQLValidator']['password'] 205
$cfg['SQLValidator']['username'] 205
$cfg['SQP']['fmtColor'] 203
$cfg['SQP']['fmtType'] 203
$cfg['SuggestDBName'] 70
$cfg['TextareaAutoSelect'] 199
$cfg['ThBgcolor'] 86
$cfg['ThemeDefault'] 48
$cfg['ThemeManager'] 48
$cfg['ThemePath'] 48
$cfg['ThemePerServer'] 49
$cfg['UploadDir'] 151
$cfg['UseDbSearch'] 161
$cfg['VerboseMultiSubmit'] 203
$cfg['WYSIWYG-PDF'] 235
cfg['ShowHttpHostTitle'] 45
control user 29
CREATE ROUTINE privileges 262
CSV files, importing
    CSV export options 148
    CSV method 148
    CSV using LOAD DATA 149

D

data
    deleting 95
    editing 89
    functions, applying to data 92
    import feature, accessing 143
    importing 143
    importing, CSV files 147, 149
    importing, file size limits 144
    importing, memory limits 145
    importing, other limits 144
    importing, SQL files 146
    importing, time limits 144
    importing, transfer limits 144
    partial imports 145
    searching 153
    single row, deleting 95
database
    additional table, creating 87
    creating 69
    Data dictionary 231, 232
    deleting 98
    Inside field option used 161

multi-table operations 170
multi-table query generator 209
operations tab 171
Print view 230
searching 160
Structure subpage 229
table attributes 165
table, creating 71
table maintenanace 164
database, creating
about 69
additional table, creating 87, 88
authorized database creation 70, 71
CREATE privilege 69
homepage, MySQL 69
no privileges 69
database export
about 118
CodeGen choice 137
Comma-Separated Values
    (CSV) format 119
CSV format 129
CSV for MS Excel 130
exporting in, NHibernate Object relation
    mapping (ORM) 137
LaTeX format 133
Microsoft Excel 2000 format 131
Microsoft Word 2000 format 132
Native MS Excel format 134
open document spreadsheet format 135
open document text format 136
PDF format 131
Save as file subpanel 126
SQL 119
SQL, options 122
subpanel 119
Text! format 137
YAML format 137
database information, MySQL server
about 288
database, dropping 289
enable statistics 288
priveleges, checking 289
statistics. sorting 289
database, left panel
handling 60
interface limitations 60

speed configuration parameters 61
database operations
database, copying 172
database, renaming 172
rename database 172
data, deleting
about 95
Empty option 98, 99
multi-rows, deleting 96
rows, deleting 97
single row 95
row, deleting 89
data, editing
Ctrl +arrows keys, using 91
data navigation 90
edit icon 90
edit mode 89
function names display, restricting 92
functions, applying to data 92
multi-row editing 94
null values, managing 91
row, deleting 89
row, editing 89
rows of data, duplicating 93
data manipulation
data, deleting 89, 95
data navigation 90
functions, applying to data 92
multi-row editing 94
multi-row, deleting 96
null values, handling 91
rows, deleting 97
rows of data, duplicating 93
single row, deleting 95
defined relations, benefits
browsable foreign-table window 192
foreign key drop-down list 191
foreign key information 190
metadata, automatic update 193
referential integrity checks 192
Designer
menu icons 186
PBXT relations 189
PDF schema, exporting 190
relations, defining 187
relations, defining with 185
Show/Hide left menu icon 187

display options 242
documentation, phpMyAdmin
  database, Print view 230
  Data dictionary 231

E

Edit PDF feature 239
Empty option 98, 99
ENUM field 107
error messages, phpMyAdmin
  BLOB related errors 308
  cannot add header information 308
  cannot load MySQL extension 306, 307
  can't connect to MySQL server 307
  config authentication, using 308
  error 404, page not found 309
  generating, components 306
  http authentication, using 307
  IIS, no input file specified 309
  MySQL, access denied 307
  MySQL, table must be repaired 308
  named pipe problem 307
  password transmission problem 308
  socket problem 307
event scheduler, MySQL 5.1
  activating 272
  event, creating 273
  event, exporting 274
  event, manipulating 273
  event permission, granting 273

F

field
  adding to table 101, 102
  attributes, editing 103
  bit-field 110
  BLOB fields 104, 105
  DATE field 108
  DATETIME field 108
  ENUM field 107, 108
  horizontal mode, using 103
  SET field 107, 108
  TEXT field, layout controlling 104
  TEXT field, using 104
  TIMESTAMP field 108, 110
  vertical mode, using 102

foreign key
  drop-down list 191
  information 190
functions, MySQL 5.0
  creating, manually 265, 266
  exporting 266, 267
  testing 266

G

garbage collection process,
    Query window 202
GD2 library 245
general options, SQL 122-123
global privileges, MySQL server 283

H

hexadecimal representation,
    transformation 252
history, phpMyAdmin 297

I

iconv module
  data recoding 128
image generation, requirements
  about 244
  GD2 library 245
  JPEG and PNG library 245
  memory limits 245
importing data
  CSV files 147, 149
  file size limits 144
  file uploads 145
  LOAD DATA INFILE statement 143
  memory limits 145
  other limits 144
  partial imports 145
  SQL and CSV formats, comparing 147
  SQL files 146
  time limits 144
  time limits, factors 144
  transfer limits 144
index management 74
  EXPLAIN command 115
  full Text indexes 113
  index, editing 113

index problems, detecting 115
multi-field indexes 112
MyISAM tables 113
single-field indexes 111
table optimization 114
InnoDB
about 174
advantages 174
foreign key feature 174
relations 182
status in MySQL server 291
tables 174
tables, without linked-tables
    infrastructure 185
Internet Protocol. *See* **IP-based access
control**

J

JPEG and PNG libraries 245

K

Kanji support 128

L

LaTeX format, database export
about 133
options 133
XML format 134
left panel, phpMyAdmin
about 43
additional table, creating 87
customizing 53, 54
database, handling 60
database names, tree display 56
database, selecting 54
elements 53
full mode 55
light mode 55
light mode, database view 56
light mode, form 55
logo, configuring 54
nested-level feature 58
server-list 59
table, quick browsing 58
table short statistics 57

tables, nested display within database 58
LIKE operator, using 156
linked-tables
bookmarks 219
functions 177
infrastructure 174
infrastructure, aim 175
infrastructure, installing 175
infrastructure, location 175
InnoDB tables, without linked-tables infra-
    structure 185
multi-user installation 176, 177
multi-user installation, table functions 177
relation view 179
single-user installation 178

M

metadata 173
column-commenting 193, 194
MIME
attributes 242
browser transformations 244
column settings 242, 243
transformation, options 244
transformation settings 241
types 243, 244
Multipurpose Internet Mail Extensions. *See*
    MIME
multi-row editing 94
multi-table operations
about 170
in-use table, repairing 171
multi-table query generator
about 209
automatic joins, between tables 217
column criteria, editing 211
columns in result, displaying 212
criteria columns, adjusting 216
criteria rows, adjusting 214
criteria rows, removing 215
field selector 211
LIKE criteria 212
query, executing 217
query, updating 212
selecting 210
sorting 211

use 209
MySQL
  about 8
  backup 117
  BLOB fields 104
  browse mode 78
  character set 50
  collations 50
  database 69
  dump 117
  export 117
  functions, applying to data 92
  index management 114
  InnoDB 174
  mysqldump utility 117
  PrimeBase XT storage engine 174
  relational data structure 173
  relational MySQL 173
  table, creating 71
  version 4.1.x 50
MySQL
  views 257
MySQL 5.0
  about 257
  functions 265, 266
  information_schema 269, 270
  procedures 262
  profiling 270, 271
  triggers 267, 268
MySQL 5.1
  event scheduler 272
  partitioning 271
MySQL server
  about 289
  binary log 294
  charsets 294
  collations 294
  copying user 287
  database creation, privileges 282
  database information 288
  database-specific privileges 284
  effective privileges 281
  global privileges 283
  host 282
  InnoDB status 291
  login information, changing 287
  new user, adding 281

password 282
password, changing 286
privileges management 279
processes 292
removing 287
status page 290, 291
status, verifying 290
storage engines 293
user management 279
username 282
user overview page 279
user, resource limits 283
variables 292
MySQL-Webadmin 297

N

**Native MS Excel format, database export
    134, 135**

O

**open document spreadsheet format, data-
    base export 135**
**open document text format, database export
    136**
operators
  != '' 155
  = ''
    155
other problems, phpMyAdmin
  authentication window, displayed more
      than once 311
  blank pages 309
  can't store value greater than 127 311
  column size changed 311
  database, not able to create 309
  duplicate field names 310
  MySQL, root password lost 310
  problems, importing large files 310
  problems, uploading large BLOB files 310
  unknown databases 311
  weird characters 309

P

panel, phpMyAdmin
  homepage 44

language selector 51, 52
left panel 43
login panel 43
query window 44, 66
right panel 43
partioning, MySQL 5.1
exporting 272
operations sub-page 272
table, creating 271, 272
PBMS 274
PDF pages
Automatic layout feature 234
displaying 236, 237
displaying, options 236, 237
editing 236, 234
embedded fonts 238
font location 238
font, using 238
new page, creating 233
planning 233
TrueType font 238
PDF, relational schema
about 232
PDF layout, designer feature using 239
PDF pages,editing 233
table, adding 232
table, linking with other tables 232
PHP 8
PHP Hypertext Processor. *See* **PHP**
phpMyAdmin
about 7
advanced features 10
Ajax-based Designer 185
arbitary server 35
authentication 29
awards 302, 303
backup 117
base configuration 306
basic features 9
BLOB streaming 274
bookmarks feature 173
calendar pop up, for data entry 108
character set, selecting 128
color picker feature 49
compression file, problems 127
config.inc.php file 14
config.inc.php file, permissions 14

configuring 13
configuring, principles 15
CSV files, importing 147
database 69
database, sorting 46
data, importing 143
data, partial imports 145
data structure, documentation 229
Deja VuSans font used 238
DELIMITER separator 143
distributors 300
downloading 11
error messages 306
feature 155
features 9
future versions 314
GD2 library 245
GoPHP5 301
header and footer, displaying 46
history 297
icon, configuring 45
index management, options 111
information_schema 269
input field, displaying for CHAR 77
input field, displaying for VARCHAR 77
installation using Apache IIS 13
installing 10
installing, on Linux server 13
installing, on local Windows server 13
installing on remote server, Window
    client used 12
installing, prerequisite information 11
interface 43
internal relation view 180
japanese encoding 128
Kanji supprot 128
language, selecting 51
linked-tables 174
MIME-based transformation 241
multi-dimensional array used 204
multi-server configuration 34
multi-statement queries 202
MySQL authentication 27
MySQL documentation links, displaying 47
need for 10
official version 299
other problems 309

panel 43
parameters, MySQL servers 21
partioning 271
phpMyBookmark 300
PmaAbsoluteUri parameter 23
Print view 229
profiling 270
Query window 200
relational MySQL 173
security 36
selective exports 139
server administration features 10
server management features 279
servers, configuring 34
server-specific configuration 23
server-specific configuration, parameter 27
server-specific sections 23
sliders 50
SQL files, importing 147
SQL query box 197
starting page 45
support 311
syntax-highlighting 203
system requirements 11, 305, 306
table names, sorting 46
temporary directory 145
themes 48
Unicode 51
unofficial version 299
version 1.3.0 298
version 2.2.7-p11 300
version 2.3.0 300
version 2.4.0 300
version 2.5.0 300
version 2.6.0 300
version 2.6.2 300
version 2.7.0 301
version 2.8.0 301
version 2.9.0 301
version 2.10.0 301
version 2.11.0 301
version 3.0 301
version 3.1 301
views 257
warnings, web-based setup script 18
web-based setup script 16

web-based setup script, other
    configuration parameters 22
Windows title configuration 45
phpMyAdmin project contributions
code base 314
patches 314
translation updates 314
primary key 74
PrimeBase Media Streaming. *See* **PBMS**
PrimeBase XT storage engine
about 174
advantages 174
tables 174

Q

QEB
about 209
initial page 209
page, elements 209, 210
queries
editing 202
history and bookmark, comparing 219, 220
multi-statement queries 202
multi-table query generator 209
Query by example. *See* **QEB**
query by example, single-table search
empty values, searching 155
non-empty values, searching 155
searching 154, 155
query window
dimensions 67

R

recode module
data recoding 128
relational MySQL
about 173
InnoDB 174
PrimeBased XT storage engine 173, 174
relation view
about 179, 180
column-commenting 193, 194
display field, defining 181
field, relating 180
foreign key system, defining 180
foreign key system, InnoDB 183

InnoDB storage engine 182, 184
internal relation view 180
PrimeBase XT storage engine 182, 184
relation, removing 181
uses 179
right panel, phpMyAdmin
about 43
database view 63
default server page 66
homepage 44
icons, for homepage and menu tabs 66
server view 65
table view 65

S

Save as file subpanel, database export
compression file 127
File name template 126
remember template 127
searching data
single-table search 153
searching database 160
search options, single-table search
display fields, selecting 158
Display order dialog 158
distinct results, obtaining 159, 160
logical operators used 159
where clause used 158, 159
security, phpMyAdmin
database list, restricting 39
directory-level protection 36
error handler 37
in-transit data, protecting 40
IP-based access control 37
levels 36
rules, IP-based access control 37, 38
Swekey hardware authentication 40
selective exports
about 139
exporting and checkboxes 140
partial query results, exporting 139
server-specific configuration, phpMyAdmin
about 23
config authentication type 28
connection, testing 28
content_type 25

MySQL, extensions 24
persistent connections 25
port 25
socket 25
SETfield 106
single-table search
about 153
case sensitivity 157
multiple criteria for same query, using 157
phpMyAdmin used 153
print view 155, 156
query by example, searching 154, 155
search options 158
search subpage, accessing 153, 154
wildcard, searching 156, 157
SQL
and CSV formats, comparing 147
files, importing 146
history, database-based 201, 202
history, session-based 201
LIKE operator 156
query box 197
Query window 200
upload directories 151
Validator 204
views 257
SQL query box
about 197
database view 198
SQL Validator
about 204
configuring 205
non-standard-conforming queries 206
reports 205
standard-conforming queries 205
SUPER privilege 267
support, phpMyAdmin
answering, to questions 312
bug tracker 313
FAQs 312
help forums 312
home page 311
SourceForge account, creating 312
support tracker 312
thread tittle, choosing 312

T

table
  additional table, creating 87, 88
  appending, data to table 170
  attributes, changing 165
  copy operation 169
  creating 71
  data insertion, manually 76
  input field, displaying for CHAR 77
  input field, displaying for VARCHAR 77
  move operation 169
  Operations sub-page 163
  renaming 169
table attributes
  about 165
  changing 165
table attributes, changing
  auto-increment, table options 169
  checksum, table options 168
  delay_key_write, table options 168
  other attributes 168
  pack_keys, table options 168
  row_format, table options 168
  table collation attribute 167
  table comments attribute 165
  table options 168
  table order attribute 166
  table storage engine attribute 165
  transactional page_checksum,
      table options 169
table collation attribute, table attributes
  about 167
  connection collation, switching 168
table, creating
  additional table 87
  additional table, creating 87
  field names 73
  fields, choosing 71
  first table 72
  index, adding to field 75
  primary key 74
  table names 73
table exports
  about 138
  split-file exports 138
table maintenanace

  about 164
  analyze table 164
  check table 164
  defragment table 164
  flush table 164
  optimize table 164
  repair table 164
table operations
  appending data to table 170
  copy 169, 170
  move 169
  multi-table operations 170
  rename 169
tables
  deleting 98
  selecting 210
table view, SQL query box
  clicking into query box 199
  field selector button 198
transformation
  about 242
  cell sort, external applications 254
  clickable thumbnail 246, 247
  date formatting 247, 248
  download link 251
  enabling 242
  examples 246
  external applications 253
  hexadecimal representation 252
  IP (v4) address 252
  links fron text 248
  link to an image 247
  original formatting, preserving 250
  parts of text, displaying 251
  source code, beautifying 252
  text/plain imagelink 249, 250
  text/plain link 248, 249
triggers, MySQL 5.0
  about 267, 268
  creating, manually 268
  testing 268, 269

U

Unicode
  about 51
  advantage 51

transformation formats 51
Unicode Transformation Format (UTF) 51
UTF-8 51
Universal Coordinated Time (UTC) 248
user, MySQL server
copying user 287
database creation, privileges 282
database-specific privileges 284
edit privileges 284
global privileges 283
host 282
login information, changing 287
new user, adding 281
new user, editing 284
password 282
password, changing 286
removing 287
resource limits 283
username 282
user overview page, privileges management
about 279, 280
reload 280, 281
user's list columns 280

V

vertical mode, field
using 102
views, MySQL 5.0
about 257

creating, from results 260, 261
creating, manually 258
operation on views 259
renaming 261
right panels 259, 260
uses 257

W

Web
about 7
Web application
about 8
Web server
upload directories 151, 152

X

XML format, database export 134

Y

YAML Ain't Markup Language. *See* **YAML**
format, database export
YAML format, database export 137

Thank you for buying
Mastering phpMyAdmin 3.1 for
Effective MySQL Management

Packt Open Source Project Royalties

When we sell a book written on an Open Source project, we pay a royalty directly to that project. Therefore by purchasing Mastering phpMyAdmin 3.1 for Effective MySQL Management, Packt will have given some of the money received to the phpMyAdmin project.

In the long term, we see ourselves and you—customers and readers of our books—as part of the Open Source ecosystem, providing sustainable revenue for the projects we publish on. Our aim at Packt is to establish publishing royalties as an essential part of the service and support a business model that sustains Open Source.

If you're working with an Open Source project that you would like us to publish on, and subsequently pay royalties to, please get in touch with us.

Writing for Packt

We welcome all inquiries from people who are interested in authoring. Book proposals should be sent to author@packtpub.com. If your book idea is still at an early stage and you would like to discuss it first before writing a formal book proposal, contact us; one of our commissioning editors will get in touch with you.

We're not just looking for published authors; if you have strong technical skills but no writing experience, our experienced editors can help you develop a writing career, or simply get some additional reward for your expertise.

About Packt Publishing

Packt, pronounced 'packed', published its first book "Mastering phpMyAdmin for Effective MySQL Management" in April 2004 and subsequently continued to specialize in publishing highly focused books on specific technologies and solutions.

Our books and publications share the experiences of your fellow IT professionals in adapting and customizing today's systems, applications, and frameworks. Our solution-based books give you the knowledge and power to customize the software and technologies you're using to get the job done. Packt books are more specific and less general than the IT books you have seen in the past. Our unique business model allows us to bring you more focused information, giving you more of what you need to know, and less of what you don't.

Packt is a modern, yet unique publishing company, which focuses on producing quality, cutting-edge books for communities of developers, administrators, and newbies alike. For more information, please visit our website: www.PacktPub.com.

PUBLISHING

Mastering phpMyAdmin 2.11 for Effective MySQL Management

ISBN: 978-1-847194-18-3   Paperback: 340 pages

Increase your MySQL productivity and control by discovering the real power of phpMyAdmin 2.11

1. Effectively administer your MySQL databases with phpMyAdmin.

2. Manage users and privileges with MySQL Server Administration tools.

3. Get to grips with the hidden features and capabilities of phpMyAdmin.

Learning PHP Data Objects

ISBN: 978-1-847192-66-0   Paperback: 200 pages

A Beginner's Guide to PHP Data Objects, Database Connection Abstraction Library for PHP 5

1. An overview of PDO

2. Creating a database and connecting to it

3. Error Handling

4. Advanced features

Please check **www.PacktPub.com** for information on our titles

PHP 5 CMS Framework Development

ISBN: 978-1-847193-57-5   Paperback: 328 pages

Expert insight and practical guidance to creating an efficient, flexible, and robust framework for a PHP 5-based content management system

1. Learn how to design, build, and implement a complete CMS framework for your custom requirements

2. Implement a solid architecture with object orientation, MVC

3. Build an infrastructure for custom menus, modules, components, sessions, user tracking, and more

4. Written by a seasoned developer of CMS applications

Learning Joomla! 1.5 Extension Development

ISBN: 978-1-847191-30-4   Paperback: 200 pages

A practical tutorial for creating your first Joomla! 1.5 extensions with PHP

1. Program your own extensions to Joomla!

2. Create new, self-contained components with both back-end and front-end functionality

3. Create configurable site modules to show information on every page

4. Distribute your extensions to other Joomla! users

Please check **www.PacktPub.com** for information on our titles

Made in the USA